THE NOVELS OF SAUL BELLOW

THE NOVELS OF

SAUL BELLOW

AN INTRODUCTION

Keith Michael Opdahl

THE PENNSYLVANIA STATE UNIVERSITY PRESS
University Park and London

The author is grateful to Professor Sherman Paul.

The following Bellow novels are quoted with permission of the Viking Press, Inc.: *The Adventures of Augie March,* Copyright © 1949, 1951, 1952, 1953 by Saul Bellow; *Seize the Day,* Copyright © 1951, 1954, 1955, 1956 by Saul Bellow; *Henderson the Rain King,* Copyright © 1958, 1959 by Saul Bellow; *Herzog,* Copyright © 1961, 1963, 1964 by Saul Bellow, all rights reserved.

Dangling Man, Copyright © 1944 by The Vanguard Press, Inc., and *The Victim,* Copyright © 1947 by Saul Bellow, are quoted with permission of The Vanguard Press, Inc.

Printed in the United States of America by
The Colonial Press Inc.

Designed by Marilyn Shobaken

to my wife

CONTENTS

THE NOVELS OF SAUL BELLOW

1 INTRODUCTION

A literary proverb holds that every writer has but one story to tell. Perhaps it is more accurate to say that every writer is compelled by a single issue. The novelist's plots and characters, however different, express the same human dilemma; he continually struggles to solve a problem that haunts him. This problem is personal, of course, but it is also—in the novelist who commands our attention —a reflection of the larger society. We are compelled as Lionel Trilling says by the writer whose inner struggle "provides us with the largest representation of the culture in which we, with him, are involved." [1]

Saul Bellow is clearly such a writer. His critics lecture him with the intensity of men who have been hit where they live; his readers feel that he is on the frontier of their own lives. That Bellow has so far answered almost no one's idea of the great novelist and everyone's idea of the potentially great novelist, that he is so clearly searching for his proper form, heightens his relevance; his critics often write as though Bellow's quest were their own. Highly praised, his novels still elicit less criticism than admonition and less analysis than scold; the critic, many reviews imply, knows the true path to greatness—if Bellow would only listen. Whatever Bellow's final position in literary history, he creates in his present readers a deeply personal response; he too, as he has said of Hemingway, "has found out some of the secret places of our pride and trouble." [2]

If this relevance to our time explains Bellow's current position as our leading novelist, it also creates several problems for the reader. The chief of these is Bellow's ambiguity. Realizing that his novels invite contradictory interpretations, reviewers complain that his final meaning is unclear. Part of this difficulty, I think, is the result of our own confusion: Bellow's novels are less ambiguous than they seem. Part of it too, derives from his continual experimentation: while many writers develop a predictable manner and substance, Bellow has restlessly sought a new milieu or a different structure, a new kind of character or a different style. But Bellow's ambiguity also results from the very ambition of his quest for meaning. He has in recent years played down the ideas in his fiction, warning against symbol-hunting, insisting that "the meanings are the comet's tail—when there is a comet," but his intention has remained intensely moral.[3] His hero always seeks some revelation; Bellow himself always shares that quest. His novels often begin with a brilliant conception—the idea of the ambiguous victim, say, or the character of Henderson—and his protagonist's claim of having solved a problem. Henderson tells us at the outset that "living proof of something of the highest importance has been presented to me," [4] and Herzog feels "confident, cheerful, clairvoyant, and strong." [5] Bellow's novels often end with Bellow laboring to keep his hero's promise. Henderson decides to reject the evidence; Herzog rejects the conditions which inspire his well-being. Their claims, we discover, were less a foreshadow of Bellow's denouement than a statement of his intention. Critics complain that Bellow's novels drive toward a revelation which seems imminent, generating excitement, but then lose that revelation in the final pages. To those who demand a tidy art, of course, this is a serious shortcoming. To those who enjoy his rich characterization and event, his moral purpose is a *donnée* happily granted. To still others, however, Bellow's difficulties are the result of an ambition that recommends him.

But Bellow's difficulty in ending his novels does suggest an art divided against itself. His protagonists find their pain in division and seek the revelation that synthesizes. Bellow's use of debate and dialogue, contrasting pairs and parallel plots, his penchant for summary and his repetition of situation all imply an attempt to resolve conflict. My purpose in this study is to define that conflict and offer a reading of the novels in light of it.

All of Bellow's novels, I think, express a single issue. To study Bellow's fiction is to study a writer's attempt to reconcile two opposing visions. This conflict may be symbolized by an image he used as the title of a novel abandoned in the late forties, "The Crab and the Butterfly." He later wrote in *Augie March* of "the horizon sea rising to grip after a cloud like a crab after a butterfly, with armored totter, then falling and travailing" (492). Bellow here defines the absurd discrepancy between human aspiration and achievement. Man reaches for his dream "with armored totter," but then falls defeated. His armor tortures his movement; his defenses rob him of joy. The image also suggests a conflict between two opposing attitudes toward the world: Bellow is torn between his admiration of militant struggle and his insistence upon a less willful, and defenseless, joy. To control or to give, to master or to revere, to survive or to enjoy, to will or to love—the center of Bellow's fiction lies within this general tension. The contrast between his recurrent pairs, between Augie and the Machiavellians or Wilhelm and his father, is that between a man of love who seeks joy within the limits of his nature and a hard-boiled man of will who would impose his desires upon the world. Defining both characters in his early fiction by their defects, Bellow works toward healthy versions of each. The man of will is defensively self-contained, incapable of community, and adolescent in his self-assertion. The man of love is overly dependent on the world and too willing to suffer. Assuming something of both Hemingway and Malamud, Bellow has sought to portray a will that is strong without monomania and a love that is open without masochism.

The opposition of these two characters also defines the psychology of the protagonist himself, for both attitudes war within a single character. Bellow's heroes are ostensibly men of love, dependent on the world, but they are at bottom alienated. Joseph of *Dangling Man* is "a person greatly concerned with keeping intact and free from encumbrance a sense of his own being" (27). Leventhal is "short and neutral" with others, Augie March "resistant," and Herzog, for all his meekness, "a difficult, aggressive man." Joseph speaks for them all, explaining the extremes of their dependence and isolation, when he says that "while we seem so intently and even desperately to be holding on to ourselves, we would far rather give ourselves away. We do not know how. So, at times, we throw ourselves away" (153–54). Bellow's plot usually insists that his hero help, emulate, or otherwise join forces with another person. Because of his "resistance," the hero must struggle to achieve community; he is locked within himself, divorced from the world. That the party to that community is the man of will, however, makes the decision a difficult one. The willful character makes unreasonable demands; he proselytizes; he may be anti-Semitic, dishonest, solipsistic, or insane. He dominates, betrays, and even attempts to murder the protagonist. Bellow insists that his hero stop holding on to himself, but he creates a situation in which the victory of love is a throwing away of the self. He creates protagonists who desperately need community, but portrays a community in which the price of admission is destruction.

It is this basic pattern, I think, which provides the underlying plot of all of Bellow's fiction and thus many of his strengths and difficulties as a novelist. Because the "community"—the people, society, or cause the protagonist longs to join—is the external world, Bellow's specific meaning may shift in the course of the novel, creating a story that is multilayered and not always consistent. In that community means society, as Allbee steps out from the city masses or Dahfu speaks for his tribe, Bellow's starting point is his protagonist's social experience—his trouble with bigotry or greed. The man of will's oppression of the hero is our culture's oppression of the individual. Bellow's protagonist is also an American hero groping toward manhood. Vacillating between a need to be loved and withdrawal from a world which does not love him as he wishes, he is immature and a victim of himself. The man of will plays adult to a childish protagonist. But Bellow's imagination, I shall argue, is basically metaphysical and religious,[6] passing from the historic fact to the larger, universal issue. In that society is actually destructive—a view Bellow intellectually rejects but continually imagines—Bellow shifts from social issues to the ultimate problems of evil and death. Bellow's heroes are childish, masochistic, and anti-social, but they are also the most difficult of all characters to create, men who are convincingly good and interesting because of it.[7] As they cope with evil—the destructiveness of the world and within themselves—and struggle with their softness, they find their problem to be these very layers of meaning. Their confusion is that of an age of competing ideologies, and their struggle finally that of such different writers as Faulkner, Cary, Yeats and Lowell: man's continuing religious need and experience. One of the most striking characteristics of Bellow's work is his view of the personal and the metaphysical as a continuum, in which personality finds justification in a universal principle or moral order which it reflects. Although I shall examine Bellow's social and psychological stories, I would emphasize that the problem and the goal of all of Bellow's heroes is religious transcendence—the problem in that their rages derive from balked religious longing and the goal in that only transcendence will finally answer the problems they face.

Transposed into aesthetic terms, the conflict of will and love is also the "story" of Bellow's aesthetic development. By writing in the first person and using such devices as Joseph's diary and Augie's memoir, Bellow finds his story in the hero's search for the meaning of his experience—a search which is Bellow's own quest for form. Bellow's aesthetic difficulties thus parallel his thematic problems. Bellow is torn between an art that is conscious, social and didactic, and one that is unconscious, subjective, and a form of "play." His delight in individual scene often conflicts with the structural demands of the total work. His relationship with his protagonist is as ambivalent as his protagonist's relation with the world. Bellow has been accused of identifying too closely with his hero and of being too detached from him. He often alternates between empathy and irony, identification and distance—between imaginatively surrendering to his character and consciously manipulating him. His protagonist's inability to break out of himself parallels the most criticized fault in his work, the fact that the mind of the protagonist is that of the novel. Bellow creates one of the most fully realized physical worlds in fiction, and his use of irony implies a standard outside of the work, but the vision of the novel is ultimately that of the central character. In that this criticism is based upon a distrust of the personal, or the assumption that a "true" point of view cannot be a subjective one, Bellow's growing confidence in subjective perception is itself an answer. So too is the religious nature of his vision: the protagonist turns inward *to* reality rather than away from it, and this criticism is merely the complaint that Bellow does not share the critic's view of reality. In that the hero is unable to reconcile his vision with the daily world, however, the issue is the thematic and aesthetic problem that the hero, and Bellow, would resolve.

Bellow's place on the current literary scene is defined by the correspondence between the conflict in his vision and a larger conflict in our society. Bellow has on the one hand been praised for his fidelity to the tradition of social realism; he has attempted what David L. Stevenson says other recent novelists have not—"to create the large, usable social images of American life" found in the fiction of the twenties and thirties.[8] Born in 1915 of Russian-Jewish immigrants, raised in one of the poorest sections of Montreal until he was nine, when his family moved to Chicago, Bellow came of age in the Depression. He spent his college years, three at the University of Chicago and one at Northwestern, in the sociological atmosphere of the thirties. These early influences—the chaos of Chicago, the suffering of the Depression, the national faith in social reform—find expression in the cultural relevance of his work.[9] Influenced by the proletarian novel, Bellow assumes a direct connection between art and society. He examines the injustice of religious prejudice and the effect of war on the middle class. He explores the place of the individual in a capitalistic society and the meaning of a vast population to the private life. His third novel, *The Adventures of Augie March,* combines the proletarian and picaresque traditions to examine the full range of American social experience. Bellow remains, says Maxwell Geismar, in the tradition of Dreiser and Farrell: he is "one of these few surviving figures of the 1930's who have not repudiated their heritage and their link with a central literary tradition of the past." [10]

Bellow also remains within a broadly social tradition in his flirtation with the formal or aesthetic bias of James and Flaubert. His first two books are slight, intense, and "well-written." When a character in his first novel claims that "the real world is the world of art and of thought," Bellow's hero, a university man, finds that "an attractive idea" (91). While the Flaubertian novel does not demand a social message, it does insist on a social aesthetic; Bellow might be said to apply the techniques of the novel of manners to the purposes of proletarian fiction. All of his characters exist in a carefully defined social context. He evokes not New York or Chicago, but neighborhoods within those cities. His characters play out their lives in coal yards, funeral parlors, police courts and aquariums. If his characters have no school tie they have telling occupations; if they find little tradition or class structure in America, they have the traditions of Judaism, the rigidity of colorful relatives, the nationalistic jealousies of a mixed community. Bellow substitutes the clash of ideologies for the intrigues of class, the pressures of money for the subtleties of social position. He is as conscious of the "high quality" as James and as aware of the telling detail as Flaubert; he uses the rituals of ordering a meal, the protocol of the boarding house, the "picturesque gloom" of the Elevated to place his character firmly within society.

We have only to read the complaint that Henderson's Africa is not sociologically accurate, on the other hand, to perceive by how far these views miss Bellow's accomplishment. Malcolm Cowley is correct I think in including Bellow among those writers who have passed "from sociology to psychology, from political to personal problems, in a word, from the public to the private." [11] The assumption that Bellow is a social novelist may actually lead to a misunderstanding of his work. Overwhelmed by his vivid surface detail, we first assume that his subject is society. We plunge into a magnificent welter of detail and event, follow a tangled plot, live intense physical sensations, and then emerge dazed and bewildered. The plot is still knotted and the social issues unreconciled. To read Bellow for the brilliance of his social scene, we discover, is comparable to reading Hemingway as a sportswriter; the major drama of the Bellow novel is psychological. However real their society, Bellow's heroes are strikingly free from it; Bellow uses a sluggish draft-board or a grandfather's million to place his hero outside of the usual social context. There, turned back upon himself, the hero faces biological and metaphysical issues which are inherent in his nature. He complains that he is a victim of society, but discovers that he is a victim of himself. He pleads cultural determinism, but wrestles with problems that are psychological and religious. Bellow often contrasts the social and biological worlds, dramatizing the repressive artificiality of our culture, but he more often interweaves the two: society embodies the limitation and destructiveness of the world at large. If Bellow fulfills Alfred Kazin's prescription that "depth of description demands that the writer identify himself with a social force to which he can give symbolic significance," [12] he does so by subordinating the social force to what it symbolizes. Because Bellow's point of view is almost always that of his protagonist, the society he describes may be a reflection—and projection—of his hero's consciousness. His portrayal of it is often an exploration of the psychology of the character who sees it.

If Bellow came of age in the thirties, he reached maturity in the fifties. If he is praised by an older generation as an example of what can be done in these confused and asocial years, he is more justifiably cited as a productive example of what many critics have recognized as an important shift in the novel. His subordination of public issues to personal salvation and a "social force" to its symbolic meaning makes his work an example of what Cowley calls the "personalist" novel. And yet even this view of Bellow's fiction, true though it may be, is incomplete. Bellow in one sense illustrates the inadequacy of these categories. Man is a social creature, defined by his social loyalties, but he is also a biological, psychological, philosophical, and religious creature; "depth of description demands" as much of as many of these as the novelist can imagine.

In the practical sense, however, such categories are real; the novelist's emphasis among them determines his choice of character, the nature of his story, and the way he tells it. Here Bellow's fiction embodies in itself the conflict between the social realists and the personalists. His novels play out within themselves the larger conflicts of our culture. As Ihab Hassan points out, Bellow's novels exemplify "the difficulty of a novelist who, like some novelists of the Thirties, gives great credence to social facts yet, unlike them, finally embraces a meta-social view of man." [13] Bellow's hero yearns to join society but is held back by his psychology; he works hard to be "human" but is distracted by social pressures. As he seeks to understand and resolve his individual problem, he wrestles directly with the relative importance of social and personal elements. In the early novels he begins with the assumption that man is a social creature, and then passes to a metaphysical view; in *Henderson the Rain King* and *Herzog* he shifts from a personalist bias to a social one. In both cases, his choice is qualified by the more ambivalent context of the novels themselves.

Bellow's dramatization of this larger conflict is exemplified by his first short story, published in *The Partisan Review* in 1941.[14] Entitled "Two Morning Monologues," it juxtaposes in its nameless characters Bellow's man of love and man of will. It also identifies them as opposing generations—that of the thirties and that now attributed to the fifties. Both characters, a boy and a gambler, are "mourning" because they are unable to live in the world in which they find themselves—a shocked nation mobilizing for World War II. Both consider the draft which threatens them a sign of their helplessness before the forces of history. The boy's reaction to this loss of freedom is to turn inward from the public realm. Unable to find a job while he waits for the draft, he has given up looking and now loafs aimlessly about Chicago. His "chief difficulty is in disposing of the day." It isn't easy, he says, "but you find unusual resources, learning to eat your sandwiches, ordering only coffee, to lounge several hours in one place, to suck a maximum from each straw and pull the marrow out of a cigarette." The boy's withdrawal from the world, his dismissal of ideology, and his emphasis on personal experience relate him to the "new" American generation. He is well-educated and worldly-wise; he feels that ideologies have offered increasingly temporary respite from despair. As Philip Rieff describes his type, "he is antiheroic, shrewd, carefully counting his satisfactions and dissatisfactions, studying unprofitable commitments as the sins most to be avoided." [15] Because he no longer seeks a faith, but to be "human"—to accept the inevitable weakness of himself and others—he is also related to David Riesman's "other-directed man." His largest complaint is that his joblessness alienates him from family and friends; intensely sensitive to the opinions of others, he would find his greatest satisfaction in community.

The gambler, for his part, is intensely active. He is very much concerned with making his way in society, and hopes to dodge the draft for which the boy waits passively. It is difficult to outwit fate, but he insists that man's helplessness is not absolute. "To get around it counts," he says. "Slipping through. . . . There's a way through the cracks. This city, this country, is full of them and it's up to people like me to find a way through them." Although the gambler is not public minded in the usual sense, he is related to the old-fashioned hero who exerted himself, at least in the thirties, within a social context. He is a "pure" embodiment of man's faith in the autonomy of will—the prerequisite of the hero. His contrast to the boy is implicit, for Bellow presents the monologues without comment, but the characters meet indirectly in the boy's confrontation with his father, who shares the gambler's faith in will. The boy complains that "it's my father's fault that I'm driven from the house all morning and most of the afternoon." Just as the gambler hopes to establish the difference between himself and the suckers who are drafted, believing that it would be "funny to come out a loser with so many fall guys in," so the father insists that the son evade the fate of his fellows. He tells of other sons who find work; he secretly publishes his son's name in a newspaper ad requesting employment. The boy pleads that he is a victim of his time, like the rest of his generation, but the father insists that he is free—if he has the will to struggle.

Bellow's use of "boyish" protagonists has been one of the

largest sources of criticism of his work. Norman Mailer complains that before *Henderson* Bellow failed to create heroes who have "the lust to struggle with the history about them." Alfred Kazin feels in Bellow's work "the lack of someone big enough to fight with life." [16] Because a passive hero tends to create a novel of revelation rather than of action, these comments are aesthetic as well as moral: the elusiveness of epiphany and the seeming insignificance of its circumstance tend to break down the novel's traditional structure. Bellow's formal difficulties relate him to those novelists who, as David L. Stevenson says, present the "individual intensity of a series of moments in the lives of their characters rather than in a progression of events toward a sharply defined denouement." Alfred Kazin complains that the novel is no longer "a series of actions which [the protagonist] initiates because of *who* he is, but a series of disclosures, as at a psychoanalyst's, designed to afford him the knowledge that may heal him." [17] Bellow's portrayal of the gambler—the character desired by Mailer and Kazin— suggests that his fiction is less an acquiescence to the fifties than a debate about it. All of Bellow's fiction contains a gambler telling a younger protagonist "to fight with life." But Bellow does write here, as elsewhere, in the manner of the boy rather than the gambler; he uses the monologue to reveal *who* his characters are rather than the actions they take. The story is plotless, a "series of disclosures" portraying two states of mind. "Two Morning Monologues" thus reflects Bellow's participation in the new aesthetic. It also suggests, I think, an answer that might be made to these complaints. The boy and the gambler are not as unlike as they appear; Bellow's tale lies in the revelation of a psychology shared by both characters. In his way the boy is as intensely active as the gambler. For all their differences, Bellow suggests, and for all the threat outside of themselves, both characters are responsible—in similar ways— for their own defeat.

The boy could end his pain by requesting induction, but, he says, "I know a great deal about myself, in as well as out—privately, that is, as well as statistically. I'm very nearly sunk. What sort of getting away would that be?" He is sunk not because he has given up but because he attempts to "save" his life. Bellow's description of how the boy spends the day calls to mind Thoreau's desire "to front only the essential facts of life . . . to live deep and suck out all the marrow of life." [18] The boy withdraws from a hostile world—the "essential fact"—to an internal one, where he hoards what little life he has. To him the sun outside is "nothing more important than a paper seal on a breakfast-food box." He prefers an empty, private existence to the exhaustion of either working or fronting the facts of life. He himself, Bellow shows, willfully chooses an existence no better than the physical death he strives to cheat.

The gambler also destroys his life by attempting to save it. "Manage right and never die," he says. "Fight him back with a stick; blow back in his face. It's in your hands to do it and in your power." The hysterical quality of this statement suggests the hysteria of his struggle; he is so obsessed with "managing right" that he too relinquishes his life. His long days at the bookie are a burial, for he is cut off from "the real races" of life. He has a wistful desire to "see them run off one of these days. Far from the book in the tobacco shop, beyond the room where the smooth billiards run." The very excitement of the race, "the last minute without air, without breath, without end," is also a kind of death. Far from "living deep," the gambler gives up what life he has in order to prove his freedom and immortality. His last remarks cast his denial of all human limits in an ironic light. "Money owing, rent postponed, hole in your glove . . . Then you hear the swishing in the heart like a deck riffled, and the stains grow under the arm."

Although the boy withdraws from the world and the gambler attempts to master it, both characters are self-destructively willful. Both attempt to "match" the world by the ingenuity or force of the self, and both defeat themselves by intensely hanging on to themselves.[19] In still another sense, however, the boy and gambler suffer not from too much self but from a lack of it; that they deliver monologues explaining *who* they are is very much to the point. Their intense rejection of external reality belies their dependence on it; both find definition only in their relationship to the world. The boy had been horrified by his father's advertisement of his name. "I didn't want my name in the paper," he explains. "I can't remember a time in my life when I didn't swallow before saying it." He will accept the identity the world gives him. When he is deprived of a job, he finds definition in modest sensation. The gambler appears to shout his name for all to hear, but his compulsion to do so reveals his fear that it means nothing. Because he finds identity only in the exertion of his will upon the world, he too is dependent on it for a sense of self.

Bellow's final rejection of both the boy and the gambler in this story reflects his early pessimism: neither acceptance nor struggle is adequate. Norman Mailer has recently suggested that "the serious novel begins from a fixed philosophical point—the desire to discover reality—and it goes to search for that reality in society, or else must embark on a trip up the upper Amazon of the inner eye." [20] Bellow's two characters—reflecting the poles of his own conflict—suggest his attempt to travel in both directions. The path of the gambler is toward success in asserting his will; he is the Hemingway hero who can affirm his value in the external world by occasional moments of self-determination. In him Bellow celebrates man's unconquerable zeal. The path of the boy is inward, toward a state of being in which all human limitation fades before the simple joy of existence. He senses a greater reality behind the physical, worships it by suffering, and finds that it sustains him. Bellow's view that both characters are dependent on the world, however, that they need very much to know *who* they are, suggests that the Amazon is the more serious of his journeys. Bellow seeks for his man of will an identity he won't have to prove, and for his man of love one he won't swallow before asserting. Bellow's use of monologue in this story, like his use of the first person in his novels, is an attempt to close in on his character's inner self, an attempt, finally, to discover a self not contingent upon the external. It is in this center, which is ultimately the object of a religious quest, that Bellow's two characters approach each other—that Bellow glimpses a transcendent reality in which strength and weakness, the active and the passive, become superfluous.

Bellow's psychological bias reflects another influence on his art, the psychological novelist, Dostoevsky. Like that of the great Russian, Bellow's largest gift is the clarity and directness with which he examines man's internal, underground existence. *Notes from Underground* inspired the form and content of *Dangling Man; The Eternal Husband* provides the situation of Bellow's second novel, *The Victim.* Augie March has some resemblance to Prince Myshkin while his friends, "those Machiavellis of small street and neighborhood" (4), owe a debt to Raskolnikov. In *Winter Notes on Summer Impressions,* Dostoevsky takes special note of the polarity of will and love. He criticizes Western Europe for the vice "of intense self-preservation, of personal gain, of self-determination of the *I,* of opposing this *I* to all nature and the rest of mankind as an independent, autonomous principle entirely equal and equivalent to all that exists outside itself." [21] Dostoevsky views this egotism as a source of evil, to which he opposes love based on religious insight. Bellow too associates extreme willfulness with evil and seeks an opposing, transcendent vision—a giving of the self to a higher reality. But this polarity, perhaps the closest similarity between the two writers, is also their most important difference. Bellow's heroes perceive a metaphysical evil they are reluctant to accept; they enjoy visions of transcendence which in the early novels only embarrass them. What in Dostoevsky's novel is the *donnée,* the occasion of the story, is in Bellow's a painful issue with which he wrestles—a truth which his stories must somehow demonstrate.

Whatever other issues they embody, the men of love and will are divided by the world views in which each finds his justification. They contrast an imaginative, believing frame of mind and a hard-boiled, skeptical one. Living in a destructive universe, what Augie's grandma calls "a fighting nature of birds and worms, and a desperate mankind without feelings" (10), the man of will survives by emulating the inhuman forces which would destroy him. He out-maneuvers a destructive society by mastering its ways and withstands a world of force by means of a forceful personality. He stands before the protagonist as the spokesman and embodiment of the practical, rational, social and destructive world—one the protagonist is reluctant to accept as finally real. The protagonist walks about a center traditionally occupied by religious faith. His desire "to know what we are and what we are for," as Joseph puts it (154), his attempt to account for evil and death, and his search for a more abiding reality beneath the temporal are all religious issues. His temporary withdrawal from the world, his sense of its mystery, and his quest for grace are attributes of the religious man. All of Bellow's protagonists suffer from a sense of incompletion or disunity; all seek some sort of rebirth or redemption. If, as William James suggests, the "fundamental mystery of religious experience" is "the satisfaction found in absolute surrender to the larger power," [22] Bellow's examination of the man of love is an examination of the religious mystery.

Bellow has become increasingly certain of his protagonist's transcendent vision, but he has to date portrayed not the victory of faith but its difficulties. His heroes enjoy a sense of transcendence which they are unable to make count in their lives. Their belief in a moral order is belied by the cruelty of the world and their own malice—and the fact that Bellow's ambivalence between belief and skepticism is found first of all in his view of evil. Because his heroes are good men "tested" by a destructive world in which they participate, Bellow's novels are studies of evil. Bellow's difficulties in portraying and understanding evil—in reconciling his views of it as a naturalistic and a spiritual force—are suggested by an unsuccessful device he used in "Dora," a short story published in 1949.[23] Dora is a simple and self-reliant old maid whose small room faces the back court of three apartment buildings. As she lies in the darkness on hot summer nights, she overhears the private lives of the tenants. She must listen to "a married couple who have been storing it up for each other like bad, horrible grease." In the night "all that hate begins to burn and stink." Her greatest horror is to overhear not two people but "*one* . . . who shouts and screams by himself, screams so thick you can't even tell who it is screaming, whether it's a man or a woman or even an animal, because you're so accustomed that a human voice should mean something." She would like to help the person, but in the maze of apartments she wouldn't know how to find him. "So you just lie there and listen, and you know that everyone else is lying and listening." The screams express the agony of the human condition: a vicious circle of "pain that causes you to make the mistakes, from which comes pain and then more mistakes again." Dora hears, in an internal darkness, the "language everybody knows but never uses."

Like Dostoevsky, Bellow faces the fearful strategies and flights of the inner man. But Dora's experience, which is a small part of the story, is only partially convincing. The screams are anonymous; we are startled but do not share the victim's pain. At the time that Bellow wrote this story, he sought to maintain a distance from the oppressive suffering he dramatized. He found his portrayal of human agony too grim—and abandoned "The Crab and the Butterfly," in which the screamer is intensely real. Bellow's development as a writer is in many ways determined by his search for distance from the suffering in his fiction. He has brought his heroes into ever closer contact with pain at the same time that he has sought to temper its immediacy. His ironic treatment of his heroes, his use of caricature and comedy, and his invention of other, similar devices are all based on his need for distance. If Bellow has difficulty in portraying human pain, however, he has even greater difficulty in explaining it. His need for distance is intensified by the ambivalence of his view of evil. The married couple overheard by Dora exemplify a frustration and spite we take literally; theirs is the painful but acknowledged malice of daily life. The man who screams by himself, with "screams so thick you can't even tell who it is screaming," expresses a more intense, "imaginary" experience of evil. Bellow associates man's simple cruelty—the malice of the ambitious and the threatened—with the biological struggle for life; as such it reflects a principle of destruction inherent in the physical world, what Augie March calls "this mighty free-running terror and wild cold of chaos . . . which does not welcome your being" (403). Like the screamer, Bellow's "good" men suffer in an impersonal, predatory world. From Augie's "terror," literally true but imaginatively expressed, however, it is but a step to view it as a spiritual entity. Bellow often assumes a moral order in which evil is not just an impersonal physical force but a principle in its own right. Bellow's heroes suffer daily from the spite of their relatives and themselves, they suffer even more from the impersonality of the physical world, but they are also haunted by a view of evil which is imaginative and metaphysical, embodied in dreams and sudden insights—a "free-running terror" which goes beyond mechanical destructiveness to become a metaphysical force. Bellow interprets these visions as paranoia, but in the act of writing he accepts them as true. His plots posit an evil that is biological or psychological, but his imagery—the concrete experience of his protagonist—is often Manichaean. Bellow would reject a demonic view of evil for a more rational one, but the imaginative logic of his fiction assumes evil to be a spiritual or metaphysical force. If Bellow's search for distance is an attempt to cope with the pain of portraying such a reality, it is also an attempt to cope with his ambivalence—to stand far enough away from the promptings of his imagination to control and understand them.

Bellow's confrontation of evil is made particularly difficult by his refusal to withdraw into a Flaubertian world of art for art's sake. He demonstrates his allegiance to Dostoevsky, reputedly an indifferent stylist, by his final rejection of Flaubert's attempt to overcome the despair of his subject by language. The Flaubertian obsession with language is a retreat from the harsh truth of modern existence. "With their care for the poetry of detail," Bellow writes,

> and in their craving for stability, [such novelists] have not made much progress toward the greatest contemporary facts. . . . When they lack the strength that can encompass and lift up these details—facts of our American, modern reality—they are inclined to put into accomplishments of style what is really a helplessness or recoil.

In spite of his own verbal skill, Bellow prefers a novelist such as Dreiser, whose "poor writing" makes him nonetheless a powerful writer. Dreiser had "no need for this use of language because of his greater lifting power." He had the "important knowledge of how life could be supported," a "passion for the subject"—a profound and powerful sense of life.[24]

Dostoevsky, of course, felt he knew "how life could be supported." Bellow's difficulty in portraying the evil he perceives is due in part to his difficulty in affirming the religious insight by which he might transcend such evil. Here Bellow's language, far from being a compensation for despair, reflects the issue he confronts. Bellow has been praised for his realistic description of the American city, but the most striking quality of his style is precisely his lack of a literal realism. He continually equates the human and the inanimate. The city streets in *Dangling Man* are "creased and with thin side-locks of snow" (23). The houses contain "the ravaged throats of entry halls and the smeary blind eyes of windows." In the spring, opened to the weather, the houses are "like old drunkards or consumptives taking a cure" (172). Tommy Wilhelm looking down on the Hudson River sees "tugs with matted beards of cordage" and "the red bones of new apartments rising on the bluffs" (106). The tiles of Herzog's bathroom are "like the cells of a brain." [25] Living in a world in which the usual distinctions between things and people are blurred, Bellow's heroes complain that their world is strange. Joseph of *Dangling Man* "suffers from a feeling of strangeness, of not quite belonging to the world, of lying under a cloud and looking up at it" (30). Augie March says that "you do all you can to humanize and familiarize the world, and suddenly it becomes more strange than ever" (285). Henderson's adventure is difficult, he says, because "it happened as in a dream" (22). Although this sense of strangeness is never the overt issue of Bellow's story, it forms in the background the issue upon which the novel's action depends. It accounts for the alienation, the bad temper, the compulsive action, the fear or the dependency which are the major issue. "If it makes for wonder," Joseph says, "it makes even more for uneasiness, and one clings to the nearest passers-by, to brothers, parents, friends and wives" (30). It drives Joseph into the army, intensifies Leventhal's fear of Allbee, and sends Henderson to Africa. It is, as Augie implies at the end of his travels, the hidden motivation of all of Bellow's heroes: whatever their particular goals, Bellow's protagonists seek to overcome the fact that they are "in the bondage of strangeness for a time still" (523).

Leventhal's sun-baked New York offers one explanation for this feeling of strangeness. "The walls were flaming coarsely," Bellow writes in *The Victim,* "and each thing . . . came to him as though raised to a new power and given another quality by the air; and the colors, granular and bloody, black, green, blue, quivered like gases over the steady baselines of shadow" (179). Under a hot sun colors do run and shapes do waver; like Augie's Mexico or Henderson's Africa, Leventhal's city is strange because of intense sensation. The world is strange, too, as Bellow says in a story in *Seize the Day,* because our cities are ephemeral and arbitrary. When Grebe in "Looking for Mr. Green" examines the Chicago Elevated, with its massive stilts and "confetti of signals," he realizes "how absurd it looked; how little reality there was to start with" (155).

A more important explanation, however, lies in the protagonist's estrangement from physical existence. The hero feels like Joseph that "the real world is not here at all and what is at hand is spurious and copied" (30). Because of "the peculiarity of my mental condition," Henderson says, "the world was not itself; it took on the aspect of an organism, a mental thing, amid whose cells I had been wandering" (156). If Bellow has wrestled with an ambivalent view of evil, he has wrestled even more with the contradictory interpretations of this "mental condition." He interprets this experience first of all as a sign of illness. The world is unreal to the protagonist because he denies that he is a part of it; seeking to evade the limitations of physical existence, he divorces himself from it and thus divorces himself from reality. His attempts to become "artificial"—to be free from evil and death—create an artificial world. As Schlossberg points out in *The Victim,* "paper grass in the grave makes all the grass paper" (256). Like D. H. Lawrence and Norman O. Brown, Bellow believes that our society is over-intellectualized. Afraid of life and even more afraid of death, man attempts to overcome limitation by dedicating himself to abstract—and therefore limitless—idea; he alienates himself from the flesh and blood that are his being. Bellow's hero must learn to live for its own sake, to find joy in his physical nature. He must emulate Augie March's ability to "look out like a creature," to feel, in the midst of all living things, that "it was enough to be among them, released on the ground as they were in their brook or in their air" (330).

But Bellow also suspects that this physical world is not real after all. Bellow's heroes are strangers in a world whose illusions they have penetrated; Joseph's feeling of strangeness is not aberration but perception. When Herzog claims that "we have ground to hope that a Life is something more than such a cloud of particles, mere facticity," Bellow adds that the insight is "far more substantial than anything he saw in this intensely lighted telegraph office" (266). In such statements Bellow shares the interpretation of strangeness described by William James. To those who experience it, James says, "the strangeness is wrong. The unreality cannot be. A mystery is concealed, and a metaphysical solution must exist." In his search for an answer "the sufferer is often led to what becomes for him a satisfying religious solution." So the Bellow hero, in passages scattered throughout his works, mentioned so casually that we pass over them, achieves what can only be described as a transcendent or religious experience. When he does so, as James points out, the "dreadful unreality and strangeness in the appearance of the world" disappear.[26] Leventhal's insight that "everything without exception, took place as if within a single soul or person," brings "a rare, pure feeling of happiness" (169). Augie March's discovery of the "axial lines of life," which reflect "the oldest knowledge, older than the Euphrates, older than the Ganges," brings with it "truth, love, peace, bounty, usefulness, harmony!" If Augie is joyful as a creature—a joy the total novel discredits—he finds even greater joy in transcendence. The world ceases to be oppressive, he says: "And all noise and grates, distortion, chatter, distraction, effort, superfluity, passed off like something unreal" (454).

Bellow has found increasing confidence in this second view of strangeness, but even in his latest novel, *Herzog,* it remains an issue. Bellow's religious perspective satisfies many of the critical questions we have about his fiction and often provides, I think, the only possible answer to the issues he confronts. But it remains an implicit rather than overt element of his plots—what Alfred Kazin calls the need to "yield with a kind of furtive reverence to the ultimate power which one can only call God." [27] As Bellow explores the many ways in which man dangles or is a victim, the transcendent vision must hold its own against other, perhaps more convincing, definitions of man. Bellow places the hero's vision in a fully defined society and contrasts it with an explicitly drawn psychology —factors which compete with it for our attention and "test" it by virtue of the conviction they contain. That the issue is imporant to Bellow's fiction as well as to our age, however, is exemplified by its importance to those influences on Bellow's work which remain to be mentioned. Two of these, the Existentialists and the Romantics, are also concerned with the "strangeness" that defines alienation.[28] Bellow is of course influenced in varying degrees by specific Existentialists and Romantics, by Nietzsche and Dostoevsky, say, rather than Kierkegaard, but he also takes a general "place" among them. In such themes as the superiority of the concrete to the abstract, the importance of subjectivity, and the rejection of reason for intuition, Bellow is both an Existentialist and a Romantic. But these general categories also represent opposing poles which correspond to Bellow's contrasting views of strangeness. Both are concerned with alienation, but in the views of such men as Sartre and Emerson the meaning of alienation—and the nature of the self— is diametrically opposed.

Sartre gives an extreme statement of the claims of the world upon the self when he argues that identity is found exclusively in man's appearance in the world, or in those conditioning factors he calls "facticity." Because we cannot conceive of a self in pure form, separate from the temporal facts of environment and identity, Sartre denies that it exists. Man has no essential self created by God and imbued with purpose, and thus he must create himself by action within the historical world. Bellow's psychological interpretation of strangeness, of course, is a recognition of just such facticity. His hero is intensely sensitive to historical conditions and feels that man finds his true self only in communal action. King Dahfu in *Henderson* seems to share Sartre's view when he says that "what Homo sapiens imagines, he may slowly convert himself to" (271). Sartre's beginning premise, however, is that there is no God; "existence precedes essence" because there is no discernible source of that essence. Bellow's transcendent interpretation of strangeness allies him with Emerson, Wordsworth, Whitman and Thoreau, who clearly believe in God. These Romantics reject orthodox dogma to base their faith on what is perhaps the source of all religious belief—man's infrequent but persistent intuition of a spiritual reality. They rediscover the personal religious experience of daily life, and in doing so feel they discover the spiritual self, which is essential. Henderson answers Dahfu when he says "I've just got to stop Becoming. Jesus Christ, when am I going to Be?" (191). He pleads for a sense of the self that is given rather than invented— the self that is essential. Bellow's heroes all speak in terms of discovering themselves rather than inventing themselves, they all withdraw from the world to simplify their lives, and they all—for all their awareness of facticity—gain glimpses of that identity which retains some element of spiritual autonomy.[29]

Like the "realism" of the man of will, Sartre's view of the self provides a foil to the romantic man of love's quest for an essential self. "Modern literature is not satisfied simply to dismiss a romantic, outmoded conception of the Self," Bellow writes. "In a spirit of deepest vengefulness it curses it." Rejecting this self-hatred, Bellow is "not convinced that there is less 'selfhood' in the modern world."[30] Herzog's hope that "a Life is something more than . . . mere facticity" (266) reflects Bellow's attempt to work out a modern version of the transcendent or essential self. Something of this same polarity between facticity and the essential may even be discerned in the most pervasive influence on Bellow's work, his Jewish heritage. Many critics have seen the Jewish experience as symbolic of modern alienation. The problems of alienation, identity, mobility, and powerlessness all form a link of kind, though not of degree, between the oppressed Jew and the faceless modern man.

Bellow describes the Jewish experience in terms that make it representative of historical alienation and determinism when he says that the Jews of the ghetto "found themselves involved in an immense joke. They were divinely designated to be great and yet they were like mice. History was something that *happened* to them; they did not make it." Bellow describes here both the extreme power of facticity and a source of the Jewish ethnic spirit. His comment that "the most ordinary Yiddish conversation is full of the grandest historical, mythological, and religious allusions" reflects a quality central to his own vision and style.[31]

The joke exists, however, because of the divine promise; if Bellow sees the Jewish heritage as one of alienation, he also sees it as a religious one. "Indeed," he says elsewhere, "the Jewish imagination has sometimes been found guilty of overhumanizing everything, of making too much of a case for us, for mankind, and of investing externals with too many meanings."[32] Bellow's participation in the Jewish imagination is reflected in Chester Eisinger's insight that "Bellow's basic attitudes—the overwhelming need for love and the joy in life—bear a remarkable similarity to the principles of Hasidism,"[33] the Jewish movement which feels the presence of the divine within the factual world. Bellow's celebration of the temporal world, his emphasis on community and love, and his rejection of the formal for the spontaneous and individual all unite his fiction with Hasidism. His love of the particular scene or event at the expense of larger form, conveying the sense that the particular may contain the larger mystery, may owe something not only to the Romantics but to the faith and the anecdotal, aphoristic literature of the Hasids.

Eisinger goes out of his way to disclaim Bellow's participation in the Hasid's spiritual faith, but the appropriateness to Bellow's fiction of another literary discussion of Judaism, Lionel Trilling's essay "Wordsworth and the Rabbis," suggests not only the coincidence of Romanticism and Judaism[34] in Bellow's religious concern but also the logic of his quest for an essential self. Once one admits the obvious difference between the English poet and the Jewish theologians, Trilling says, one sees that they share an awareness of divinity that leads to a "quietism, which is not in the least a negation of life, but, on the contrary, an affirmation of life so complete that it needed no saying." As we have seen, Bellow is suspicious of quietism: his thematic difficulties are due in part to the difficulty of reconciling his hero—"a difficult, aggressive man"—with the "wise passivity" contained in his affirmative ideas. Religious insight in Bellow's fiction requires the hero to surrender to God or to involuntary perception; psychological insight in his fiction requires the hero to "give" himself to the physical world, accepting the limitation of life; and even the emphasis on society in Bellow's work requires a surrender of the self to history or the limiting community. Whether to serve his community or assert his self, the hero must act. But as the boy and the gambler demonstrate, some element of quietism —with its strong sense of the self—is a prerequisite to healthy action. Although our militant culture is suspicious of it, Trilling continues, quietism enjoys advantages which are the deepest goal of our fiction. "There is scarcely a great writer of our own day who has not addressed himself to the ontological crisis, who has not conceived of life as a struggle to be—not to live, but to be." Quoting Hegel and Wordsworth, Trilling sees "an intention which is to be discerned through all our literature—the intention to imagine, and to reach, a condition of the soul in which the will is freed from 'particular aims,' in which it is 'strong in itself and in beatitude.' " [35] Before Bellow's man of love can lose his fear of the world, he must achieve a sense of the self which cannot be absorbed by it; a self which is "strong in itself" is in many ways a prerequisite to a goodness which is not weakness or masochism. The man of will, enslaved by his attempts to establish the sovereignty of the self by personal effort, and thus enslaved by the world he would master, needs even more a "condition of the soul in which the will is freed from 'particular aims.' "

Aside from personal experience, there is perhaps no greater argument for the existence of an essential self than an intensely alive fictional character. While many talk of the disintegration of the self, novelists such as Bellow create characters who live for us with a presence we feel more deeply than their factual identities. Bellow's novels are clearly the vehicle of his thought or thematic concern, and he might be accused of subordinating his story to this concern, but his ultimate theme—as in his characterization—lies in the story itself. "For a short while," Bellow says of the story in general, "all the strength and all the radiance of the world are brought to bear upon a few human figures." [36] In such scenes as Herzog watching Gersbach wash June or Wilhelm's final collapse, some of us may catch a glimpse of such a radiance, a quality possibly related to Martin Buber's claim that "God can be beheld in each thing and reached through each pure deed." [37] Such a sense—related also to the aura of moral significance which pervades Bellow's fiction, and described by Bellow in Dreiser's fiction as "a sense of life"—is Bellow's ultimate answer. Bellow is embroiled in the quest of his hero, but he also draws back to see that quest as drama. He is aware of the buoyancy of man, and takes it as a cause for celebration; he is aware of the ultimate helplessness of man before fate and takes it, without sentimentality or apology, as something mysterious; but his final appeal is not to the resolution of man's conflict with fate but to the spectacle of man seeking resolution.

CHAPTER 2 THE GENERALIZED MAN

We are oppressed at being men—men with a real individual body and blood, we are ashamed of it, we think it a disgrace and try to contrive to be some sort of impossible generalized man.

DOSTOEVSKY, *Notes from Underground*

Intellectuals have often used the major catastrophe of their age—its plague or war or fire—to describe the human condition. Joseph, the *Dangling Man* of Bellow's first novel, is no exception. He views his imminent draft into World War II as the epitome of death and determinism. "We are called upon to accept the imposition of all kinds of wrongs," he complains, to be "those at the gates when they are locked, to be of no significance, to die." Before this inevitable "imposition" one must bow his head: completely determined, Joseph must accept himself as "one of a shoal, driven toward the weirs." But man must also see himself as an "inestimable prize." To lose one's faith in self-determination is to lose one's faith in life. "There are, then," Joseph says, "these two preparations: one for life and the other for death" (119). Man dangles between the need to assert his freedom—to rebel—and the wisdom of acquiescence; he must simultaneously reject and accept his death.

The opposition between an enslaving world and man's desire for freedom is of course a common literary theme. The conflict which Bellow defines, however, lies not between the self and the world but two attitudes toward the world. Joseph speaks of "preparation" rather than action; he admits the victory of the world over his physical being and seeks a source of value that is inherent in his inner self. He seeks not to do battle with the world, like the ordinary hero, nor to make those symbolic gestures by which the Hemingway hero proves his dignity, but to discover within himself the reality which renders such conflict superfluous. If *Dangling Man* is "our best war novel," as Irving Kristol claimed in 1944,[1] then it is significant for what it does not portray. *The Naked and the Dead* examines World War II in naturalistic terms that look back to the thirties, while *Dangling Man* examines a civilian's private quest for an autonomous self—a quest that looks to the fifties. If "I had a complete vision of life," Joseph says of the war, "I would not then be affected essentially" (168). He objects to the draft because it interferes with his search for this vision, which he sees as a search for his essential identity. "Who can be the earnest huntsman of himself," he asks, "when he knows he is in turn a quarry? . . . But I must know what I myself am" (119).

Joseph's peculiar position in society gives him both the leisure and the impetus to discover his self. He is a "dangling man" because he had quit his job to prepare for induction into the army. When that induction was delayed, he was unable to get another job. At first he had looked upon his leisure as an opportunity to write some biographical essays he had planned. His wife Iva, sharing this view of his predicament, had cheerfully moved into a rented room with him to live on her salary alone. But Joseph had soon discovered the truth of Bellow's later warning to writers that "you must manage your freedom or drown in it." [2] He had found himself unable to read or write. Alone all day, he had become Dostoevsky's Underground Man, "a sick man . . . a spiteful man." "It is perfectly clear to me," Joseph says, "that I am deteriorating, storing bitterness and spite which eat like acids at my endowment of generosity and good will" (12). Like the Underground Man, who also had problems of identity, not knowing "how to become anything: neither spiteful nor kind . . . neither a hero nor an insect," [3] and whose *Notes from Underground* are an act of self-definition, Joseph begins a journal, the "record of inward transactions" which forms the novel. He must admit defeat, however, after five months. Unable to discover his identity, he accepts that offered by society; unable to stem his growing maliciousness, "a bad, harsh mood which I despise in others—the nastiness of a customer to a waiter or of a parent to a child," he joins the war by requesting induction (142).

The reason for Joseph's failure is both the substance of his story and the critical problem of the novel. In that Bellow's metaphor of the dangling man captured the intellectual bankruptcy of the time, providing what Edmund Wilson called "one of the most honest pieces of testimony on the psychology of a whole generation," it was a brilliant stroke for a first novel in the early forties.[4] As Chester Eisinger suggests, "the quest for the self was intensified in the fiction of this decade in such a way as to assume the proportions of a movement."[5] Joseph's loss of his social identity provides the reduction to essentials with which the quest for the self might well begin. But Bellow's metaphor also permitted him to include too much, almost all the novels he had in him, in a single book. Although it is short and intense, *Dangling Man* is as episodic as *The Adventures of Augie March*. Joseph ranges over the philosophic and the trivial, the past and the future, his guilt and his dreams, his walks and his boarding house neighbors. Out of this welter of event and idea grow several explanations of Joseph's failure, several definitions of the self, and thus several stories. Joseph's many distinctions between the old Joseph and the new, his mind and his will, his mildness and his nasty temper, his enslavement by history and his struggle for freedom—all conflicts which might define his failure—raise the suspicion that he is defeated as much by Bellow's inventiveness as by his disillusionment. As Bellow develops his metaphor, discovering ever new ways in which man dangles, he provides no single controlling view of his protagonist. Thus at least two critics have argued that Joseph's final request for induction is not a defeat at all but rather a victory over his self-imposed isolation. Rather than the culmination of his despair, they claim, Joseph's end is a rejoining of the society he has rejected.[6]

As a dangling man, of course, Joseph might well dangle among interpretations of his end, and his various stories suggest this is the case. But taken together, I think, the stories portray a larger tale which grows out of the peculiar relationship of *Dangling Man* to the social realism of the thirties. Joseph is a victim of his society, suffering from the malaise that followed disillusionment in Marxism, and a victim of his own psychology, or his flight from natural human limitation. In these two views *Dangling Man* embodies, if in its irony, many of the values and purposes of social realism. Joseph's problem is that he no longer has a consistent view of society from which to act, and his paralysis is a "usable social image" of a community thrown back upon itself. If Joseph's rejection of Marxism belongs to his time, however, it also belongs to his sensibility, which is a religious one. His concern with "preparation" rather than action—his search for the self which will not be "affected essentially"—raises another level of identity and a different perspective on the novel. As a social and psychological man, Joseph must find his real identity outside himself; he is defeated because he turns inward, away from the world, and his final request for induction might well be the first step toward salvation. But Joseph is ultimately defeated not because he turns inward but because he is unable to. Here *Dangling Man* forms a telling contrast with another first novel which grows out of *Notes from Underground,* Sartre's *Nausea.* Both Roquentin and Joseph end their stories of spiritual crisis by joining society, but Sartre sees victory where Bellow sees defeat. Roquentin feels that he can define himself only by action within a social context; Joseph volunteers because he fails to find the self which exists separately from its actions. "That what men created they also were, through some transcendent means," Joseph says, "I could not bring myself to concede" (24–25). Bellow's form and his occasional echo of Sartre give reason to believe that he has *Nausea* in mind. Joseph's search for an autonomous self is a rejection of the assumption—belonging to both the thirties and French Existentialism—that man is defined exclusively in external or historical terms. Joseph fails to make his rejection stick because he is nevertheless a part of his time; he dangles, finally, between religious impulses which point to the "new" fiction of the fifties and the limitations of his heritage from the thirties.

Bellow designed *Dangling Man* first of all as a vehicle for cultural criticism. Joseph's paralysis makes him a spectator rather than a man of action—a keen observer through whom Bellow can criticize society. Bellow's use of the journal form, which is as "formless" as the human mind, permits him to subordinate the complexities of plot or story to his social insight. Believing man to be socially determined, Joseph speaks for himself as well as the tailor who overcharges him when he says that "Mr. Fanzel is innocent. I blame the spiritual climate" (110). That climate is the capitalistic one of fearful acquisition and the despairing one of a society which has lost a sustaining vision. Bellow's social criticism is not economic or sociological, however, but psychological. He examines the psychology of a people who compensate for the loss of shared belief with a host of desperately held ideologies. Bellow takes his cue from Dostoevsky's Underground Man, who says that "we are oppressed at being men—men with a real individual body and blood, we are ashamed of it, we think it a disgrace and try to contrive to be some sort of impossible generalized man." [7] Joseph is surrounded by underground men—Communists, songwriters, businessmen, actors, even peddlers of religious pamphlets—all spiteful and self-absorbed, all seeking to be born from an idea. "I could name hundreds of these ideal constructions," Joseph complains, "each proclaiming: 'This is the only possible way to meet chaos' " (140). The large number of ideals and the obsession with which people hold them destroys community. Living in worlds of private fantasy, people have gone underground where they are "dispersed into separate corners, incommunicado" (139). When they meet their ideologies create a fearful struggle: they are "ready to fly at one another," Joseph says, "from confused motives of love and loneliness" (147).

Bellow reveals this communal battlefield by a party Joseph had attended several months before the diary opens. Joseph too, at that time "the old Joseph" as he calls himself, had had an ideal. He had admitted that man might be "full of instinctive bloody rages, licentious and unruly from his earliest days, an animal who had to be tamed," but "he could find in himself no such history of hate overcome." He had believed "in his own mildness, believed in it piously," and with his friends had formed " 'a colony of the spirit,' or a group whose covenants forbade spite, bloodiness and cruelty" (39). But it was at a gathering of the colony that Joseph discovered the falsehood of his ideal. Minna Servatius had become drunk because of marital troubles and had demanded to be hypnotized by Abt, an old suitor she had rejected years before. When she was under, Abt proceeded to humiliate her. He pinched her hand, claiming she would feel no pain, but "the skin, where he had twisted it, remained white long afterwards" (52). He made her shiver from the cold and asked her how many drinks she had had, knowing she would be unable to answer. Perhaps "aware of the insult," she suddenly sat up and screamed for her husband. Joseph then discovered that his own wife, Iva, was drunk. He had recognized, he says, that "the human purpose of these occasions had always been to free the charge of feeling in the pent heart," but he is shocked and disillusioned. Abt and Minna reveal a modern corruption: "We did these things without grace or mystery, lacking the forms for them and, relying on drunkenness, assassinated the Gods in one another and shrieked in vengefulness and hurt" (46). Referring to Hobbes, Joseph is forced to conclude that "one was constantly threatened, shouldered, and, sometimes invaded by 'nasty, brutish, and short,' lost fights to it in unexpected corners. In the colony? Even in oneself" (56).

Joseph's analysis of this corruption provides one of the basic insights of the novel. He sees that it is the ideal construction—the means by which we seek salvation—that corrupts us. Our many conflicting ideals preclude any communal form for the expression of scorn and anger. The ideal itself, moreover, is a source of anger. Because we fear that we will fall short of our ideal, Joseph says,

> we hate immoderately and punish ourselves and one another immoderately. The fear of lagging pursues and maddens us. The fear lies in us like a cloud. It makes an inner climate of darkness. And occasionally there is a storm and hate and wounding rain out of us [89].

Abt had humiliated Minna because of his fear of failing to become "great in anything he chose" (86). The members of the colony had turned against each other because each had turned against himself, bitterly aware of his probable failure to achieve salvation. That most of these people assume that "there is no limit to what a man can be" heightens their fear of failure and makes their hate and wounding inevitable (88). The ideal construction, Joseph sees, is self-defeating: the obsessive and fearful effort by which the ideologist attempts to be more than human is all too human after all.

Bellow portrays this self-defeat most clearly in the underground men's attempt to evade mortality. Surrounded by death in the war, in his rooming house, where his landlady is dying, and on the street, where he sees a man fall from a heart attack, Joseph takes death as a symbol of all human limits. Because "death is the abolition of choice," he says, "the more choice is limited, the closer we are to death" (148). By enslaving themselves to their ideal, and thus limiting their choice, those seeking to become generalized create a living death. Joseph's friend John Pearl gives one result of this process when he complains that "everything is peeling and scaling in South Brooklyn. . . . It's the treelessness, as much as anything, that hurts me. The unnatural, too-human deadness." Joseph knows "what he feels, the kind of terror, and the danger he sees of the lack of the human in the too-human" (153). The deadness of the city is too-human because it represents our society's attempt to avoid death by embracing stone and metal. The ideologist who forms Joseph's society invests his whole life—his freedom, energy and happiness—in either an idea, which is abstract, or an object, which is inorganic. He identifies himself with "things" because they are beyond the limits of the human condition: through them he can transcend himself. But these things—our ideologies and our cities—evade the limits of life by virtue of the fact that they are not concrete or alive; the individual invests his life in death. Joseph instinctively knows what Norman O. Brown points out, that "death is overcome on condition that the real actuality of life pass into . . . immortal and dead things." [8]

One of the most striking examples of such too-human deadness is a woman Joseph meets while walking about the neighborhood. Evangelizing for Christian Science, the woman sells pamphlets containing the testimonials of soldiers who have survived "the maiming fire only because of their faith" (161). The futility of her hope that man can transcend physical limits by religion is revealed by her own desperate illness. "Yesterday," Joseph reports, "she was sicker than ever. Her skin was the color of brick dust; her breath was sour." Every time he sees her he is struck by her wasting illness. "Her lips come together like the seams of a badly sewn baseball. Her face burns and wastes under your eyes; the very hairs at the corners of her mouth seem already to have shriveled" (162). Her pathos is heightened by the way she attempts to stop passersby.

> She rushes to block you with her body clumsily, almost despairingly. If she misses, she is incapable of following up, and if you succeed in eluding her—if you want to elude her, if you have the heart to continue doing so time after time—she can only stand, defeated, staring after you [161].

The woman is killing herself to prove her dedication as well as the validity of her faith, and the sicker she becomes, the more intense her effort. She seems in a trance, for her speech is memorized and while she talks "the hard brown shells of her eyes do not change" (161). The last time Joseph sees her she momentarily loses "all sense of her whereabouts" (163). Sacrificing her life to her faith that man can evade death, the woman appears to be destroyed by the very ideal that sustains her.

Bellow's portrayal of this society fulfills Lionel Trilling's later suggestion that "social class and the conflicts it produces may not be any longer a compelling subject to the novelist, but the organization of society into ideological groups presents a subject scarcely less absorbing." [9] But Bellow's prime interest is the disastrous results of such organization. Joseph defines himself in broad social terms, saying that "my talent, if I have one at all, is for being a citizen" (91). Whenever he seeks community he finds an Abt venting frustration or an evangelist insisting he affirm some ideal construction. His friends, his in-laws, even his brother demand that he play a supporting role to the ideologies that "save" them. They are able only to "see things as they wish to see them," and subordinate Joseph, the person, to their obsession (39). If Joseph contradicts their ideal, they deny he exists. When Joseph tries to cash a check, the banker looks up from Joseph's identification to ask "how do I know you're this person?" (174). Joseph doesn't have a job; he is outside of the business community. The banker decides he doesn't know who Joseph is. When Joseph meets Burns, who remained a Communist after Joseph left the Party, Burns looks right through his former comrade, pretending he isn't there. "This is always happening to me," Joseph complains (33). Like the Underground Man, who shoved an army officer to force recognition, Joseph loudly insults Burns to force him to look at him. Without a job or an ideology, Joseph is without an identity. No one mentions his surname, even though he has many conversations in which it might be used. Having forsaken the ideal construction, he becomes to his community only a physical presence: his friends are "ashamed of him" and "think he is a disgrace" and view him as "some sort of impossible generalized man." Joseph perceives the evils of a society of ideal constructions because he is a victim of those evils.[10]

Joseph's increasing social isolation provides one source of form in the novel. Having become isolated from "the old Joseph," Joseph describes his growing alienation from other people. He begins with the city of Chicago, his society, and proceeds to lose increasingly personal relationships. The actual chronology is mixed, for some of the events are recalled from previous months, but as Joseph records them the scenes represent an ever narrowing circle. By the middle of the novel he is alienated from his in-laws, his friends at the party, his brother, his mistress, and his wife; because Joseph is solitary except for a few minor acquaintances and an alter-ego he calls *Tu As Raison Aussi*—a second self with whom he quarrels alone in his room—the novel narrows from society to the self. The rest of the journal records the disintegration which culminates in Joseph's desperate reunion with society. He ends his journal by reversing the Underground Man's shout, "it is better to do nothing! Better conscious inertia! And so hurrah for underground!"[11]

Joseph exults that he is at long last "in other hands, relieved of self-determination, freedom cancelled." He shouts "hurray for regular hours! . . . Long live regimentation!" (191). Having "not done well alone," he welcomes the annihilation of the self that he had been trying to preserve.

As a victim of society who gives voice to Bellow's own insights, Joseph is treated sympathetically. The ironic tone of his defeat, however, adds a second dimension to the novel. Bellow began Joseph's diary with a rejection of the code "of hardboiled-dom . . . that curious mixture of striving, asceticism, and rigor, the origins of which some trace back to Alexander the Great" (9). He had rejected it first of all because the code denied any expression of man's inner life and thus an examination of "most serious matters." Behind this dismissal of the code lay Bellow's criticism of obsessive striving, for all ideologists are Hemingway heroes in their dedication and self-sacrifice. Bellow also seemed to reject Hemingway's usual distance between character and author. Just as Joseph declared that he was going to close in on his inner life, so Bellow seemed to declare that he was going to close in on his character. But this implied declaration leads to misunderstanding and disagreement. It led reviewers in 1944 to judge the book, and Bellow's own attitude toward Joseph, by their reaction to the hero rather than to his story. Several reviewers disliked Joseph and accused Bellow of too little critical distance from him; *Time* wished that Bellow had suspected that "as an object of pity, his hero is a pharisaical stinker," and Herbert Kupferberg described Joseph as "a spineless young man, hardly worthy of the thought and careful writing that Mr. Bellow lavished on him." N. L. Rothman, who admired Joseph's "rare, cold, clarity of vision" and "gift of prophecy," also assumed Bellow's identification with Joseph. Later commentators, on the other hand, have complained that Bellow is too distant from his character; Rueben Frank notes that "the author vanishes from the area between the reader and Joseph's consciousness, only to be perceived *behind* the latter, too artfully directing that which we take to be a free and spontaneous movement." [12]

These contradictory remarks testify to Joseph's complexity as a character, but they also point to Bellow's own ambivalent attitude toward him. If Bellow sympathizes with Joseph, he also treats him with irony. *Dangling Man* is a criticism of its protagonist as well as society. Joseph claims to be the victim of his age but he is the victim of himself. He claims to be victimized by the underground men, but he too is an underground man, able "to see things only as he wishes to see them." Insisting on his mildness with increasingly bad temper and denying his death by withdrawing ever farther from life, Joseph is the victim of his striving rather than his despair—of his attempt to evade the limits of his life. Bellow reveals this self-defeat by means of a simple ironic contrast. On February 22, for example, Joseph realizes that "differences in our personal histories . . . become of minor importance" because the quest of all mankind is one and the same (154). But on the next few pages he records quarreling with a friend because they were "temporarily in different classes." "You get it," he says. "You're not stupid. . . . We *are* in different classes. The very difference in our clothes shows it" (157, 158). During this incident and his relation of it, Joseph has completely forgotten his theory of the past week.

Bellow uses the same technique to reveal Joseph's more damaging denial of malice or evil. After dinner at the home of his brother Amos, during which his niece Etta makes some disparaging remarks, Joseph retreats to their music room where he listens to a favorite record. The music tells him that he is "still an apprentice in suffering and humiliation" and that he must learn to meet them "with grace, without meanness" (67). He realizes that he will not be able to do so until he has become a "whole man." His thoughts are interrupted by Etta, who insists on listening to another record. Although he has now heard his record twice, Joseph childishly argues with the teenager and ends up spanking her. When her screams bring the others, Etta claims Joseph attacked her. She also reports that Joseph had looked through her mother's dressing table. Joseph had only spanked her, and he had only looked in the table for a pin, but he assumes they believe the worst and flies into a rage. He is indeed unable to meet humiliation "without meanness." He fails to see that the squabble began over the music which called for grace.

Joseph is even less perceptive in his thoughts the next day. Etta bears a striking resemblance to him, and he had always assumed that "a similarity of faces must mean a similarity of nature" (75). As he recalls the history of his superstition, he remembers a boyhood fear that he "concealed something rotten" or evil behind the face he considered handsome. Etta's spite might reflect a mutual corruption. But, Joseph says, "I have long ago freed myself from this morbidity. It is because of Etta that I undertook to trace it back. . . . There is no reason to believe that there is any parallel between us" (77–78). Still believing "in his own mildness" Joseph is happy to find that it was Etta who was depraved in their quarrel and that they have nothing in common—in spite of the fact that he had wondered if any of the others "were capable of observing how exactly alike we looked at that moment" (71). Joseph concludes his entry by noting that he now has "additional proof" of his "inability to read people properly, to recognize the likelihood of baseness in them." Truly the man who is facing reality, he adds, "I shall have to begin schooling myself in shrewdness" (78).

These ironic revelations create a second rough form to the novel. By including Joseph's memories along with events of the day, Bellow is able to arrange the journal according to the human limits Joseph struggles to deny, regardless of their actual sequence. Bellow establishes Joseph's rejection of his age in a visit to his in-laws and his quarrel with Burns. He then turns to Joseph's concern with evil in the colony party and the dinner with Amos. In the last third of the journal Joseph makes the largest denial of all—the fact of death. When a man dies on the street, he takes it as a prevision and despite claims of acceptance is unable to eat dinner. Bellow depends chiefly upon Joseph's dreams—which are more reliable than his conscious mind—to reveal the result of Joseph's denial of death. Joseph describes two dreams, the first of which places him "in a low chamber with rows of large cribs or wicker bassinets in which the dead of a massacre were lying." There had been a revolution, and he is there to reclaim a body for some friends. He makes it clear to the "guide" that he is an outsider, "not personally acquainted with the deceased." This denial of any connection with death leads to one, for the keeper, "brisk as a rat among his charges," also stands for death. He feels that Joseph's denial forms a conspiracy between them: they both understand that "it's well to put oneself in the clear in something like this" (120, 121). When the keeper smiles at Joseph with an offensive air of understanding and complicity, Joseph finds that he has exchanged one alliance with death for another.

In his second dream Joseph is a "sapper with the Army in North Africa." He crawls through a window into a room in which a grenade is wired to the door. Afraid to cut the wires, he decides to explode the grenade by shooting it, and when he misses he sees that "if I had hit the mark I would have killed myself" (121). By attempting to avoid death he had put himself into jeopardy. Joseph's dreams point to a lesson that he refuses to accept and a truth about himself that he is unable to see—Bellow's later insight that "we can keep death too near us by secret care." [13] In his withdrawal from society and his inner striving, Joseph has clung to himself too intently, has thrashed about too wildly: he has imprisoned himself by his effort. By the end of the novel his increasingly frequent rages approximate the depravity he fears and his growing isolation is itself a form of the death he denies.

Bellow heightens the irony of Joseph's self-defeat by a motif which corrects Joseph's fault but which he is pointedly unable to accept. Near the beginning of his journal, Joseph quotes Goethe's statement that "all comfort in life is based upon a regular occurrence of external phenomena. The changes of the day and night, of the seasons, of flowers and fruits, and all other recurring pleasures that come to us . . . —these are the mainsprings of our earthly life." If we ignore the external world, "then comes on the sorest evil, the heaviest disease—we regard life as a loathsome burden" (18). Joseph's complaint in later months of "still no fruits and flowers" is made ironic by the biological joy that is very much available. Bellow sandwiches Joseph's dreams of death, perhaps the most despairing passages in the book, with two passages of just such joy. Joseph is in bed with a cold, and Iva, "at her most ample and generous best," quits work to nurse him. They read for a while and then doze off. Joseph awakes first and, he says, "heard the slight, mixed rhythm of her breathing and mine. This endeared her to me more than any favor could." He continues,

> the icicles and frost patterns on the window turned brilliant; the trees, like instruments, opened all their sounds into the wind, and the bold, icy colors of sky and snow and clouds burned strongly. A day for a world without deformity or threat of damage, and my pleasure in the weather was all the greater because it held its own beauty and was engaged with nothing but itself. [118–119]

Joseph, who had been ignoring Iva because she had failed to live up to his "plan," is able to feel the full weight of her existence, divorced from any action or favor. She is valuable to him because she is there, her breathing mixed with his. Joseph is also able to feel the full measure of his own existence and the value that simple fact provides. His quest for a basis for life—for an identity—should have ended before it began; Joseph is unable to accept the gift of life, which need be "engaged in nothing but itself." Joseph blames his lack of such a gift on society: "What would Goethe say to the view from this window," he asks, "the wintry, ill-lit street, he with his recurring pleasures, fruits, and flowers?" (78). But Bellow himself blames Joseph's lack on his efforts to transcend a limited physical existence: the acceptance of the biological is the antidote Dostoevsky as well as Goethe prescribes for the "loathing of life."

In the last part of the novel, Joseph realizes that he cannot control his inner self because it is not completely his own. He begins a conversation with *Tu As Raison Aussi* by complaining that he is "harried, pushed, badgered, worried, nagged, heckled" by "the public part of me. It goes deep. It's the world internalized, in short" (164–65). He sees that he can't get along without the illusions he had rejected, and that his withdrawal has intensified his need. Echoing the Underground Man's description of "that hell of unsatisfied desires turned inward," [14] Joseph perceives that "what we really want is to stop living so exclusively and vainly for our own sake, impure and unknowing, turning inward and self-fastened" (154). His desire for freedom from the ideal construction is itself an ideal which creates effort and rage: his struggle to overcome the evils of ideology corresponds to the very faults he would reject.

Bellow's use of irony to establish this theme partially explains our feeling that he is *behind* Joseph, manipulating him. So too does Bellow's difficulty in reconciling his irony with the limited point of view of the first person. Without a perceptive second character or information supplied by an omniscient author, Bellow tries to rely on the irony inherent in Joseph's self-contradiction. He reveals this contradiction in the first part of the novel solely by the juxtaposition of journal entries—by the discrepancy between Joseph's description of an action and his later thoughts about it. Because the action and the meditation are both given straight, and seem reasonable enough in their own context, we often fail to perceive their ironic contrast. Sensing this difficulty, Bellow uses other devices: Joseph's conversations with *Tu As Raison Aussi,* criticism of Joseph by his friends, and Joseph's own knowledge of his self-deception. Bellow relies almost exclusively on this last device as the novel draws to a close. But when we perceive Bellow's original intention in the final pages, and shift into the necessary ironic attitude, we are too conscious of Joseph's self-deception to trust his self-knowledge. The result of this confusing shift is that even though Bellow bases his form upon an ironic juxtaposition of thought and action, we are never sure how to take Joseph's journal entries.

To this difficulty in the novel we must add a second, even more important one. Joseph realizes that he has defeated himself, but he isn't conscious of the whole story. *Dangling Man* is ultimately puzzling, I think, because Joseph's withdrawal makes such good sense after all. Bellow sympathetically deplores Joseph's isolation as the symptom of cultural bankruptcy; he ironically deplores it as the result of Joseph's obsessive psychology. But Joseph's withdrawal is also a simple search for health. As Augie March puts it, "the reason for solitude can only be reunion" (447). Like many American figures ranging from Thoreau to Ellison's *Invisible Man*, Joseph withdraws from society to prepare for re-entry, in this case recruitment by the army. His "retreat" from life is analogous to the religious retreat, for he seeks the strength and insight to surmount the death and determinism that await him. He hopes to discover, he says, "whether I can claim the right to preserve myself in this flood of death that has carried off so many like me." The "self" he hopes to preserve is not his physical being, which he realizes is determined by external forces, but "the mind. Anyway, the self that we must govern" (167). He hopes to be "a member of the Army, but not a *part* of it" (133–34). Painfully aware of his external helplessness, Joseph continually returns to his need for a self which exists in its own right, whatever its dependence on the world, a self which is essential rather than contingent. He even finds some evidence of such a self by turning inward from the actions of men to their motives. The old Joseph had tried but failed "to find clear signs of their common humanity" in the acts of men, "in their businesses and politics, their taverns, movies, assaults, divorces, murders" (25). The new Joseph sees that while these external elements are hopelessly diverse and inhuman, the human purpose behind them is the same for all. By investigating the inner man, Joseph is able to perceive that "all the striving is for one end . . . the desire for pure freedom." And if that is the case, "the differences in our personal histories, which hitherto meant so much to us, become of minor importance" (154).

Such insights as these might provide Joseph with the community he seeks. They offer him a tempering perspective on his struggle and a possibly healing sense of the human condition. They also suggest a third way in which Joseph dangles—the conflict between his need for faith and his rational skepticism. "My beliefs are inadequate," Joseph complains, "they do not guard me" (123). When he defines the "desire for pure freedom" as "to know what we are and what we are for, to know our purpose, to seek grace," he defines his quest as a religious one (154). Like the boy and the gambler, Joseph needs very much to know *who* he is; acceptance of the world may be wisdom, as the social and psychological stories suggest, but as Bellow defines Joseph's need—and Joseph's world —acceptance alone is not really an answer. Here Bellow's use of Dostoevsky's *Notes from Underground* is particularly appropriate, for Dostoevsky viewed the experience of his anti-hero as a demonstration of the need for faith. The censors "left in the passages where I railed at everything and *pretended* to blaspheme," Dostoevsky wrote his brother, "but they deleted the passage where I deduced from all this the *necessity of belief.*" [15] Bellow likens Joseph to the Underground Man, provides him with the questions and insights from which we might deduce the *necessity of belief,* but clings to the rationality Dostoevsky rejected. Perhaps the most striking fact of *Dangling Man* is that Joseph talks a great deal about turning inward but is really unable to do so. He withdraws from the social and physical world, but he also withdraws from his deepest self. He records not his "inner transactions" but his reflections on them. When he says that at night "the heart, like a toad, exudes its fear with a repulsive puff," he gives not the moment of fear but a metaphor (123). This tendency is natural to the journal, but it also reveals Joseph's insistence that he think himself to clarity. Joseph is an imaginative man trying to be rational, a rationalist overthrown by his imagination. He defines his problems intellectually and abstractly, but like Leventhal facing Allbee or Herzog in the New York courtroom, he is overthrown by his concrete experience. He clings to his conscious mind, which tells him that evil is not absolute and matter is real, but he is haunted by visions of horror and a sense that the world is illusion.

Joseph's experience fulfills many of the "proofs" for faith apparent in *Notes from Underground.* His paralysis exemplifies the psychological danger of rationality, and his rages fulfill Dostoevsky's definition of evil as an inevitable human malice. Man needs faith, Dostoevsky says, because the rationality by which he would save himself leads to the very ills from which he needs saving. But Joseph also perceives an evil of even greater force than that in *Notes from Underground*. He describes the sunset of his day of joy in terms that reject the biological serenity he had just felt. He sees "apocalyptic reds and purples such as must have appeared on the punished bodies of great saints, blues heavy and rich" (124). Joseph directs his attention to social and psychological issues, but evil—malice and death, even a sense of the world as corruption— is never far from his thoughts. "The world comes after you," he complains. "It presents you with a gun or a mechanic's tool . . . cuts off your future, is clumsy or crafty, oppressive, treacherous, murderous, black, whorish, venal, inadvertently naïve or funny" (137). When he remembers his childhood neighborhood, where he saw "a cage with a rat in it thrown on a bonfire, and two quarreling drunkards, one of whom walked away bleeding" he thinks that "it is the only place where I was ever allowed to encounter reality" (86). He sees a disturbing sensuality in such people as his sister-in-law, who reminds him of the Biblical women who "walk with stretched forth necks and wanton eyes, walking and mincing as they go" (60). The visits of Alf Steidler, a cynical former schoolmate, make him feel "as tired as though I had spent the day in dissipations of a particularly degrading sort with Steidler as my accomplice" (133). In the world of sensuality, as in Etta's accusation of rape, in the world of affairs—"the lies and moral buggery, the odium"(91) —and even in the physical world—"the green, menacing air" (30) —Joseph is intensely sensitive to the presence of evil.

Unsustained by vocation, alone all day, Joseph himself colors the world he fears will take his life. As a Marxist, he had viewed the bourgeois world as corrupt, and he may have retained this vaguely Manichaean view. But there is also evidence, in spite of the novel's limited and thus obscuring point of view, that Bellow takes Joseph's vision of evil as more than paranoia. Like the dreams of his Biblical ancestor, Joseph's dreams become real. Bellow links the imagery of Joseph's subjective visions of horror with that of his actual, daily life. The Christian Science woman, for example, with her yellow teeth, staring eyes, and a face that "burns and wastes under your eyes," is related to what Joseph describes as his first vision of death —a picture of his grandfather "supporting his head on a withered fist, his streaming beard yellow, sulphurous, his eyes staring and his clothing shroudlike" (75). Even the streets of Joseph's city, lined with yellow grass, overlooked by the "ravaged throats of entry halls and the smeary blind eyes of windows" and appearing "burnt out," are related to this vision (172). Joseph associates his grandfather and the guide of the first dream with the "ancient figure" who appears in a third dream. He had been walking in a back alley, he says, when he heard "another set of footsteps added to mine, heavier and grittier." He had turned to see "that swollen face" come forward to kiss him on the temple, and then had run, "hearing again the gritting boots. The roused dogs behind the snaggled boards of the fences abandoned themselves to the wildest rage of barking. I ran, stumbling through drifts of ashes, into the street" (122). When a man falls on a city street, the policeman who appears has the guide's pointed face, and Joseph thinks of "the last breath which comes like the gritting of gravel under a heavy tread" (116). The climax of *Dangling Man,* in which Joseph retreats to the alley after quarreling with Iva and the others in the rooming house, is a complete reenactment of the dream.[16] Joseph stands in the darkness for a minute, and then rushes to the street. Instead of the guide, "brisk as a rat among his charges," he hears something "among the cans and papers. A rat, I thought and, sickened, I went even more quickly, skirting a pool at the foot of the street where a torn umbrella lay stogged in water and ashes" (183). Unable to take the terror of the alley, Joseph rushes to the street; unable to take the horror of his lonely existence, he rushes to request induction into the war.[17]

Bellow's sympathetic tone in these passages, their pervasive position, and their fulfillment of Joseph's "paranoia" in his daily life, all suggest that Bellow takes this vision seriously. In doing so he creates a world which cannot be accepted in itself. If the world is inherently destructive or evil, only transcendence—if it can be affirmed—is an answer. But Joseph is also overthrown by the very visions which might suggest transcendence. He often uses religious images, as in his description of mankind as "the feeble-minded children of angels," or his description of his rooming house as "the hospital of a religious order" (137, 142). He describes his problem as his confrontation of "the craters of the spirit," from which such conforming people as his friend Myron are "safe," and defines them by saying that "we are all drawn toward the same craters of the spirit—to know what we are and what we are for, to know our purpose, to seek grace" (154). Occurring as it does within the context of these questions and terms, Joseph's sense of strangeness might well be taken as the beginning of a religious intuition that the material world is not absolutely real. Joseph gropes, in his own way, toward Dahfu's view in *Henderson* "that nature might be a mentality" (269). He is subject to hallucinations in which he manipulates the appearance of the world. By "isolating a wall with sunlight on it," he says, "I have been able to persuade myself, despite the surrounding ice, that the month was July, not February." Such powers, which he fears may "damage the sense of reality" (13), account for his experience of "strangeness, of not quite belonging to the world, of lying under a cloud and looking up at it" (30). He suspects that the world is a "conspiracy"—or what Herzog calls "a system of prevention, a denial of what every human being knows" (289). At the end of the novel, in the last scene before he leaves for the army, Joseph has an experience which he says "put the very facts of simple existence in doubt" (190–91). His boyhood room, "delusively, dwindled and became a tiny square, swiftly drawn back, myself and all the objects in it growing smaller." He takes this as a revelation of "the ephemeral agreements by which we live and pace ourselves," and has perceived "an element of treason to common sense in the very objects of common sense. Or that there was no trusting them, save through wide agreement." Because his withdrawal from the world had divorced him from "the necessary trust, auxiliary to all sanity," Joseph turns to the "wide agreement" he will find in the army (190).

It is true that Joseph's request for induction fulfills the thematic requirements of the social and psychological stories, and thus may be an affirmative decision. Joseph's sense of strangeness, as we have seen, may be taken as a symptom of his alienation from the world. In joining the army Joseph joins society, accepting historical limitation, and takes his place among other mortal men, accepting physical limitation. But the issue in *Dangling Man* is not Joseph's evasion of the army but his preparation for it. When Joseph hopes that "the war could teach me, by violence, what I had been unable to learn during those months in the room," he confesses that he has failed in his goal (191). Bellow's portrayal of an evil world which cannot merely be accepted, his sympathetic treatment of Joseph's instinctual answer to that world—the need for an essential, transcendent self—and the evidence that Joseph is close to just such a sense of the self, all seem to rule out the optimistic interpretation. Such passages as Joseph's meditation in Etta's music room reveal Bellow's sympathy with his religious struggle as well as its relationship to Bellow's general conflict between will and love. Joseph's music tells him of the need for grace, and then "named only one source, the universal one, God." The music goes "easily to . . . the seldom-disturbed thickets around the heart," he says, but "was there no way to attain that answer except to sacrifice the mind that sought to be satisfied?" Joseph associates the intellect with willful control and the imagination or faith with a passive surrender of that control: "Out of my own strength it was necessary for me to return the verdict for reason," he concludes, "in its partial inadequacy, and against the advantages of its surrender" (68). Describing himself at different times as a "good man" and a "Machiavellian," dangling between his rationality and what Gooley MacDowell later calls "feelings of being that go beyond and beyond all I ever knew of thought," [18] Joseph embodies within himself the polarity of Bellow's later contrasting characters. He gives himself to society and possible death because he is unable to give himself to imagination or faith. That Bellow fluctuates between idea and drama in the novel, and between identification and manipulation in regard to Joseph, suggests that he too in his art shares Joseph's conflict.

We may now say with hindsight that Bellow's instinct in *Dangling Man* was sound. His declaration for the inner life is a rejection of the externalization which belonged not only to Hemingway but to the proletarian novel. We now see that the radical novel produced a mediocre fiction because it subordinated character to economic and social doctrine. Bellow in his first novel would return to character, and especially inner character, as the center of his fiction. But Bellow was also a product of the thirties. Sharing Joseph's insistence upon rationality, Bellow too at this time dangled. In that Joseph is torn between a self-sufficient rationality and a surrender to a higher power, he—and Bellow—dangle between two works which influenced *Dangling Man, Notes from Underground* and *Nausea*. Bellow and Sartre both write their first novels out of *Notes from Underground,* both create rational heroes who suffer symptoms similar to Dostoevsky's anti-hero, and both insist, ironically enough, upon the rationality Dostoevsky rejects. Roquentin works through the rationality, finding transcendence of the absurd world by an act of will. He feels joy when he sees that a singer and a song writer "have washed themselves of the sin of existing" by the purity of their art, and decides that he too will create an art that will be "beautiful and hard as steel and make people ashamed of their existence." [19] Although Joseph finds such a solution attractive, he dangles between it and Dostoevsky's stand. His rejection of the Marxism which Sartre accepts parallels Dostoevsky's rejection of rational utopianism. Joseph seeks the freedom to be found in meaning rather than meaninglessness. Seeking a reality higher than the self, finding none in a society which, as Bellow has said [20] of "the greatest human qualities," has "no vocabulary for them and no ceremony (except in the churches) which makes them public" —Joseph might well argue that only the self is proof of the greatest reality. Joseph dangles, he is rational, he is defeated because he withdraws from society to the self, but he also sees that it is the self which is morally aware and thus representative of whatever moral order may exist.

CHAPTER 3 THE IFRIT
AND THE FELLAHIN

Though in many of its aspects this visible world seems formed in love, the invisible spheres were formed in fright. . . . All deified Nature absolutely paints like the harlot, whose allurements cover nothing but the charnelhouse within.

MELVILLE, *Moby Dick*

The reviews of *Dangling Man* were encouraging, even if they were buried among the war-bond ads of the supplements' final pages. All of the critics found fault with the book—it was crabbed in style, too narrow, too pessimistic—but they also found a talent much greater than the usual, too-consciously attributed promise of first novels. Bellow's metaphor went far toward expressing the era, and his protagonist was decidedly alive. In creating a living situation and character, however, Bellow had sacrificed qualities which were less important than his achievement and yet essential to a polished novel. The journal form by which he examined Joseph permitted him to avoid the development of a real plot. Except for a very general pattern, he had treated each entry as a separate entity without subordinating it to a preconceived design of the whole. The life of the novel was also uneven. Joseph stood out in part because the other characters were a pale background for the sharp lines of his own character. The novel's striking flashes of color and texture contrasted with a dominant black and white of abstraction. Bellow had to show that he could tell a more inclusive, varied story, that he could breathe life into more than one character and evoke a physical world larger than a single room. He had to tighten his control over his imagination and broaden its scope.

Bellow apparently worked hard on *The Victim*: he had already written two drafts by 1945, and he published nothing else until it came out in 1947.[1] The book is carefully planned, almost as if Bellow designed it to overcome the shortcomings of *Dangling Man*. He attempted to avoid the formlessness of a novel of "subjective brooding" by writing about a major social problem, racial and religious prejudice. His idea was both simple and profound. Most novels protesting prejudice are themselves guilty of denying the victim's humanity, for they condescendingly idealize minority-group members. Meek, faithful, and forgiving, the Jew or Negro has only those minor faults which make him "lovable." The victim of prejudice is capable of good and evil, of course, and may even be driven by prejudice into the faults that are attributed to him; the weak man may be warped by fear into fitting the bigot's distorted image of his race. He himself, in fact, may share the paranoia which lies behind prejudice. Bellow perceived in the minority-group member the psychology Sartre attributes to the bigot: anti-Semitism is "fear of the human condition" and is "at bottom a form of Manichaeism." The bigot's hatred is an "explanatory myth," in which he prefers a world ordered by "the struggle of the principle of Good with the principle of Evil" to a world of accident.[2] The anti-Semite's projection of evil onto the Jews is his attempt to order the world by giving tangible shape to his fears. The Jew, for his part, facing senseless persecution or the "sufferance" of others, may have as many fears and as deep a need for order as the bigot; he too may be tempted to posit an absolute evil and locate it—perhaps in a second minority. Both persecutor and victim might live in a Manichaean universe, both victims of fear, both oppressed by their own humanity.

To dramatize this point Bellow carefully developed the ironic juxtaposition of *Dangling Man* into a series of parallel plots and characters that nicely suited the purposes of irony. This technique, together with his social theme and painstaking style, placed *The Victim* in the James-Flaubert tradition of conscious artistry. It also earned Bellow critical praise. *The Victim* was hailed by many of those reviewers who remembered his first novel as an "advance in every way." Diana Trilling wrote that "one has only to compare it to Mr. Bellow's earlier *Dangling Man* to have a striking lesson in the way in which intellect has the power to alter the quality of a novelist's feeling and even enhance his art." But not all critics agreed. Several complained of an "artificial and heavy-handed" symbolism and a last chapter that is "disastrously out-of-key." They sensed that Bellow's conscious design—far from enhancing or clarifying his art—is a flaw that obscures his meaning. Rueben Frank noted in 1954 that a large part of the story "comes off more as an intellectual statement than as the problems of living human beings." Alan Downer held that "so much contrivance in a realistic novel is acceptable only if it contributes to an understanding of . . . the novel," and then stated what even those who praised Bellow's plot had reluctantly confessed: "It is never clear what *The Victim* is about." [3] Bellow had created living characters in a brilliantly evoked physical world, it seemed, but he hadn't told a clear story; he had designed a plot to overcome the obscurity of *Dangling Man,* but for some reason had failed.[4]

The Victim is not completely clear, I think, because Bellow transcended his original subject. The image of the victim, like that of the dangling man, permits various definitions and thus a shift in theme. Viewing anti-Semitism as "fear of the human condition," Bellow passed from an immediate social problem whose limits would help him control the novel to the larger, metaphysical problem of evil. *The Victim* shifted from a novel about man in society to one about man in the physical world, it outgrew its form, and Bellow found himself at the end struggling to reconcile his original conception of parallel plots with a deeper, contradictory level. We notice Bellow's ironic detachment—one source of our sense of contrivance—because it is not consistent; we miss the expected denouement of a realistic novel because *The Victim* is finally not realistic. Bellow's plot is social and ironic; his physical description—the world he creates by detail and metaphor—converts the social issues into metaphysical or religious ones and belies Bellow's conscious detachment. Because of this thematic escalation, Bellow's achievement lies in the intensity and complexity of individual scenes rather than in the neatness of plot. When we recognize the perspective as a religious one, however, the novel becomes clearer. The characters are in fact victims of the very complexity that blurs the story—a complexity that derives from the very real tension or paradox which makes man feel his existence is mysterious. If Bellow's complexity creates aesthetic difficulties, it also gives almost perfect support to his theme and gives another, final dimension to the many ways in which man is a victim.

To understand Bellow's achievement we must first examine the "intellectual statement" implicit in his parallel plots. His basic idea is reflected in the changes he made in the situation borrowed from Dostoevsky's *The Eternal Husband*. His protagonist Asa Leventhal is related to Dostoevsky's Velchaninov, who is forced to remain in St. Petersburg by a dispute over an inheritance—one of Bellow's major themes. Oppressed by the heat and loneliness, Velchaninov develops vague feelings of guilt or "hypochondria." Leventhal too, left alone in New York by his wife's visit with her mother, suffers from "hypochondria" or a fear of imminent ruin. His anxiety, however, is much more specific than Velchaninov's. As a Jew, Leventhal feels himself an outsider at the trade magazine where he works. He feels a "guilty relief" about his job and a "sense of infringement"; he had made mistakes in his life which should have cast him among those who "did not get away with it—the lost, the outcast, the overcome, the effaced, the ruined" (20). The loss of his first job in New York had forced him to clerk in a flophouse for derelicts. Saved by a civil service job in Baltimore, he had quit it in anger at his fiancée's infidelity, and in New York had again almost touched bottom. He had become "peculiarly aggressive" in job hunting, taking a quarrelsome, "exaggerating, illogical, overly familiar" attitude toward prospective employers. An especially bitter scene with Rudiger, a powerful editor, made him fear he had been blacklisted. He had finally found his present job as editor, and had married Mary, the girl in Baltimore, but he feels himself an impostor. At any time, he fears, chance might restore his job to its rightful owner.

Kirby Allbee, the man who had introduced Leventhal to Rudiger, claims to be that rightful owner. Like Dostoevsky's Pavel Pavlovitch, who appears out of the city to beg help from Velchaninov, Allbee appears one summer night to threaten Leventhal. Pavel and Allbee are both widowed and alcoholic; both have an impudent, secretive, and threatening manner. Allbee, however, is much more aggressive—and obnoxious—than the meek Pavel. A member of a venerable New England family, Allbee blames his ruin on the displacement of his class by the Jews, the "new" people who are "running everything," and believes Leventhal is the particular Jew who deposed him. "The world's changed hands," he says. "I'm like the Indian who sees a train running over the prairie where the buffalo used to roam" (232). Allbee had been fired by Rudiger soon after introducing Leventhal to him. He claims that Leventhal, knowing Rudiger would dismiss Allbee, had provoked the editor purposely to avenge Allbee's anti-Semitism. The loss of that job had insured Allbee's decline. Convinced that Leventhal is "entirely to blame" for the death of his wife as well as his career, Allbee emerges from the city masses to accuse Leventhal of his crime and to let him "clear himself" by saving his victim.

Related to Pavel, Allbee is also an elaboration of Steidler, the unsavory actor in *Dangling Man* who had reminded Joseph of "Rameau's nephew, described by Diderot as '. . . *un* (*personnage*) *composé de hauteur et de bassessee, de bon sens et de déraison*'" (127). Much of what Allbee says, especially about the plight of man in a mechanical culture, makes good sense. And yet he is obviously unbalanced. There is a "note of impersonation" in his accusations, and a discrepancy between his conversational tone and the look in his eyes makes him seem like an impostor who doesn't believe his own words. He shifts crazily from "something clear, familiar, and truthful," a sincere remorse for his own failings, to wildly inconsistent charges; he assumes a determinism that precludes his own moral responsibility and a free will that makes Leventhal accountable and thus guilty (75). Confused by Allbee's inconsistency, angered by his anti-Semitism, and weakened by the absence of the stable Mary, Leventhal refuses his demands and is himself victimized. Allbee invades his previously secure existence. The alcoholic persuades Leventhal to put him up when he can't pay for a room. He reads Leventhal's intimate mail, sleeps with a whore in his bed, and even uses his oven for a suicide attempt. Outraged and yet paralyzed with bewilderment, Leventhal finds himself driven out of his own house. His deepest fears, it seems, are about to be fulfilled.

Although Pavel Pavlovitch too encroaches on Velchaninov, Dostoevsky finds his story in the ironic revelation of Velchaninov's continued malice: having cuckolded Pavel years before, Velchaninov now proceeds to destroy him. Bellow finds his story not in Leventhal's malice toward Allbee, but in the ironic revelation of Leventhal's "fault," the reason he is unable to help or ignore Allbee. As his troubles mount up, Leventhal feels that the "showdown" is coming. "Illness, madness, and death were forcing him to confront his fault. He had used every means, and principally indifference and neglect, to avoid acknowledging it and he still did not know what it was" (158). This fault, Bellow shows, lies not in the difference between Leventhal and Allbee, but in their similarity. Dostoevsky contrasts two types, each of whom is doomed to his fate by his character: Velchaninov is the "predatory man" who victimizes others, and Pavel is "the eternal husband" or cuckold who permits himself to be used. Leventhal and Allbee appear to be opposites, the secure and the ruined, the victim and the oppressor, but both suffer from a sense of persecution based on the fear that they don't deserve the social position they claim. Leventhal refuses to help Allbee because he suspects that Allbee is really out for revenge, hoping to ruin him rather than save himself. He is closer than he realizes to his father, who had hoped "to be freed by money from the power of his enemies. And who were the enemies? The world, everyone. They were imaginary" (111). This same kind of suspicion lies behind Allbee's bigotry: deeply fearful of a world in which he finds himself an outcast, Allbee creates an imaginary enemy to whom he can attribute malice. Leventhal believes that he has "an unsuspicious character," Bellow tells us; Allbee is "happy to say" that suspicion is "not in my make-up" (96, 192). But each man victimizes the other because he is a victim of himself: Jew and Gentile, victim and bigot, both men suffer from the self-persecution of imaginary fears.

Bellow reveals this parallel between characters by means of the ironic juxtaposition he used in *Dangling Man*. A few pages after Allbee attributes his own spite to "you people," the Jews, telling Leventhal that "if somebody hurts you, you hit back in any way and anything goes," Leventhal remembers a woman who had insulted him and Mary at a movie: "Hit them!" he thinks. "That was all they understood. . . . His father had believed in getting his due, at any rate. And there was a certain wisdom in that" (141, 149). "Why," a friend tells Leventhal, "you're succumbing your-self to all the things that are said against us" (130). But Bellow's chief means of revealing this parallel is by a structural pattern simi-lar to that of *The Eternal Husband*. Dostoevsky alternates, chap-ter by chapter, two kinds of scenes: his characters alone together, in an oppressively subjective atmosphere that seems to justify Velchaninov's fear, and the two men in public, where Velchaninov persecutes the harmless Pavel Pavlovitch. Bellow interweaves Leventhal's claustrophobic meetings with Allbee with a second plot—a second issue of moral responsibility—which takes him into the city. Leventhal's sister-in-law Elena phones him and with "terrible cries" begs him to rush to Staten Island. His nephew Mickey is sick: he must assume the responsibility his brother Max abandoned to work in Galveston. Although Elena is superstitiously afraid to part with the boy, Leventhal persuades her to send him to a hospital. They are too late, Mickey dies, and Leventhal guiltily fears Elena's blame. At the funeral parlor she gives him a look of "bitter anger"; he wonders "what would he do if then and there— imagining the worst—she began to scream at him, accusing him?" (181–82) She herself, he believes, is at fault. She delayed getting medical help; she is a slovenly housekeeper; she has "a sug-gestion of distraction or even of madness" in her eyes (7). When Max arrives, Leventhal suggests that Elena is an unfit mother for their other son and warns against her Italian mother whom he suspects of anti-Semitism. "She's full of hate," he tells his brother. "It's as clear as day to me that she thinks the baby's death was God's punishment because Elena married you." Max admits that his wife is upset, but he denies her insanity as well as the threat of her mother. "You've sure turned into a suspicious character," he tells Leventhal. "I never heard anything so peculiar in all my life" (240).

Having established a parallel between Leventhal's suspicions of Allbee and Elena, Bellow bases Leventhal's (and our) knowledge of his fault upon the truth of his warning to Max. "If he were wrong about Elena," Leventhal thinks, "the mistake was a terrible and damaging one; the confusion in himself out of which it had risen was even more terrible" (240–41). He later tells himself that "the reason for a mistake like that could not be neglected; it had to be dug out" (265). But when he finds himself locked out of his apartment and Allbee in bed with a strange woman, he takes it as proof of Allbee's malice and throws him out. "He hated me," he thinks. "He hated me enough to cut my throat. He didn't do it because he was too much of a coward. That's why he was pulling all those stunts instead" (277). Allbee had slept with the whore to humiliate him. When Max shows up, however, Leventhal realizes that he had been mistaken about Elena and the old woman. Wrong about Elena, Leventhal could well be wrong about Allbee. Although it is puzzling, the final action of the chapter—the climax of the novel—suggests that he is. Allbee sneaks back late that night and attempts suicide using Leventhal's gas oven. Leventhal awakes in time to stop him, and Allbee flees. Far from wishing to destroy Leventhal, Bellow suggests, Allbee needed help to keep from destroying himself. His request for help had been sincere; the "note of impersonation" in his bearing had been caused by fear rather than by malice—by his dread that he was unentitled to the aid he hysterically demanded.

Dostoevsky's Pavel Pavlovitch had stood over Velchaninov with a razor in the climax of their story, but he had done so only after Velchaninov had wronged him several times over. And he had only stood there. Velchaninov thinks that "Pavel Pavlovitch wanted to kill him, but didn't know he wanted to kill him." [5] Leventhal thinks that Allbee had planned murder. He reaches the end of his agony without realizing the fault within him. Bellow supplies that knowledge in the final chapter in which Leventhal and Allbee accidentally meet several years later. Time has softened Leventhal's "sense of infringement," Bellow says, and he senses that "Allbee had no real desire to be malicious" (292). Allbee too has made "peace with things as they are" and can admit that Leventhal had helped him after all (294). He also explains his suicide attempt. "I wasn't thinking of hurting you. I suppose you would have been. . . . But I wasn't thinking of you. You weren't even in my mind." He then states one of the major themes of the novel: "When you turn against yourself, nobody else means anything to you either" (293). Although Bellow leaves the suicide attempt ambiguous, with Leventhal's rejection of Allbee's explanation, he reveals that Allbee hadn't consciously sought revenge as Leventhal had suspected. Each man had victimized the other, Bellow suggests, because each was victimized by his own imaginary fears. No longer on guard against enemies who hate him, Leventhal fulfills Joseph's hope that time would give him what he had been unable to find by himself. "Something recalcitrant seemed to have left him," Bellow tells us. "His obstinately unrevealing expression had softened" (285). The passing years had gone far in healing his fault.[6]

Such is the story Bellow seems to have planned. That many have felt the novel to be more than this suggests the presence of other levels of meaning. So too does the feeling that the last chapter—in which Bellow states his theme—is "disastrously out-of-key." We might explain this charge by the sudden leap in years after an almost day by day narration, or by the purgation or relief that follows the suicide scene. But there is also a sense in the conclusion that Bellow turns back upon previous events to impose an order that had somehow been lost. In a similar coda to *The Eternal Hus-*

band, Dostoevsky uses the leap in years to demonstrate the permanence of his types: despite the interval and different circumstances, Pavel Pavlovitch and Velchaninov are still cuckold and adulterer, still trapped by their respective characters. Bellow uses his leap in time to introduce—and justify—a change in character. He introduces this change partly out of emulation of Dostoevsky's tone, partly out of his insistence against despair, but also, I think, partly out of doubts about his clarity. Having denied Leventhal and Allbee any perception of their fault as a result of their experience, he uses an unjustified change in character to insure our perception of it.

This clarification was necessary and yet "out-of-key" because Bellow saw more complexity in Leventhal's world than that inherent in the parallel plots. If *The Victim* is about the dangers of man's illusions of evil, it is also about the reality of evil. If Bellow's two plots contrast an imaginative, subjective level of experience with a "real" one, giving the decision to the real, Bellow's imagery imbues the literal city with imaginative value and gives the decision to the subjective. Instead of showing up illusion against hard literal fact, Bellow overshadows the literal facts with what they come to represent—their symbolic truth in his character's imagination. Leventhal too, like Joseph, struggles with a conflict between the imaginative and the rational. He too is paralyzed by a figure of death. Just as Joseph's dreams of death become real, so Allbee becomes a real threat. What takes place entirely within Joseph's private world, however, forms in *The Victim* a complex psychological relationship between two characters. Behind the moral issue of Leventhal's debt to Allbee lies the question of what each man represents to the other. Leventhal is unable to help Allbee and Allbee persecutes Leventhal for a reason more profound than their fear of social displacement: Bellow subordinates the theme of man's fear of imaginary evil to that of man's denial of the real evil in the world and himself. Each of the characters, Bellow shows, views the other as a symbol of the evil he would deny. The moral issue between the two men becomes an issue concerning the nature of the world and man's ability to face it.

Bellow introduces the evils Leventhal and Allbee fear in his epigraphs from *Thousand and One Nights* and De Quincey's *The Pains of Opium*. In the first, a merchant, throwing away some date seeds, accidentally kills the invisible son of an Ifrit who promptly executes him. The merchant is the vehicle and the victim of coincidence or chance. Bellow's second quotation—of De Quincey's vision of a sea of faces, "imploring, wrathful, despairing; faces that surged upward by thousands, by myriads, by generations"—portrays the loss of the individual in the oppressive, suffering masses of people. Allbee complains of the masses—he feels he has been usurped by an immigrant horde—but it is the destruction of the individual by chance which terrifies him. Unable to cope with the senseless "blind movement" in which the individual is "shuttled back and forth," he has to find a particular reason for his ruin— anything but accident. "We don't choose much," he complains. "We don't choose to be born, for example, and unless we commit suicide we don't choose the time to die, either" (193). Leventhal's plea of coincidence in Allbee's firing is an appeal to the truth Allbee cannot accept. Allbee wants Leventhal's help, but he must have Leventhal's confession of malicious intent: only by discovering a human purpose behind his ruin can Allbee endure the senseless forces which determine man.

Leventhal, on the other hand, accepts the impersonal evil of accident, but fears the evil within the human heart. Allbee's claim that he has maliciously ruined him charges Leventhal with the very malevolence he denies. De Quincey's faces are "wrathful"; the merchant, oppressed by the heat, throws away the stones "with force." Like Joseph frightened by his rage, Leventhal stands accused of a malice that only one of Bellow's heroes before Henderson can admit. But Leventhal also fears the irrationality and sensuality he associates with the masses. Unable to face these elements within himself, he projects them onto the people around him, converting a fear of his own nature into a fear with which he can cope, a fear of the outside world. When he witnesses a furious argument between a cuckold and his wife, he realizes that "he really did not know what went on about him, what strange things, savage things. They hung near him all the time in trembling drops, invisible, usually, or seen from a distance." His deepest fear is that sooner or later "one or two of the drops might . . . fall on him" (94). Part of his difficulty with Elena is the emotionality she shares with his mother who had died in an insane asylum. Allbee, who cheerfully confesses to "a fallen nature," is the epitome of sensuality: the shadows under his eyes are like "the bruises under the skin of an apple"; he has an air about him that suggests "the decay of something" (160, 292). Allbee represents the potential depravity of "all physical being" to Leventhal, "a depth of life in which he himself would be lost, choked, ended. There lay horror, evil, all that he had kept himself from" (277). Leventhal would be freed from Allbee's demands, but he wants even more to be freed from the potential depravity Allbee represents. Only by denying the sincerity of Allbee's accusation can he deny his own malice and reject the irrationality and sensuality of Allbee's "depth of life."

Bellow's shift to this psychology is reflected in the particular use he makes of Leventhal's fears. Part of Leventhal's hypochondria is his fear that he is tainted by his mother's madness and his father's belief in imaginary enemies: he worries constantly that he is "seeing things." Alone in his apartment, Bellow tells us, Leventhal felt "threatened by something while he slept. And that was not all. He imagined that he saw mice darting along the walls" (25). Leventhal suspects what Bellow's second plot makes clear, that he has "let his imagination run away with him" (189). But in his confrontation with Allbee, on the very next page after the imagined mice, Leventhal's imagination is correct. He notices a man following him in a crowded park, watching him closely: "Instantly Leventhal became reserved, partly as a rebuff to his nerves, his busy imagination" (26). A very real Allbee steps forth. Bellow repeats this pattern in Allbee's suicide attempt. When Leventhal awakes to find his front door open and hears sounds in the kitchen, he is afraid that he imagines a nonexistent danger. "What if the chair had slid down and the door opened by itself?" he thinks. "And what if the kitchen were empty? His nerves again, his sick imagination." He holds back, "feeling that to be deceived now through his nerves would crush him" (282). But Allbee *is* in the kitchen.

Leventhal might be mistaken in his suspicion that Allbee means to commit murder rather than suicide, but he is not mistaken about the existence of a real threat. Wrong about the motives of Elena and Allbee, Leventhal is right about the deeper issue, the destructive powers of the evil that Allbee represents, the reality of "the revolting sweetness of the gas like the acrid sweetness of sewage" (283). Allbee attempts suicide to combat a meaningless universe, but in doing so he poses a real danger. By denying the evil Allbee symbolizes, and refusing to help, Leventhal makes himself vulnerable to that evil. Barring the derelict from his apartment merely intensified Allbee's desperation. Unless we face the fact of human depravity squarely, Bellow suggests, it will return to haunt and even destroy us.

This shift in the psychology of Bellow's characters also explains two chapters which are otherwise digressions. Leventhal meets his friend Harkavy and some others in a cafeteria and a few chapters later attends a party at the Harkavys'. On both occasions Schlossberg, "a large old man with a sturdy gray head, hulking shoulders, and a wide, worn face" is present (123). Schlossberg states the theme of the novel Bellow was actually writing when he says "it's bad to be less than human, and it's bad to be more than human." In neither case does the individual "have any use for life" (133). Behind these faults lies the desire to avoid death or the destructive forces in the universe and man. The individual who wants to be more than human—like Allbee—creates the illusion that he doesn't share the mortality of his fellow man. The individual who is less than human tries like Leventhal to avoid all exhausting engagement with life. Both retreat in their own way from the limiting world and the limited self. "I have to be myself in full," Schlossberg says. "Which is somebody who dies, isn't it?" Reminded of a funeral where "they had paper grass in the grave to cover up the dirt," Schlossberg points out that "paper grass in the grave makes all the grass paper" (255, 256). Hardly relevant to a novel about the threat of an imaginary evil or death, Schlossberg's comments play a direct role in The Victim because they define Leventhal's real fault as well as Allbee's, the inadequate humanity of the individual who refuses to face and accept the evil and death that are part of life.[7]

In accomplishing his second task, broadening the scope of his imagination, Bellow intensely evoked the city. "On some nights New York is as hot as Bangkok," *The Victim* begins. "The whole continent seems to have moved from its place and slid nearer the equator, the bitter gray Atlantic to have become green and tropical, and the people, thronging the streets, barbaric fellahin among the stupendous monuments of their mystery" (3). The "unnatural, too-human deadness" of the city in *Dangling Man* had been at once the creation of a society which denies the limits of physical existence and—by virtue of Bellow's metaphors—an "imagined swamp where death waited in the thickened water," or the physical force which creates those limits (105). Bellow expanded this use of metaphor in *The Victim* to use the city the way earlier American writers used the forest or sea: the city symbolizes the world's destructive power. The stainless steel and glass, the ringing of bells, the "trains rushing by under the gratings" setting off "charges of metal dust" all give a sense of the lifeless, mechanical world Allbee fears (22). The "barbaric fellahin," the brilliant sensation, and the heat, "thickening the air, sinking grass and bushes under its weight," all evoke the oppressive, teeming life feared by Leventhal (108). The city, having "slid nearer the equator," reflects the tropical intensity of too much life. Having planned the hallucinatory quality of his city to be a reflection of Leventhal's suspicious state of mind—a creation of his sick imagination—Bellow shifts to an urban primitivism in which the city represents reality itself.

This physical description is, I think, one of Bellow's finest achievements in the novel. He never lets us forget the stifling heat or the mute, pressing crowds. If we take Schlossberg's comments as Bellow's own, we might assume a relationship between this physical evocation and one of Bellow's recurrent affirmative themes—the peace man finds in accepting the physical world. Man's gloomy struggle is unnecessary, Bellow suggests, because man can obtain "salvation" by merely accepting the richness and multiplicity of the physical world. Schlossberg's claim that "paper grass in the grave makes all the grass paper" holds out the promise that real grass in the grave makes all grass real—that man may find a home in the world if he accepts its inevitable limitations.

But one of the striking facts about *The Victim* is that its world is overwhelmingly oppressive. Bellow succeeds in expanding Joseph's narrow world less by leaving Joseph's room than by expanding its four walls to encompass a city. Leventhal's New York is claustrophobic: the sky presses down, the sensation fatigues, and the crowds jostle. Bellow's description of the sky gives some substance to Leventhal's feeling that he is threatened by something. The sun is like "the flame at the back of a vast baker's oven; the day hung on, gaping fierily over the black of the Jersey shore" (22). Leventhal walks through streets "deadened with heat and light" and before buildings which "smoulder and faced massively . . . into the sun and across the hot green netting of the bridges" (36). While the sun plays a simple role in fraying tempers and intensifying sensation—a perfect background for Leventhal's bizarre encounter—it is also an important presence in its own right, a force that dominates the city. In that it encompasses both the tropical richness and the lifeless world Bellow's protagonists fear, it suggests that *The Victim* is actually about a single evil—one which Bellow often speaks of as a principle of nature. When Leventhal looks at the sun, he sees a light "akin to the yellow revealed in the slit of the eye of a wild animal, say a lion, something inhuman that didn't care about anything human and yet was implanted in every human being too, one speck of it, and formed a part of him that responded to the heat and the glare" (51). Although we might pass over this as a mere figure of speech, Bellow's subsequent fiction shows that it is one of his most persistent and serious concerns. He describes a similar light in Augie's Mexico, in the story "By the Rock Wall," and in Henderson's desert—where Henderson feels "something between the stones and me" (46). Bellow often conceives of evil— that mentioned by Allbee, say, or Herzog—as a force which is impersonally destructive in the universe and malevolent in animals, reflected in the eyes of Henderson's lions as "clear circles of inhuman wrath" and "rings of black light" (261). He also sees, like D. H. Lawrence, an analogous quality in man: he equates this force with the instinctual drives of the species and the impersonal force and cruelty of the human will. Just as Allbee fears the loss of human value in a universe of "hot stars and cold hearts," and Leventhal fears it in the evolutionary or reproductive drives of the masses, so each man fears in his way what Rogin, "A Father-to-Be" in that story, calls "the life force" which "occupied each of us in turn in its progress toward its own fulfillment, trampling on our individual humanity, using us for its own ends like mere dinosaurs or bees." [8]

Both the intensity and the meaning of this world belie Schlossberg's plea and represent a third level in the novel which is the most important of all. As he does in *Dangling Man,* Bellow argues for the acceptance of the world, but creates one which can hardly be accepted. He passes not only from Leventhal's imaginary fear to the need to accept evil as real, but from the wisdom of acceptance to the need for transcendence. Although Bellow does not conclusively affirm religious experience in *The Victim,* he comes much closer to it than in his first novel. Here too the final chapter provides a focal point for the issue. Among the many reasons for our impression of a shift in tone is the fact that Leventhal cautiously affirms transcendence. Everyone in our society, Leventhal thinks, assumes that "a promise had been made" entitling him to a particular economic position or seat in the social theater. Most people either feared they didn't deserve their "ticket," as he had, or were frustrated like Allbee at not receiving the ticket they felt they deserved. Many feared they would get no ticket at all. But "the reality was different. For why should tickets, mere tickets, be promised if promises were being made—tickets to desirable and undesirable places? There were more important things to be promised." Leventhal loses his fear of ruin when he sees that the real promise of life lies deeper than social arrangements. Having made this leap, he concludes that "possibly there was a promise, since so many felt it. He himself was almost ready to affirm that there was" (286).

This "promise" refers in part to the serenity Schlossberg finds in acceptance of our limited humanity. By stating it in teleological terms, however, as a promise that is more than the potential of the given world, one that "had been made . . . at the start of life, and perhaps even before," Leventhal implies a larger reality behind the physical (286, 287). Exploring the many ways in which man is victim, Bellow reaches a perspective that is broadly religious. Formal religion, of course, plays a large part in *The Victim*; as one of the bases of prejudice it is, with the revivalist bands that play in the park and the religious references in discussion, always in the background. Behind Allbee's drinking, we are told, is the fact that there "were ministers in his family, influences to throw off" (42). Because the characters do not embrace a formal faith, sharing Joseph's lack of "sustaining beliefs," they are thrown back into the fearful bewilderment of superstition. Their fear and struggle, like Joseph's, are the result of their unsatisfied need for religious meaning. Sensing what Norman O. Brown points out, that "power was originally sacred, and it remains so in the modern world," [9] Leventhal and Allbee have no response to it other than crude "magic"—the source of their difficulties. Allbee's prejudice is a form of superstition "from the middle ages," and Leventhal's paralysis is caused by his superstition that Allbee's charge means total ruin.

Although not changed by them, Leventhal enjoys glimpses of transcendence far more definite than Joseph's. He feels at one point that "there was not a single part of him on which the whole world did not press with full weight," and is "bewilderingly moved": the emotion is "a disguised opportunity to discover something of great importance." When the discovery does not arrive, "it came into his head that he was like a man in a mine who could smell smoke and feel heat but never see the flames" (257, 258). On another occasion, having dreamed that he had cried unashamedly when he was barred from a train, he awakes in "a state of great lucidity" and with "a rare, pure feeling of happiness." He sees that "everybody committed errors and offenses. But it was supremely plain to him that everything, everything without exception, took place as if within a single soul or person" (169).

Such insights foreshadow Leventhal's affirmation of a transcendent promise. They also explain a more important religious perspective implied in the relationship of the two characters and in Bellow's description of the city. Dostoevsky's major theme in *The Eternal Husband* is the community that Velchaninov and Pavel Pavlovitch discover in the mystery of their roles. Each man, sadist and masochist, adulterer and eternal husband, is enslaved by his own character. At their final meeting Pavel Pavlovitch, married again and cuckold again, finds himself once more in danger of being cuckolded by Velchaninov. Aware that they are still playing out their individual psychologies, the two men are bound by the mystery of their seemingly predestined fates. Leventhal and Allbee in their final meeting feel a similar though more general sense of community. They have both touched bottom, suffering their deepest fears before one another, and this experience gives them a shared sense of the difficulty and "strangeness" of existence. Stripped of rational poses and social protections, both men find themselves thrown back on personal resources, outside Joseph's "wide agreement." They achieve a larger or primitive perspective in which they question not just the social order but the arbitrary arrangements of the physical world. Allbee represents the social ruin which terrifies Leventhal; he represents the "overwhelming human closeness and thickness" of all being, the "innumerable millions, crossing, touching, pressing"; but he also represents an asocial, metaphysical perspective in which man is a victim of the complex physical world (183, 184). It is at the park where he met Allbee that Leventhal, looking at the crowd, is reminded of a story about "Hell cracking open on account of the rage of the god of the sea, and all the souls, crammed together, looking out" (184). Hesitantly realizing that each is an instrument by which the world victimizes the other, Allbee and Leventhal see that they are both victims of the inherent confusion and mystery of existence. Their calm in their final meeting, like that of Dostoevsky's antagonists, is based on this shared perspective: when Allbee confesses that he is now content to be a passenger on the train he hoped to run, Leventhal asks him, now trying to detain him as he now rushes away, "wait a minute, what's your idea of who runs things?" (294)

Leventhal's feeling that he can "smell smoke and feel heat but never see the flames" is a statement of Bellow's dominant effect in *The Victim*. Behind all of the description, conversation, and action lies a sense that there is more, that the "actual" reality is a symptom or sign of something deeper. Allbee and Leventhal fear the elements which victimize man because they imply a meaningless universe, but Bellow himself senses a purpose in the nature of that victimization. Leventhal's world implies what Wilhelm suspects in "Seize the Day," that his mistakes "expressed the very purpose of his life and the essence of his being here. Maybe he was supposed to make them and suffer from them on this earth" (56). Bellow returns to a sense of an unseen power, sometimes explainable, as in the subway door which automatically closes on Leventhal or in the door held closed by Elena's mother, but often unexplainable and more than hypochondria. As his heroes suffer, each feeling like Leventhal that "there was not a single part of him on which the whole world did not press with full weight," they gain a glimpse of a world which is not empty but "full," which is not an open void but a closed and somehow meaningful whole. This may be viewed as a projection of Leventhal's mind, but it is also Bellow's vision of a living, organic universe. In such a world, likening "the mass of passengers" to "a crowd of souls, each concentrating on its destination" is more than metaphor (64). Leventhal's charged, overheated city gives substance to the view that "everything, everything without exception, took place as if within a single soul or person."

That such a possibility exists, that man needs it to exist, and that, as Leventhal says, "tomorrow this would be untenable. 'I won't be able to hold on to it,' " all contribute to man's victimization (169). So too does the presence of the many reasonable and yet contradictory interpretations of Allbee and the world he represents. In one sense the issue of the novel is not whether Leventhal should help Allbee, but where he might find the strength to help or ignore him. When Leventhal thinks that it is necessary to open oneself to others but that "you couldn't find a place in your feelings for everything, or give at every touch like a swinging door," he too is Bellow's dangling hero, withdrawing from and giving himself to the world (98). In another sense, there is no question but that Leventhal should help Allbee. Leventhal is also Bellow's typical hero in that he is called upon to be a good man in the face of great difficulty. Leventhal suffers, like Henderson, from "the good that I would that I do not" (124). Creating heroes who desire or are forced to act compassionately, Bellow tests that compassion by a threatening world. Leventhal is called upon not to be kind or decent, but to be moral—to risk his own interest for the sake of another who is not only obnoxious but who may be beyond help. Leventhal discovers in his difficulty, like the hero of the story "By the Rock Wall," that "everything that was not firm, everything the least bit false, not strict—the being loosely humane, relatively considerate, fairly decent—everything like that was knocked down on the first serious consideration." [10] Whether he is to dispose of Allbee or risk his own security to help him, Leventhal needs the same sense of self as Joseph, one which is "strong in itself" rather than in its social role and which can accept or reject the world as it wills. Leventhal too finds that an externally derived identity is inadequate: the real threat in Allbee's hatred, the fact that his claims are unreasonable, and the fact that the highest morality requests that Leventhal help him—all of these factors raise the issue above our practical social standards and require a morality and strength that lie deeper than the external world. Allbee himself, of course, needs a similar confidence in his identity. In that Leventhal retreats from the world to his secure but limited existence, and Allbee would "be-all,"—asserting an unlimited will—the two characters play out the drama implicit in the boy and the gambler in Bellow's first short story. They also play out the two sides of Joseph's character.[11] And they also suggest, more directly than those previous works, the necessity for—and perhaps the possibility of—an essential self which accepts inevitable victimization because it glimpses something higher.

CHAPTER **4** "LIFE AMONG THE
MACHIAVELLIANS"

Sin has educated Donatello, and elevated him.
Is sin, then, . . . is it, like sorrow, merely
an element of human education, through
which we struggle to a higher and purer state
than we could otherwise have attained?

HAWTHORNE, *The Marble Faun*

As George Grebe in the short story "Looking for Mr. Green" wanders about the "giant raw place" that is Chicago, he feels a "huge energy, an escaped, unattached, unregulated power." He then states an idea important to Bellow's intention in *The Adventures of Augie March:* "Not only must people feel it," he thinks, but "they were compelled to match it. In their very bodies." [1] Grebe associates this energy with "the war of flesh and blood" or the violence and sensuality which Leventhal fears in the city masses. In his first two novels, Bellow examined this war in moral terms, defending subjective value by means of a transcendent vision, but he reversed his tactics in *Augie March.* He sought not to transcend those elements which destroy personality but to meet them on their own terms—to "match" them by the very force, the Whitmanian gusto, of his prose. The best defense is an offense; Bellow attempted to celebrate man and the world by the very qualities his early protagonists abhor. As Irving Kristol says, Bellow wrestled with demons in his first two novels; in *Augie March* he "jumped in their midst, bussed them, and inquired if they had read any good books lately." [2] Having created two characters who were strangers in a frightening world, Bellow turned in 1953 to a hero who joyfully feels at home in a colorful Chicago.

This new approach earned Bellow critical and popular acclaim. His portrayal of Chicago in the thirties caught the spirit of

America in the fifties. To J. B. Priestley, "this is the place, these the people." To Norman Podhoretz, Augie's adventures reflect "the intellectual's joyous [new] sense of connection with the common grain of American life." [3] Augie's happy acceptance of his time and place expresses the acquiescence of the Eisenhower decade at the same time that it breaks through the narrow world of the alienated hero. The "huge energy" which Bellow matches is at once the force of the physical world and the force of society, particularly one that is exploding in population and technology. It is also—in spite of Bellow's use of an earlier setting—the negative force of what many considered the inertia of the fifties, what Bellow himself calls elsewhere "the reign of the fat gods" which "subverts everything good and exalts lies, and . . . wears a crown of normalcy." [4] By portraying a vitality and color that is antithetical to "normalcy" and yet is the very fabric of our nation, Bellow celebrates America at the same time that he rejects false values. While other writers struggled to discover a new ideology, and felt themselves disarmed by the size and lethargy of their culture, Bellow turned from ideology to a world justified in itself. He argued for accommodation not by the usual indirect means of an alienated hero, but by a forthright example of engagement. "Those days," Augie says, "whatever touched me had me entirely" (315). Having progressed from Joseph's rejection of the world to Leventhal's qualified acceptance, Bellow now made another leap, rejecting Flaubertian polish and despair to create a rough-hewed, energetic new world.[5]

If *Augie March* caught the spirit of the fifties, however, it did so by embodying some of that era's difficulties. Norman Podhoretz goes on to say that in "the willed spontaneity of the writing, the abstractness of the hero . . . we can also detect the uncertainty and emotional strain that lurked on the underside of the new optimism." The conflict between Augie's announcement that he will write catch as catch can—promising an episodic novel—and his assumption of moral growth—claiming a *Bildungsroman*—suggests that this "uncertainty" exists in the novel's form. If Bellow worked to contain an unruly story within his planned structure in *The Victim,* he works to impose order upon an ostensibly "open" story in

Augie March. Because it involves Augie's education or change, the question of the novel's form is also the question of Augie's character. Augie presents himself as a man of love open to any and all experience. As Chester Eisinger describes him, he is "an uncommitted wanderer upon the face of the earth, savoring experience for its infinite variety and cherishing his independence to seek it out where he may." But other critics describe a different Augie: they feel that Augie's joy is spurious, that he is not the affirmative hero he appears to be. Augie ventures into the world, but he is not a part of it; his constant movement is an evasion rather than an engagement of life. Podhoretz says that Augie "goes through everything, yet undergoes nothing," and V. S. Pritchett calls Augie "a neutral, the indifferent man." [6] Because there is a close relationship between commitment and characterization, as Robert Penn Warren has pointed out, this issue becomes one of the fullness or "life" of Augie's characterization. Some critics claim that Augie's character is thin because he lacks those commitments which might give it substance.[7]

There are of course many possible answers to this problem. Part of the issue lies in the complexity of Augie's character: he contains "something adoptional" about him at the same time that he is "resistant." "You've got *opposition* in you," Einhorn tells him. "You don't slide through everything. You just make it look so" (117). This ambivalence belongs to all of Bellow's heroes, as we have seen, but it also belongs to the thought of the fifties. The difference of opinion over Augie's character is based in part on the critic's interpretation of "commitment"—an issue still with us. To Eisinger, Augie's lack of a concrete, specific commitment is his glory; Augie is engaged in the broad spectacle of life rather than a small corner of it. To others, engagement means concrete commitment: to talk of "life" or "experience" is too abstract, too easy, too much of a rationale for rejecting what lies at hand. There is a sense in which *Augie March,* like other contemporary novels, pays lip service to engagement but celebrates our real day-dream of invulnerable self-containment. Then too Augie may be neutral precisely because of his health. His claim that it is "enough to be among [the animals], released on the ground as they were in their brook or in their air," is a claim to a connection with the natural world—a major theme in our fiction—but it is also a confession of innocence (330). If Augie embodies the values implied in much of our wasteland literature, including Bellow's first two novels, he may well reveal a potential shortcoming of those values: he is heartless or neutral in the way that all innocence is neutral. He would lack substance as a character in the same way Hawthorne's Donatello does.

The issue of Augie's character is also an aesthetic one, arising, as do other problems in Bellow's fiction, from Bellow's use of point of view. Although *Augie March* is told in the first person, Bellow makes a clear distinction between his narrator and his protagonist. The voice of the novel is not that of the young Augie living his adventures but that of an older man looking back on them. The narrator occasionally identifies with the story, but just as often stands back from it. "I see this now," he will say. "At that time not" (285). When he mentions the young man's absorption with a lover, he complains of his present fatigue: "As I wasn't yet old enough to be tired of confinement to my own sense, I didn't appreciate this enough" (316). In one sense Augie's neutrality is really the narrator's objectivity. He views the adventures in which Augie is immersed with a cool eye that keeps them at a distance. What substance we do find in Augie's character, on the other hand, may be that of the novel's voice. As the spontaneous young protagonist speeds through his adventures, the narrator's comment provides the compassion, the analysis, the learning, and the form which are lacking in the adventures themselves. Except for the last chapters, when the protagonist catches up with the narrator, the episodic novel would belong to the boy who lives the adventures and the *Bildungsroman* would belong to the man who is reliving them.

Our psychology as readers may also be relevant: Augie's world is so intense that we are driven into identifying with whatever self Augie may have. Although all of these approaches to the problems in the novel might be fruitfully developed, I would like to advance still another. Bellow has described *Augie March* as his "favorite fantasy." He had begun a different novel after *The Victim,* entitled "The Crab and the Butterfly," but had found it rough going. "Every time I was depressed while writing the grim one," he says, "I'd treat myself to a fantasy holiday." He completed a hundred thousand words of "The Crab and the Butterfly," but suddenly "felt a great revulsion" and junked it.[8] When we view *Augie March* as Bellow's "favorite fantasy," Bellow's progression from the alienation of his first two novels to the accommodation of his third is not quite what it seems. Bellow jumped into the midst of his demons not because he had worked his way to affirmation, but because he had been unable to. As his world broadened in the first two novels, his sense of evil deepened. Joseph's vague figure of death became the very real Allbee and Joseph's sterile Chicago became Leventhal's terrifying New York. The problems of *Augie March* may be explained by the strain in Bellow's need to take a holiday. Many of Augie's limitations are due to the fact that he is the opposite of Leventhal and Joseph; much of the stylistic excess is due to the effort needed to "match" a world of force. We may also explain the problems by the author's failure to sustain his original tone. Although the change is gradual, and Bellow's attitude is mixed from the very beginning, Bellow shifts in the course of the novel from the externalization of his holiday to an internality similar to that of the earlier novels. As Augie's spontaneity and joy become circumspection and complaint, he passes from a neutrality required by the logic of Bellow's original premise to a man painfully engaged with the world: he shifts from a young man who dissolves himself in the external world to an adult who turns inward and discovers himself—and gains substance as a character.[9] This is to say that *Augie March* is a *Bildungsroman* after all, except that Bellow's shift seems unplanned. "One of my great pleasures," Bellow has said, "was in having the ideas taken away from me, as it were, by the characters." [10] One of these characters is the narrator, from whom—since the novel is his memoir—we expect a consistent moral vision. It is he who insists on an external joy, even though he has lived through the experiences which qualify it.

We may dismiss this incongruity as a necessary convention, or argue that the narrator relives his life, assuming his earlier attitudes, but the logic of the memoir points to a shift in Bellow's position. That Bellow took a holiday, that his art changes, and that the novel reverses in theme all suggest that Bellow drifted back in the course of writing to an internal, moral view of the forces he tried to match.

Bellow's need for a fantasy holiday is illustrated by "Trip to Galena," a chapter of "The Crab and the Butterfly" which he published as a short story.[11] Because its protagonist faces up to issues which Joseph and Leventhal evade, the chapter is in many ways a culmination of the labor Bellow left uncompleted in his first two novels. The story consists of a conversation on a fire escape between Weyl, the protagonist, and a humane, level-headed man named Mr. Scampi. Weyl's sister Fanny had tried to save him from his disreputable bachelorhood by taking him to visit the home of her new fiancé, a pretentious lawyer from Galena, Illinois. The trip, Weyl tells Scampi, was a disaster. Critical of the Neffs, disappointed in Fanny, and angry with the plot to marry him off to one of the family's marriageable daughters, Weyl had suddenly left. He had found there he says only "dislike, distaste, people unable to stand themselves or others; and, at the same time, practical organization, prudence, selfishness" (792). For Fanny to join these people is an abject surrender. "I demoted her a few grades in my mind for going on with Herb Neff and all that middling and ordinary stuff," he says. "She had the means to play for the highest stakes, to do and be the exceptional, live in the high quality" (791). Rejecting Fanny's retreat to a secure but unhappy existence, Weyl insists that one must embrace either the possibility or the futility of life. "Either of the extremes is worth campaigning for," he says, "but holding to the middle line is shameful" (792).

Although Weyl does all of the talking, Bellow's story lies not in Weyl's description of the trip but in Scampi's reaction to it. Like

James, Bellow makes the discussion of an event an event in itself; as Weyl discusses Fanny, Scampi—whose point of view is that of the story—struggles to understand Weyl. The story moves increasingly inward. At the beginning of their talk Scampi wants "to smooth his way . . . and be as little as possible the passive, profiting listener," but he is soon appalled by Weyl's uncontrolled labor. Weyl "was moving into something necessitous and compulsive"; Scampi "expected something truly extraordinary." When Weyl makes an embarrassing confidence Scampi thinks "here came the thing he was compelled to talk about," but then sees that "there was still more and more to be brought into place, bigger and heavier pieces of masonry." Because Scampi doesn't see Weyl's point, or how his ideas "have any practical bearing on Weyl's relations with his sister," the issue of the story becomes what Weyl means and whether his intensity is justified. Bellow raises an implicit conflict between Scampi's calm rationality and Weyl's intense emotionalism. After describing his trip, Weyl launches into a lecture about the amorality of biological impulse. "If a woman puts on the garter-belt of a woman [who was] murdered," he says, "and if it becomes the comfort of her body . . . you can't reproach the body for being what it is or ask why it lacks the germ of justice." So too with the shoes of a murdered man: "What's that, treachery from the feet?" Scampi sees the truth of these comments, but he is puzzled by Weyl's illogical suffering: "what was the outcry about. 'Why does he mix it all together?'" Scampi "could not see that there was any normal connection between Weyl's personal history and the feet and belts."

Weyl "mixes it all together" because of the intensity of his effort to accept the violence and sensuality feared by Joseph and Leventhal. Fanny had just ended an affair with a cheap racketeer, he says, and he suspects that "she threatened to kill him." Asking the same question as Gooley MacDowell[12]—"if a good idea isn't also a law of the body, then what is it to us?"—Weyl seeks to reconcile Fanny's potential for the "highest quality" with the biological amorality that is natural to her. Like many of Bellow's fictional women, Fanny combines great ability with a willful and

sensual nature: Weyl seeks to settle—once and for all—the problem Augie faces in Thea and Herzog in Madeleine. But Weyl is
intense for still another reason; at the end of the story—its climax
—Bellow provides another, the largest of all pieces of masonry. In
doing so he justifies Weyl's brooding intensity, answers Scampi's
questions, and provides a clue as to why he abandoned "The Crab
and the Butterfly." Weyl himself had once tried to kill someone.
During the war, he says, he had smashed a bottle over a stranger's
head. He had been sober; he had never seen the man before; his
act had been one of pure malevolence. As he confesses, Scampi
notes, he wears a "depressed, iron, dull look," and "it was apparent
that he was gruesomely suffering."

Weyl confesses what Bellow's previous—and immediately suc-
ceeding—heroes cannot face, the issue toward which I would guess
Bellow was working all along. Joseph's fear of the ancient figure
and Leventhal's fear of Allbee are really fear of what they suspect
in themselves. Both feel tainted, both stand accused by others of
malice, and both disclaim any fault whatsoever. Weyl, in contrast,
is painfully self-accused. He is the only one of Bellow's heroes
before Henderson who faces up to a personal capacity for evil. He
is also the only one—to judge by this chapter—Bellow does not
treat with irony. Because the rest of "The Crab and the Butterfly"
is unfinished and unpublished, we can only speculate as to why
Bellow abandoned it. The ambition of Weyl's struggle and the
sympathy with which Bellow treats it, however, suggest that Bellow's revulsion with the novel was partly due to his thematic ambition. Weyl claims that the chaos of modern times has pushed us
increasingly into the "open of our natures, nearer and nearer to the
original personal quality in people. That's bringing the fight pretty
close to the bull, it's full of risks; and if we're murdered it will be
because the original nature is murderous." Weyl attempts to define
the "original nature" of man, and in doing so hopes to prove that it
is not murderous; he seeks "something redeeming in the original
thing and a reason for all the old talk about nobility." Bellow's
other heroes feel that some sort of evil exists and yearn for "something redeeming," but they look to the external world as the

source of both evil and hope. Weyl, fulfilling Joseph's need, recognizes evil and seeks redemption within the basic, essential self.
While the other heroes never really act upon their needs, moreover,
Bellow makes Weyl's conversation an exploration of the self. As
he talks Weyl returns to "the original personal quality," creating
what Scampi calls a "primitive root occasion." Weyl seemed "taken
backward in form and voice, difficult to hear and see." His emotions are "a primitive breaker that the civilized bather is finally too
fragile for." Scampi sees Weyl's self-control "come and go, deliberately, heavily, like a heron visiting a pond, until all at once it
seemed to fly powerfully away and leave a space that anything
might occupy."

The opening pages of *Augie March,* in contrast, present a
comfortable antithesis to Weyl's intense internal struggle. By writing a picaresque novel Bellow could create a large number of epi-
sodes without worrying about thematic problems. Augie like Weyl
rejects the middle class, but he feels no compulsion to justify himself; he is too busy living to worry about the "original nature."
Again like Weyl, he refuses to settle down in Galena, but he feels
none of Weyl's bitter isolation and disappointment; he is free to
wander through all parts of our culture. As the hero of an episodic
novel, Augie needs little internal character development: taking a
"holiday" from the psychological and thematic problems of the
self, Bellow affirms the world by celebrating the color and vitality
of many different scenes and characters, all interesting for their own
sake. Augie in fact revels in the very elements that Weyl—and
Bellow's other protagonists—find disturbing.[13] If each of the other
heroes suffers before an Allbee or a Tamkin, Augie finds his youth
among a dozen such people—his "Life Among the Machiavellians,"
as Bellow considered naming the novel—a happy, carefree one.
Grandma Lausch, "a pouncy old hawk of a Bolshevik" through
whose "dark little gums . . . guile, malice and command issued,"
sets the pattern of all the Machiavellians in her rule of the March
family (7). Her influence on Augie, and that of his militant older
brother, Simon, is reflected in her comment that "the more you love
people the more they'll mix you up. A child loves, a person re-

spects. Respect is better than love" (9). Leventhal hates Elena's willful mother, and Weyl struggles with the "desperate mankind without feelings" described by Mrs. Lausch, but Augie loves Grandma—who is actually just a boarder in their home—and listens to her lectures with good humor.

Augie's real allegiance, he says, belongs to another influence in his family—and another element which disturbs Weyl—his mother and idiot brother Georgie. Mentally retarded and growing blind, abandoned by the laundry driver who fathered her children, Mrs. March suffers a "love-originated servitude" with simple serenity. Georgie is "chaste, lummoxy, caressing, gentle and diligent" (9). Leventhal fears the city and watches himself for signs of his mother's madness; Weyl broods over his sister and labors to keep from "blowing his top." Augie March—a bastard—boasts of his sensuousness and cheerfully accepts the mental weakness of his family: he himself, he confesses, is not particularly level-headed. Surrounded by colorful lechers, receiving a trip to a whorehouse for his high school graduation present, Augie happily accepts the "strange things, terrible things" that Leventhal fears in the city masses and Weyl suspects in his sister.

Bellow's celebration of these qualities, and the implications of that celebration, are reflected in his style. Just as Augie accepts all people and experience, so Bellow piles detail upon detail and mixes poolroom slang with erudite quotation. Bellow's metaphors especially provide the selfish Machiavellians with vitality and nobility. Bellow punctures the Machiavellians' denial of their physical existence by comparing them to animals. As the cripple Einhorn attempts to "suck a pierced egg," he illustrates "something humanly foxy, paw-handled, hungry above average need" (68). When Grandma Lausch leaves her room she comes "along the old paths of the house . . . where the trail changed to brown in the linoleum, a good part of this the work of her own feet and flint-colored slippers going steadily along this fox run for the better part of ten years" (55). To this recognition of man's animal existence, Bellow adds a claim to man's greatness. Augie's stated view that we're not "at the dwarf end of all times" or "beings of a different kind" from those of the heroic ages—the basis of his inclusion of Einhorn in the same category with Caesar—is borne out by many metaphors based on the grandeur of government (60). Describing Grandma's loss of influence over Simon and himself, Augie proclaims that "new days were pushing out the last of an old regime, the time when counselors and ministers see the finish of their glory, and Switzers and Praetorian Guards get restless" (55). He tells us that "when you believed you had tracked Einhorn through his acts and doings and were about to capture him . . . here he came from a new direction—a governor in a limousine, with state troopers around him, dominant and necessary, everybody's lover" (83).

In that these metaphors look to our life as creatures and as kings, they reflect the dichotomy between the biological and the Machiavellian implicit in Mama and Grandma. They also reflect the thematic implications of Bellow's holiday. To define the family in terms of biology or politics is to define a family based on principles other than love. Likened to animals, the Machiavellians are creatures of appetite; likened to heads of state, they are . . . Machiavellians. Einhorn tells Augie that he "should choose or seize with force . . . should have the strength of voice to make other voices fall silent—the same principle for persons as for peoples, parties, states" (183). Even the influence of Mama, ostensibly opposed to this view, matches the physical world in that her love is largely instinctual or physical. Biology and politics reduce the individual to a pawn of the external world—the fear of Leventhal and Allbee—and define a world of pure force or power. Instead of the "slight but continuous brushing and quivering of the dynamo" in "Trip to Galena," Augie March is immersed in "a tremendous high tension and antagonistic energy asked to lie still that couldn't lie still" (127). Augie's celebration of his society as "labor fodder and secretarial forces . . . an immense sampling of a tremendous host, the multitudes of holy writ, begotten by West-moving, factor-shoved parents" replaces Weyl's moral struggle with a catalogue in which mankind is merely a physical force (125). Supported by Bellow's cultural references, which refer almost exclusively to the coercive and the violent, such catalogues define the moral vision of the book.[14] Bellow matches the raw energy of Chicago by accepting the naturalistic world of power as not only real but right—a moral referent. When Augie is beaten by an anti-Semitic gang, among whom is his best friend, he dismisses it "as needing no more special explanation than the stone-and-bat wars of the street gangs or the swarming on a fall evening of parish punks to rip up fences, screech and bawl at girls, and beat up strangers."

But Bellow matches force in the novel in still another, contradictory way. When Augie says "now I know it wasn't so necessary to lie," and adds, "that maybe one didn't need to be keen didn't occur to us; it was a contest," he suggests that the world is not as formidable as Grandma and Einhorn claim (4). I think Bellow would like to demonstrate that a helpless good may endure because it is a power in its own right. To the extent that Augie's compassion is a biological instinct, Bellow's characterization implies that love is a physical force, perhaps capable of matching—and surmounting—the "terrible forces." The creaturely affection of Mama and Augie ties them to a naturalistic world, but it also raises the possibility that love is rooted in the physical. Augie's adventures prove that one must be keen indeed, heavily qualifying this idea, but his character demonstrates what Weyl would prove, that the generous and compassionate are part of the "original thing" and thus, as Gooley MacDowell says, "a law of the body."

Bellow's adoption of the form and spirit of the picaresque novel in *Augie March* admirably suited his celebration of force. As Robert Heilman suggests in his essay on *The Confessions of Felix Krull*,[15] the techniques of the picaresque novel minimize the reader's sympathy for the rogue's victims—making acceptance of a cruel world possible. The novelist precludes reader identification with the victims by sketching them vaguely or with the broad strokes of caricature. He maintains a swift pace from episode to episode so that the implications of the rogue's acts never sink in. He also creates a population that desires or deserves to be swindled: the rogue merely satisfies the victim's unconscious masochistic desires, as in *Felix Krull,* or turns the victim's greed or cruelty upon himself, converting chicanery into crude justice. Viewing his characters from the outside, where they become lost in a multitude of people, the picaresque novelist rejects the fine moral distinctions of the private self to find his perspective and value in the broad spectacle of man.

Bellow's use of these techniques to match the world of force raises still another reason for the difficulties in Augie's character. To be at home in a destructive world the *picaro* must, like Arthur Seaton in *Saturday Night and Sunday Morning,* be hard-boiled or neutral. Thus Augie is committed to an abstraction and is resistant. He searches, he says, for "a fate good enough"—a search that keeps him aloof from the world. But as a vulnerable, loving heir to Mama and Georgie, Augie is really the opposite of the *picaro*. It is not Augie who lives by his wits but the Machiavellians. Good-hearted, spontaneous, and vulnerable, Augie is in fact more of a traveling victim than rogue. His character is thin because Bellow was compelled to minimize Augie's sensitivity to the world of force if Augie was to remain an affirmative character. Bellow does this by using the techniques directed at the *picaro*'s victims on Augie himself. Augie's character is shadowy at the beginning—it is not Augie but rather the Machiavellians who enjoy sharply defined identities. Augie shifts from adventure to adventure with a swiftness that precludes any brooding over his hard knocks. So too with Augie's simplicity, his ability to lose himself in others, even what one critic has labeled his masochism—Bellow early in the novel dissolves the selfhood of his protagonist in the broad spectacle of Chicago. He succeeds in creating a hero who feels little pain, but he also gives the impression that Augie feels nothing at all. Augie himself fits a comment Marcus Klein makes about Bellow's style: by accepting everything, Augie really accepts nothing.[16]

This strategy permits Bellow to begin the novel on a note of joy. Augie recognizes evil—the beatings he receives, the selfishness of Grandma Lausch, the atrocities that made an atheist out of a local junk collector—but he sees evil externally, its horror diluted by a colorful mass of detail. But Augie finds it increasingly difficult to dismiss evil as a colorful external.[17] His resilience is tested in the first half of the novel by increasingly heavy blows, and he himself comes to see that he is a traveling victim. He lives, like Joseph, in a society in which people have gone underground. Fearful of the death or determinism inherent in physical existence, they are too self-absorbed to offer him the love he seeks. They are, as Bellow wrote in 1954, "people testing to find whether they can eat without tasting, view without suffering, make love without feeling and exist between winning and losing in an even state of potentiality."[18] Each builds a particular version of reality in place of the physical one he denies, and views Augie as an adjunct to it. *Augie March* and another distinguished novel of the decade, Ralph Ellison's *Invisible Man,* define a culture in which the generous or the human is lost in desperate ideology. While Ellison's protagonist is invisible because of race and institutions, Augie is invisible because of private ideals. What all this means, Augie says, "is not a single Tower of Babel plotted in common, but hundreds of thousands of separate beginnings, the length and breadth of America" (152).

Grandma Lausch, the first of four Machiavellians who dominate Augie in the first half of the novel, is typical of them all in her destruction of Augie's childhood world. She decides that the idiot Georgie must enter the state home. Her decision is sensible in view of the March's poverty and Georgie's maturity, but it also echoes some of the implications of Benjy's internment in *The Sound and the Fury.* No Dilsey (unlike Mama, who is), Grandma is all too ready to be practical. "There still remains the satisfaction this gave her," Augie says. She feels that Georgie's fate somehow justifies her stern ideas, and even makes it an act of revenge—"her rebuke in full for all our difficulty, disobedience, waywardness, and unmindfulness of our actual condition" (50–51). Like Faulkner, Bellow uses the idiot to suggest the basic physical self which is important to the family. "There was something missing" after Grandma's expulsion of Georgie, Augie says, and she loses her power over the two boys (55). It was almost "as though it were care of Georgie that had been the main basis of household union and now everything was disturbed." He and Simon drift off to the

Chicago streets to avoid the "dinkier, darker, smaller" house in which "once shiny and venerated things [were] losing their attraction and richness and importance" (58).

Augie is also deprived of the home he finds working for William Einhorn. Described as "the first superior man I knew," Einhorn is courageous, brilliant, ambitious and petty. He turns from large real estate deals to cheating the phone company, from lecturing on the vanity of appetite to visiting houses of prostitution. Married and crippled as he is, mounted serenely on Augie's back, he sails among the girls with a crisp dignity. Augie's job consists of aiding Einhorn in the simple physical tasks—a job the care of Georgie prepared him for—and he comes to admire Einhorn's victory over his handicap. But Einhorn's selfishness and spite destroy Augie's view of him as a substitute father: because there is something "adoptional" about Augie, Einhorn pointedly reminds him he is not one of the family. "It sometimes got my goat, he and Mrs. Einhorn made so sure I knew my place" (72). A year later, when Augie visits Einhorn to ask for advice, he finds him "too busy to give me his attention" (155).

Augie's colorful childhood breaks apart during the period he serves Einhorn. Grandma Lausch moves into a home, Einhorn's father dies, leaving the estate in confusion, and the Depression ruins Einhorn and eliminates Augie's job. It is while he is with the next Machiavellian, however, that Augie's frame of mind begins to change. Augie gets a job in a fashionable sporting goods store in Evanston and becomes the center of the "pale-fire concentration" of the owner's wife, Mrs. Renling. She seeks to polish the young clerk into a gentleman. "I'll make you perfect," she tells him, "completely perfect" (130). Under her tutelage Augie revels in a world of expensive dress and upperclass manners. "Something of a footman, something of a nephew, passing around candy dishes, opening ginger ale in the pantry," he waits on his benefactress as he had waited on Einhorn, and even takes a trip with her to Benton Harbor, Michigan (132). There he falls in love with an heiress, Esther Fenchel, and receives his first bitter shock. When she suspects he is Mrs. Renling's gigolo, Augie feels himself "trampled all over my body by a thing some way connected by weight with my mother and my brother George." For a few moments his glory becomes his corruption and he is Bellow's old hero—"as though," he continues, "run over by the beast that kept them steady company and that I thought I was safely away from" (142). The feeling passes, and when Mrs. Renling proposes that he become her son and heir, safe from the "outcast and the ruined" she vividly describes, he refuses. Although Mrs. Renling seems the opposite of Einhorn, offering him family and fortune, she is really the same. She really wants him "to consolidate what she affirmed she was" (151). She offers love and home to an object, not a person; "I had family enough to suit me and history to be loyal to," Augie says, "not as though I had been gotten off of a stock pile" (153).

From this point on Augie's rapport with the world disintegrates, with two steps backward for each one forward. It is during the breakup with Mrs. Renling that Augie is ignored by Einhorn. When Augie visits Grandma in the home, she doesn't remember him. He struggles to make a living in a depressed Chicago, unsuccessfully peddles a smelly rubber paint, and then joins a hoodlum on a trip to Buffalo in a stolen car. He barely misses involvement in a shooting, is stranded without money in upper New York, and spends a night in a Detroit jail. When he returns to Chicago, he finds that Simon, having troubles of his own, has moved their mother into a dingy room. Although Augie retains some buoyancy —telling us while in jail that he "didn't get any great shock from this of personal injustice"—his mood begins to darken (174). "There haven't been civilizations without cities," he says. "But what about cities without civilizations? An inhuman thing, if possible, to have so many people together who beget nothing on one another" (159). He has learned that "there is a darkness. It is for everyone." He himself is immersed in a "mud-sprung, famine-knifed, street-pounding, war-rattled, difficult, painstaking, kicked in the belly, grief and cartilage mankind." And it, in turn, is "under a coal-sucking Vesuvius of chaos smoke," or "inside a heaving Cal-

cutta midnight" (175). When a friend tells Augie to get an education, Augie complains that "there'd still be black forces waiting to
give me the boot" (189).

This mood colors Augie's life with the fourth Machiavellian,
and remarkably so. Augie's rejection of Grandma, Einhorn and
Mrs. Renling had been a rejection of their sterile worlds. Searching
for love, he had sought an equivalent to his original family, a goal
fulfilled when Simon makes a comeback by marrying for money.
Simon recruits Augie to help him run a coal-yard—his wedding
present. He also wants his brother to get in "on a good thing" and
marry Lucy Magnus, his sister-in-law. Augie objects to the calcula-
tion involved, but he loves his brother, and the Magnus family
might provide the community so far denied him. But Simon is even
more enslaved by his dominant idea than Augie's previous patrons,
for he has to live up to certain expectations. "He had his pockets
full of money as an advance on his promised ability to make a rich
man of himself and now had to deliver" (224). The price he pays
is "the task of doing bold things with an unhappy gut," and the cost
is shown in "the mental wounds of his face, the death of its color,
and the near-insanity of his behavior" (217, 226). During his busy
life with Simon and Lucy, Augie makes friends with a waitress
named Mimi Villars who is dominated by her idea of love. In surrendering herself to it she becomes pregnant and asks Augie, who
is merely a friend, to accompany her during an abortion. Augie
obliges, but the Magnus family learns enough of the details through
a third party to suspect him of being the father. Lucy chooses to
keep her inheritance by staying with the outraged family. To
Augie's horror, so does Simon. "This is where I shake you, Augie,"
he shouts, "before you do worse to me" (275). "Scorched, bitter,
foul, and violent," the good-hearted young man finds himself deprived of community once more (281).

"You do all you can to humanize and familiarize the world,"
Augie tells us, "and suddenly it becomes more strange than ever."
Our way of humanizing the world is to create a "small circle that
encompasses two or three heads in the same history of love," but
it is impossible for us to maintain it. "Try and stay, though, inside.

See how long you can" (285). With this summary of Augie's early experience, Bellow evidently concludes the part he once considered publishing as Volume One.[19] Augie's disillusion with Chicago is now crystallized by the injustice he sees as a labor organizer. When the professional thugs of a rival union give him the second beating of his life, his reaction is far from light-hearted. With "the dry snot of fear in [his] blood-clotted nose," he is overcome with disgust. He is "harrowed by . . . hate" for Chicago (308). And he finds himself very much in love with Thea Fenchel, Esther's sister, who asks him to go to Mexico with her. He accepts her offer.

Augie's hatred for the city and his brooding reaction to his beating suggest the changes that occur in his character. He now feels and judges his experience. This provides him with the self he lacks earlier. Bellow shifts from Augie's early joy to his later disillusionment and from the Machiavellians as a center of attention to Augie himself. He also becomes increasingly concerned with Augie's inner life. Bellow's description of Augie's life with the Coblins in the second chapter had focused almost exclusively upon the colorful family. When Augie visits the Coblins again in Chapter Twelve, they are merely a background for his despair. Augie chats with them, but spends most of his visit brooding as he stares out of the window: we are given his thoughts rather than a description of his surroundings. When Mrs. Coblin gives Augie some photographs to look at, he glances at them, he says, "only to turn my eyes at last again to the weather" (284).

This shift partially explains the dissatisfaction many feel with the Mexican episode. In the first half of the book Bellow relies on the momentum of style and invention to carry the story forward. The foreshadowing that he gives at the head of each chapter belongs to the narrator rather than the adventures, and is lost in a plethora of detail. By the beginning of Chapter Fourteen, however, Bellow has adopted a different view of Augie and a different approach to the novel. Bellow begins the Mexican adventure with Augie's own warning about the future—revealing a reversal in his character. Committed to another for the first time, Augie confesses that his alliance with Thea fills him with fear. He worries over "how I was abandoning some mighty old protections which now stood empty" (316). Uneasy over the fact that "the unit of humanity should maybe be not one but two," Augie fears that "what happened to her had to happen to me too, necessarily. This was scary" (323).

As he and Thea drive deep into Mexico, Augie discovers that he has reason to fear. Mexico too trembles with a frightening force, but it is now part of nature rather than an industrial city. Augie feels the sky grow in intensity: "it held back an element too strong for life . . . the flamy brilliance of blue stood off this menace and sometimes, like a sheath or silk membrane, showed the weight it held in sags" (338). Thea—the most open of all the Machiavellians in her obsession with force—hopes to match this environment with a primitive venture: she trains an eagle to hunt rare Mexican lizards. Augie joins her project out of love for her, but he also realizes "how ancient it was, the kind of ambition that was involved or the aspect of game or hazard" (344). He comes closer to primitive force than he cares to, for while hunting he is kicked in the head by a falling horse. "It takes some of us a long time to find out what the price is of being in nature, and what the facts are about your tenure," he remarks after the accident. He then suggests an opposition between society and truth: "How long it takes depends on how swiftly the social sugars dissolve" (362).

Augie also discovers that he has reason to worry about his "old protections." He too, like Weyl, is not the man he thought he was—a discovery that destroys the identity that supported him. The eagle proves to be a coward, and Augie and Thea drift apart, Thea to the hunting of snakes and Augie to a brooding convalescence among the expatriates in town. When Augie spends a night on a mountainside making love to Stella, another beautiful woman, Thea breaks with him and Augie suddenly confronts the truth about his impulsive nature. Sick with guilt, he sees the justice of Thea's charge that "love would be strange and foreign to you no matter which way it happened, and maybe you just don't want it" (396).

"Me, love's servant?" he cries. "I wasn't at all!" (401) Instead of being with Mama and Georgie against the Machiavellians, he had been "trying to recruit other people to . . . sustain him in his make-believe" (402). He sees with horror that he "wasn't a bit goodhearted or affectionate," and that his "aim of being simple was just a fraud" (401).[20] He had in fact used love to flee the world he had never really accepted. "Whoever would give me cover from this mighty free-running terror and wild cold of chaos I went to," he says, "and therefore to temporary embraces. It wasn't very courageous" (403). He had fled to Simon and Lucy after suffering isolation and near starvation; he had fled to Thea from the agony of his beating. No longer the happy hero of engagement, he now sees that he had fled to Stella from the difficult love of Thea.

After this discovery, which is the emotional climax of the book, both Augie and the novel go limp.[21] When Thea refuses to rejoin Augie, Bellow lays the foundation for a plot in which Augie would protect Trotsky. "But it fell through," Augie says of the venture, "and when it did I was very glad" (418). Augie mopes about Mexico and then drifts back to Chicago. In one sense this change of pace is a needed relief from Augie's intense break up with Thea and is analogous to the last chapter of *The Victim*. It derives from the rhythm of Bellow's imagination, in which he builds to a scene of violence followed by one of purgation or exhaustion. But Bellow's new tone also reflects the fact that *The Adventures of Augie March* is a changed book. Augie's recognition that he is not a man of love drives him back upon himself, where he too, as he says of Georgie, makes "the struggle that we make if we consent to live. Just as though, the time for it coming round, we left what company we were in and went privately to take a few falls with our own select antagonist in his secret room" (419). Like Bellow's other heroes, Augie broods over his past mistakes. He sees that he had used Stella to protect himself from Thea; he sees what a friend in Mexico had tried to tell him, "that I couldn't be hurt enough by the fate of other people." He now sees that his commitment to "possibility" had been no commitment at all: "Nobody gets out of these pains like a pilgrim, looking at temples and docks and smoking cigarettes past the bone heaps of history . . . there where people stayed at home and caught it in the neck" (453). No longer a larky young man in search of adventure, Augie yearns not for a Machiavellian who can love but the ability within himself.

This insight and struggle give Augie an inner life and a substantial identity. In Chicago we surprisingly learn that Augie is stingy. He is guarded with Simon, misrepresents a car he sells—for profit rather than a lark—and proves himself capable of bearing a grudge all along. "No one had been good enough for them," he thinks while visiting the Einhorns. "Now maybe was my chance to pass them by" (430). He feels toward the city what Bellow himself now felt, that "in its repetition it exhausted your imagination" (458). Complaining that "you're nothing here. Nothing," he confesses an alienation similar to Joseph's and Leventhal's (459). He is also like them in his glimpse of a transcendent reality—one which he claims has changed his life and which qualifies Bellow's celebration of the world. Augie discovers, he says, "the axial lines of life, with respect to which you must be straight or else your existence is merely clownery, hiding tragedy." It has been his continual movement which has kept him from these Emersonian lines: "When striving stops, there they are as a gift." At the "axis" of reality, the lines are the center in which the physical and the spiritual coalesce, reducing man's dependence on the world. With the lines "all noise and grates, distortion, chatter, distraction, effort, superfluity, passed off like something unreal." Because they are the "oldest knowledge, older than the Euphrates, older than the Ganges," and because by their means "life can come together again and man be regenerated," Augie feels hope for his own regeneration (454). If one can remain true to these lines, he will have the inner strength that all of Bellow's heroes seek: "even his pains will be joy if they are true, even his helplessness will not take away his power, even wandering will not take him away from himself, even the big social jokes and hoaxes need not make him ridiculous" (455).

Because the lines offer him a sense of autonomy, Augie claims that he can now live truly in the world. The vision is what he had sought all along—and what Bellow's narrative had implicitly promised—the revelation which offers "a fate good enough." Because the lines justify Augie's rejection of the social world and imply that a metaphysical purpose lies within the physical, they might well supply the novel's climax. But Bellow dismisses the vision, perhaps because it is sudden or inconsistent with his original celebration of force.

Having achieved his revelation, Augie is like the other heroes in his flight from the internal self. Joseph and Leventhal retreat from the world, but they also withdraw from their internal being: they live in the narrow thread of consciousness between the awesome reality outside and the even more frightening reality deep within. "Know thyself!" Allbee shouts at Leventhal. "Everybody knows but nobody wants to admit" (227). If Augie had fled to "temporary embraces" to avoid the world's terror, he had also fled to an external reality to avoid facing his inner being: he has almost no inner life earlier in the novel because his adventures are an evasion of that identity. He claims in Mexico that he "wanted another chance" and tells himself that he "must try to be brave again," but he runs from himself and his vision (403). World War II breaks out right after Augie feels the axial lines and "overnight," he says, "I had no personal notions at all. . . . It was just the war I cared about and I was on fire." Viewing himself as a man of sympathy and courage, he screams at newsreels, makes speeches against the enemy, and undergoes a hernia operation to qualify for service. The narrator—the older voice which now expresses Bellow's irony—realizes that this patriotism is another escape from himself. "Well," he says, "what you terribly need you take when you get the chance" (457). Having achieved the means of transcending the world, Augie throws himself into the world to flee himself.

Bellow develops Augie's ironic self-defeat in the young man's marriage to Stella, the girl in Mexico. Having met her again and fallen in love while training for the merchant marine, Augie ignores her repeated warnings. When she tries to tell him "all she could about herself," he is "just like royalty and disposed of all matters with a word" (476). When she confesses that she is not a hundred percent honest, he answers "she must be one hundred and ten, two hundred" (473). When a mutual friend tells Augie several stories about untruthful wives in a conversation about Stella, Augie asks him "how are these stories supposed to apply, just now," before his marriage, but lets the hint pass (483). Having admitted that he fled to love from the world, Augie now sees no truth in Stella's warning that "you want all your troubles to be over all of a sudden and you're so anxious for it you may be making a mistake" (474). Her warning is fulfilled, for Augie later learns that in his obsession with the external he has married the external woman. Stella's inner life is completely her own, he says: she "refuses me—for the time being, anyway—the most important things I ask of her" (522).

Bellow rounds out the novel with two self-contained chapters which portray contrasting Machiavellians. Both Mintouchian, a wealthy lawyer who befriends Augie, and Basteshaw, an eccentric scientist with whom Augie is shipwrecked, are extreme, Mintouchian in his ideas and Basteshaw in his actions. They also form an extreme and now central contrast between the internal and the external. Mintouchian's specialty is "secrets"—the hidden knowledge of the inner man. Although he takes the harshest view of human nature of all the Machiavellians, he is the most serene. There is no real fidelity, he tells Augie, and all love is adultery. Everyone, "in inner consciousness, which is outlaw and accepts no check," is a Machiavellian. "What of it? Life is possible anyhow. Except that even legitimate and reasonable things have to come through this Mongolia, or clear-light desert minus trees" (480). Because the human genius is "devoted to lying and seeming what you are not," the real truth lies within, contrary to appearance. It is this truth of the self rather than of environment which determines our fate. "You are the author of your death," he tells Augie. "What is the weapon? The nails and hammer of your character" (484).

Although Augie rejects this view at the time, it is close to Bellow's own. Augie had not been the man he appeared to be, and his failure with Thea had been a failure within himself. And in the next chapter, the most violent of all, Augie echoes Mintouchian's remarks. Now married, Augie ships out in the merchant marine. When his ship is torpedoed, he finds himself alone with what can only be termed the ultimate Machiavellian. Although he insanely claims omniscience, Basteshaw too speaks many of Bellow's ideas. Everyone searches for what Augie has sought, the "assurance of a fate worth suffering for," and almost everyone suffers from "blindness to life, secession, unreceptivity, a dull wall of anxious, overprotected flesh"—the Galena that outrages Weyl (503, 509). But Basteshaw's solution is a burlesque of the assumptions with which Bellow began the novel. Before the nightmare of mass life, Basteshaw proclaims an aggressive optimism: he had wanted to be, he says, a Renaissance cardinal. "Vigorous. Without embarrassment. Happy as a god" (503). If Augie finds peace by looking out as a creature, Basteshaw goes him one better, emulating the spontaneity and amorality of the cells. "The complex organisms get bored," he says, but "the cells have the will to persist in their essence" (505). Basteshaw too dismisses evil as an external, and his plan to eradicate it by a serum that cures boredom reduces such materialism and optimism to absurdity. When he asks Augie to drift to the Canary Islands where they can continue his research in spite of the war, Augie turns him down in terms similar to Mintouchian's. "No one will be a poet or saint because you fool with him," he says. "When you come right down to it, I've had trouble enough becoming what I already am, by nature" (509–10). Basteshaw then overpowers Augie and ties him up. When he falls ill, Augie frees himself to once again nurse a Machiavellian enemy.

In the final chapter—Augie having hailed a ship and survived the war—Bellow presents a nostalgic, brooding hero who has failed in his search for a "fate good enough." Eager to serve humanity, Augie makes his living by bribing European officials in order to sell surplus pharmaceutical goods on the black market. He has decided that love and home alone are a worthwhile fate, but he is deprived of both by Stella's obsession with a previous lover: she insists upon working as an actress in order to prove herself independent of the man who rejected her. Her fondness for her husband is overshadowed by her involvement with the past. "I don't want to give a false impression of one hundred per cent desperation," Augie says, but as he speaks his voice cracks with disappointment (526). He has learned of his wife's lover from a third party, has confronted her with his knowledge, and has discovered that she had lied to him again. When he tries to bring things out into the open, he is relegated to the painful role of confidant: "She had to harrow his memory over and over," he tells us, "and in so doing she dug me up considerably too" (527). Traveling about Europe by himself, alone even when with Stella in their Paris apartment, Augie is, as Weyl puts it, "bored sick . . . as anyone gets, crawling around on the surface of life by himself" (781). Like Joseph, he writes to save himself: "I have written out these memoirs of mine," he says, "since, as a traveling man, traveling by myself, I have lots of time on my hands" (519). The happy-go-lucky hero and colorful Chicago of *Augie March* have really been an older man's antidote to despair.

Because Augie's new maturity reverses the novel's original premise, creating the same conflict that exists in the other novels, Augie's development is more than a young man's education. The shorter sentences and paragraphs, the fewer allusions and metaphors, and the now painful internal focus of the last chapter reveal a shift in Bellow's art as well as in his theme. In a sense Bellow's fantasy turned into a nightmare. Augie is a good man tested by hostile forces, like all of Bellow's heroes, but if his goodness is biological—a morality rooted in physical impulse—he is finally as oppressed by the physical and the instinctual as Leventhal. He feels, as he said earlier, "as if I had been carrying something with special sacred devotedness and it had spilled and scalded me" (144–45). In another sense *Augie March* begins as a naturalistic novel and ends as a personalist one, for Bellow assumes an environmental determinism which he subsequently rejects in favor of the unconditioned self. Augie—and Bellow—had originally assumed that a "man's character is his fate," telling us that "all the influences were lined up waiting for me . . . which is why I tell you more of them than of myself" (3, 43). But Augie now adds that a man's fate—or what determines his life—is his character. Having sought a fate good enough, and blamed his culture for his difficulty, Augie now says "maybe I can't take these very things I want" (514). He also sees that it is the internal self which defines and contains reality: "all the while you thought you were going around idle terribly hard work was taking place. . . . And none of this work is seen from the outside. It's internally done. . . . Where is everybody? Inside your breast and skin, the entire cast" (523). At the end, when he has like Donatello become a full character, Augie defines his fate as a struggle with the world and himself. His claim that he is "a sort of Columbus of those near-at-hand" who believes that "you can come to them in this immediate *terra incognita* that spreads out in every gaze," is less a summary of his character than a recognition of what has been true throughout the novel, that he has to make a long voyage to reach his fellow man (536).

CHAPTER 5   COME THEN, SORROW

For when all is said and done, we are in the end absolutely dependent on the universe; and into sacrifices and surrenders of some sort, deliberately looked at and accepted, we are drawn and pressed as into our only permanent positions of repose.

WILLIAM JAMES, *Varieties of Religious Experience*

"Seize the Day," a novelette Bellow published in 1956, depicts the death throes of a drowning man. Tommy Wilhelm faces complete submergence in failure. He begins his day by plunging downward in a hotel elevator to a city sunk metaphorically beneath the sea. The New York streets carry a "tide of Broadway traffic" which is the "current" of the city (77, 100). The baroque hotel he sees from the lobby window looks "like the image of itself reflected in deep water, white and cumulous above, with cavernous distortions underneath" (5). Although Wilhelm struggles to keep "the waters of the earth" from rolling over him, he looks "like a man about to drown" (77, 104). He has foolishly quit his job and has no money to meet the demands of his wife, who seeks to punish him for leaving her. His relations with his elderly father, whom he has denied by changing his name, reach the breaking point; the physician denies his plea for help by calling him a slob. He finally loses the little money he has left on the commodities market, where he had speculated at the urging of a phony psychologist, Dr. Tamkin.

The waters roll over him when he stumbles, defeated, into a funeral home. There, "where it was dark and cool," his troubles end. The quiet chapel has the wavering, dream-like quality of an ocean grotto. Organ music "stirred and breathed from the pipes" and "men in formal clothes and black homburgs strode softly back and forth on the cork floor, up and down the center aisle" (116). Wilhelm feels a "splash of heartsickness" as he stands before the corpse of a stranger (117). When he begins to cry, at first softly and then hysterically, his drowning is complete. "The heavy sea-like music came up to his ears," Bellow writes. "It poured into him where he had hidden himself in the center of a crowd by the great and happy oblivion of tears. He heard it and sank deeper than sorrow, through torn sobs and cries toward the consummation of his heart's ultimate need" (118).[1]

The ambiguity of Wilhelm's drowning, which is both a failure and a triumph, is the central problem of "Seize the Day." Because the water in which Wilhelm is immersed represents the "cavernous distortions" of his own character, it reflects the conflict in Bellow's view of human nature. Bellow sees man as D. H. Lawrence does, as "hard, isolate, and a killer." Mintouchian would warn Wilhelm as he warns Augie that "you fight your malice too much" (479). Wilhelm denies the existence of the predatory in man, and in doing so exemplifies one of Bellow's most frequent themes, the destruction of man by his humane ideals. As Bellow's good doctor warns in "Sermon by Dr. Pep," a monologue published in 1949, "we are the only ones who turn our appetite on ourselves, and the most hopeful and outward-gentle the most of all." Because he is unable to accept the cruelty natural to life, or is "too gentle and abstaining to be predacious at large, with the humane eyes of civilized self-consumption," Wilhelm's ultimate need is his own death. His drowning is a suicide, the culmination of his self-pity and self-hate. As Brendan Gill puts it, he ends his day "sobbing his heart out over his plight and yet feeling rather better than usual." [2]

But Wilhelm's denial of a loveless world is also Bellow's own. The view that man is exclusively "hard, isolate and a killer" is one that Bellow would disprove in his fiction. Weyl sought to oppose the murderous in man with "something redeeming in the original thing." Having attempted to meet force on its own terms in *Augie March,* Bellow returns in this novelette to the reconciliation of his moral vision with a naturalistic world, a reconciliation that he achieves. Many critics agree with Brendan Gill that Wilhelm feels better than usual at the end, but they see it as a triumph over his masochism rather than a symptom of it: Wilhelm does indeed reach the "consummation of his heart's ultimate need." If he is a sick man, like Bellow's previous heroes, he is also—again like them—a potentially healthy one. He achieves a healing insight into himself, for he passes beneath self-pity to "the source of all tears," and then "deeper than sorrow," to a center which is beyond grief.

These contrasting interpretations—and their many published variations[3]—suggest that Wilhelm's drowning is a source of confusion much like the unresolved conflicts of the other stories—with one difference. Bellow's other novels are not clear because of a contradiction between the separate elements of plot and metaphor or speech and action, but "Seize the Day" is unclear because of the ambiguity of a single image. Bellow's effortless manner and openly mixed attitude toward Wilhelm suggest that he now uses the conflict that creates strain in the other works, that he dramatizes not the resolution of an issue but the natural ambiguity which contains it. "Seize the Day" portrays a problem rather than its solution, I think, and in doing so crystallizes the ambivalence that lies within Bellow's vision. There is no doubt that Wilhelm is weak and masochistic, but there is even less doubt that his final grief is a triumph of greater depth than purgation or self-knowledge. Bellow's water imagery contains both possibilities in that it symbolizes the rigorous life forces which destroy Wilhelm and a transcendent reality which raises him above destruction. Because of this ambivalence, Wilhelm embodies our mixed attitude toward the soft character and the religious issues he raises. He is a masochist in the same way that Malamud's Morris Bober is afraid of life and Waugh's Tony Last is a fool, but he is also like them in his achievement of a larger, and perhaps sacred, dignity. We may attribute this apparently unjustified stature to our awe before suffering, or to the fact that the passivity of these characters is our ultimate condition. By throwing themselves on the world they test it the way a child tests his parents' love, dramatizing our final helplessness. But their stature derives most of all, I think, from the religious perspective their suffering offers. Here Bellow's division between the rational and the imaginative, and his yoking of the personal and the metaphysical, is crucial: Wilhelm is related to the sacred sufferers of mythology and Jewish literature, but he is a salesman of children's play pens. He suffers not in the ancient world or a Polish village but on Columbus Circle. His problem is that he is part of Broadway, for all of his complaint: he is the suffering Jew without his faith, a visionary who wants to be a Hollywood star. His humiliating defeat is a triumph because he is finally forced to let go of the world. He too is a man of will, for all his passivity; he is finally stripped of all recourse, thrown back upon his inner self, and confronted with the mystery of self-enslavement. At the end he follows the path William James describes as that of conversion; he suspends his will, forgoes the world, and is flooded with the sense of transcendence that can set him free. That his drowning is also the culmination of his masochism adds to the impressiveness of the triumph we feel at the same time that it expresses our mixed attitude—and the paradox traditionally encompassed by faith.

"Seize the Day" is also significant because it marks a change in Bellow's art. Although much has been written about Bellow's shift from the Flaubert-James to the picaresque tradition of the novel, the most important shift in his art has been in characterization. Much like Henderson, Wilhelm is as different from Augie March as he is from Leventhal. Bellow drew Joseph and Leventhal with the fine detail that creates identification on the part of the reader, but he draws Tommy Wilhelm with the broad strokes of Dickensian caricature. Wilhelm's unadmirable personality discourages sympathetic emotion. He drinks Coca-Cola before breakfast, carries old cigarette butts in his pocket, and sobs in self-pity at the loss of a dog. He is larger than life, with a hulking body to match his gargantuan emotions. "Though he called himself a hippopotamus," Bellow says, "he more nearly resembled a bear" (23). Bellow treats him with both humor and pathos, but Wilhelm remains what most reviewers found him to be—a "despicable and dirty character." [4] Bellow's short stories suggest that the distance created by Wilhelm's characterization is essential to Bellow's art. Bellow needs this distance to portray the inhumanity he sees within man.

He also needs a Tommy Wilhelm, dirty and despicable as he may be, to achieve an affirmation of something higher.

Most of Bellow's short stories in the fifties contain the same pattern as his novels. As the protagonist wanders about the city or his summer home, he wrestles with a revelation of human or natural destructiveness. His memory serves the purpose of Joseph's diary, Weyl's conversation, and Henderson's travelogue—the play of mind over a shocking or disturbing experience. Because of this pattern, the stories represent Bellow's continued confrontation of the problems he turned away from in *Augie March*. He published almost half of his short stories between 1949 and 1951, the period in which he struggled with and abandoned "The Crab and the Butterfly." They illuminate his conception of evil and define the aesthetic problems, particularly in characterization, which arise from his struggle with it. All of the protagonists face the subject of Dr. Pep's sermon, the fact that in spring "the butterflies drink up what is left of the porcupines who passed on happy in their sleep." To live, they learn, we murder, and to deny this fact is to deny life. But the stories also suggest that Dr. Pep's sermon is Bellow's lecture to himself. If the protagonists struggle to accept the cruelty of the natural world, they are met with a final, shocking experience they cannot accept.

The significance of this pattern to Bellow's thematic problems is revealed by the only story written before 1952 included in *Seize the Day* (a collection of short fiction and a play published in 1956). Entitled "Looking for Mr. Green," [5] the story describes a quest I take to be Bellow's own and a failure which contrasts with Dr. Pep's acceptance of bloodthirsty butterflies. George Grebe is a well-educated man of thirty-five who has been caught unprepared for the hard times of the Depression. Because his study of the humanities qualifies him for only trivial and part-time jobs, he is grateful when a friend gets him a permanent position delivering relief checks in the Chicago slums. But his first day on the job is marred by his inability to find a Mr. Green. The Negroes in the chaotic tenement in which the crippled man lives are too suspicious of white bill-collectors to tell Grebe where he is. The Latin scholar knocks on several doors, talks to the janitor, and even visits a nearby grocery store. Although it is a bitterly cold day, he persists in his search until well past dinner time. He is idealistic, and knows that his client needs the money he brings. But "that was not the most important consideration": he is determined to find Mr. Green because "he wanted to do well, simply for doing-well's sake, to acquit himself decently of a job because he so rarely had a job to do that required just this sort of energy" (136).

His determination also springs from the meaning that the elusive Negro assumes in his imagination. Bellow establishes his symbolic intention in a conversation between Grebe and his new superintendent, Raynor. The superior chides Grebe for his love of culture. "Were you brought up tenderly," he asks, "with permission to go out and find out what were the last things that everything else stands for while everybody else labored in the fallen world of appearances?" (147) Raynor finds satisfaction in the fact that Grebe must abandon his search for ultimate reality and face the ugliness of an ephemeral city. Wandering about the tenement district, Grebe understands what Raynor means: the buildings which had seemed permanent fifty years before have been broken down quickly by "centuries of history accomplished through human massing." All cities, he realizes, "stood for themselves by agreement, and were natural and not unnatural by agreement" (155). But Grebe also wonders about the "reality which doesn't depend on consent but within which consent is a game." If people create their own world of appearances, why, he asks himself, should they agree to cities of misery and painful ugliness? "Because there *is something* that is dismal and permanently ugly?" (156) His search for Mr. Green is transformed by his imagination into a quest for the final reality behind man's temporary creations. Because man is part of that reality, and is "compelled to match it" in his very being, Grebe's search is an exploration of our human nature (154). His trek through the "earthen, musky human gloom" of the Negro tenements becomes a pilgrimage to the sources of human history (142). When he sees a hallway covered with scrawlings, Bellow notes that "so the sealed rooms of pyramids were also decorated, and the caves of human dawn" (140). The kitchen of an elderly colored man, who is like "one of the underground kings of mythology," is a "gloomy, heathen midden" (153). Grebe enters another room full of people "sitting on benches like a parliament. There was no light, properly speaking, but a tempered darkness that the window gave, and everyone seemed to him enormous." Before these people Grebe "entered like a schoolboy," as indeed he is, both in his search for truth and in his humility before the awesome facts of primitive humanity (141).

But Grebe seeks more than the dismal and permanently ugly. Fresh from Raynor's chastisement, he seeks something holy and permanently beautiful—a reality that man might match by benevolence and dignity. The Negroes hide Mr. Green because Grebe represents hostile urban forces which they fear will destroy their neighbor and which Grebe, to find his quarry, must somehow surmount. "It was important that there was a real Mr. Green whom they could not keep him from reaching because he seemed to come as an emissary from hostile appearances" (160). His unsuccessful search defines the *something* that is dismal and permanently ugly" rather than the affirmative reality. For in the end he finds in Green's small bungalow a drunken and naked woman. As she gropes her way down the stairs to a freezing hallway, Grebe overhears her mutter, "So I cain't ...k, huh? I'll show that son-of-a-bitch kin I, cain't I." She blunders into Grebe in the darkness, and he stumbles away from her, shocked. "See what he had tracked down, in his hunting game!" (158) The woman answers his request to see her husband with a curse and demands that he take the check up to Green himself. He refuses, feeling that the hidden man "would probably be drunk and naked, too" (159). He starts to leave, but then decides to deliver the check to the woman. "Though she might not be Mrs. Green," Bellow writes, "he was convinced that Mr. Green was upstairs. Whoever she was, the woman stood for Green, whom he was not to see this time" (160).

Although Bellow ends the story on a hopeful note, the drunken woman reflects his discomfort before the violent and the sensual, whatever Dr. Pep may advise. Like Lawrence, Bellow is intensely conscious of the destructive will and particularly sensitive to it in women. He is also like Lawrence in that he associates this will with a principle in the universe: Grebe associates the woman with Raynor's harsh world and with another fiercely willful woman, Staika, who reminds him of "the war of flesh and blood, perhaps turned a little crazy and certainly intensely ugly" (149). While Lawrence finds an answer to this element in psychological self-sufficiency—Birkin's achievement of an autonomous self, for example—Bellow here seeks an opposing principle inherent in the world. Grebe's search for Mr. Green is a search for the real man behind the name, or a physical embodiment of the something holy and beautiful. Just as Bellow would discover a way in which a good man such as Augie might survive in a world of Machiavellians, and does so by making the good a biological force, capable of withstanding other, less benevolent forces, so he searches for that moral value which is physically present, and thus a force, in the world. Evil, in Bellow's vision, is rooted in the physical world, and he would find a way in which the good too is physical. This is in part an aesthetic problem, for an imaginative analogue to human nature such as Grebe's tenements requires an image for the good as well as the *"something* that is dismal." One of the striking qualities of Bellow's fiction is the discrepancy between its many images for indifference or cruelty against almost none for compassion or charity. But the issue is also central to Bellow's conception of the world and man. When Grebe says that "it almost doesn't do any good to have a name if you can't be found by it. It doesn't stand for anything," he refers to our values and thus our humanity (157). Still, he insists, "there must be a way to find a person" (151).

"Looking for Mr. Green" ends with Grebe embarrassed but still elated that Mr. Green "*could* be found!" In another short story published the same year (1951), Bellow portrays a character without Grebe's faith in Mr. Green and a war not dismissed as easily. He contrasts our ideals and our nature in "By the Rock Wall" [6] by a simple analogy between man and animal, and in doing so brings the problem of inhuman force even closer to his protagonist. Willard, from whose point of view Bellow tells the story, has discovered that his wife had cheated on him fifteen years before. He had accepted the fact the previous night, in the rare intimacy of their confidential talk, but he is bitterly angry about it in the morning. His own infidelities heighten his disgust; each, he realizes, has swindled the other. His disappointment is not simply that of the cuckold, for as he putters about their summer home, avoiding his wife as much as possible, his mind begins to perceive a larger significance in their double disgrace. He recalls an incident which had "made him glimpse himself as only the figure of a man never seen by others except as a figure, exactly as he himself saw them, coming, mingling, rising, threatening another, running away from another." He is unable to accept such cold impersonality. His wife's infidelity is particularly horrifying because it suggests a similar impersonality at the very heart of his marriage; merely a figure in the mass of humanity, he is also a stranger in the innermost depths of his wife's being. To attempt to include another person in "the other life to which you descended by yourself," as they had done, is to be shocked by the existence of a separate self that knows no marriage. With this insight comes another, "that there was nothing in the world that was absolutely for oneself." His brooding is suddenly interrupted by some sharp screams by the rock wall on the edge of their property. There he and his wife find a mink dragging a rabbit larger than itself to a crevice in the wall. The mink "was wound so tightly about the rabbit that they could only see it as something constricting, a terrible force doubled with it, carried crookedly when the rabbit's feet found the ground." The mink has a "savage dragging force which Willard felt like violence to himself." When he attempts to save the rabbit, the harassed idealist feels "as though he had been struck two crushing blows on the shoulders." Bellow completes the analogy as Willard later meditates on the blood-splattered mink. Before such violence, he realizes, "everything that was not firm, everything the least bit false, not strict—the being loosely humane, relatively considerate, fairly decent—everything like that was knocked down on the first serious consideration." His desire to "have at least one thing for oneself exclusively"—recognition in the deepest self of his wife—was also knocked down by violence. Willard sees that it is the falsehood of his desire, based upon the humane ideal of love, that "more than anything else was injuring him." The very essence of life is its independence from, and indifference to, the life around it. The nervous savagery of the mink is a distillation of the fierce power in all living things, akin to the speck perceived by Leventhal; "it looked more roused, more awake, than any creature he had ever seen." Brooding over a past wrong and then shocked by a destructive present, Willard finds that modestly held ideals are impossible before impersonal and inhumane forces.

These short stories suggest two paths which Bellow might have taken but which fell short of his artistic purpose. "By the Rock Wall" evokes man's isolation and inhumanity with intense immediacy, but it exposed Bellow to the same despair that overwhelmed him in "The Crab and the Butterfly." Until he found Mr. Green, Bellow had to maintain an aesthetic distance from the cruelty or evil he imagined, both for his personal equanimity and the sake of artistic control. To achieve a necessary distance in such stories as "Looking for Mr. Green," however, he had to evade the experience of that truth. The drunken woman is a striking device, but she is more of an allegorical abstraction than a living character; we perceive but do not feel the destructive will she symbolizes. Because she is not a permanent part of Grebe's experience, he recognizes the terror of life without suffering from it as do Willard and Leventhal. The strength of Grebe's character is an even more important evasion, for it makes him superior to the average man. Grebe was smaller than the enormous Negroes of the primitive parliament, Bellow tells us, but "he was his own man, he retracted nothing about himself, and he looked back at them, gray-eyed, with amusement and also with a sort of courage" (142). The inner strength which allows Grebe to view the primitive terror of life with a dispassionate eye is actually an implicit damnation of the Willards and Leventhals—the mass of men—who do not share that courage. Grebe is not stiff-lipped or hard-boiled, but he is "a hunter inexperienced in the camouflage of his game"—a Hemingway hero who exemplifies precisely the type of human affirmation Bellow seeks to avoid (135). "But it is strange that Hemingway's standards . . . should be such exclusive ones," Bellow has written. "I suppose that in a game not all can play. Only those within the spell and within the rules are eligible. Manhood, as Hemingway views it, must necessarily be the manhood of the few." [7] In 1951 Bellow faced the despair of an intensely imagined world of violence or the endless spinning out of devices to keep his harsh vision at a distance. If he were to find Mr. Green, however, that elusive personification of moral reality would be available to all men, the weakest as well as the most courageous.

Bellow found the solution to his problem of aesthetic distance five years later in the characterization of Tommy Wilhelm. The oversized ex-salesman suffers an agony as personal as Willard's but the reader does not undergo the oppression of intense identification. Bellow suggested the theory behind his new use of caricature in an article he wrote about Khrushchev in power. "In the West the connections between opinion, feeling and bodily motion have been broken," he said. "We have lost the expressive power. . . . One of the privileges of [political] power seems to be the privilege of direct emotional self-expression." [8] Khrushchev, who had the large size and spontaneity of Wilhelm and Henderson, is himself a Bellow hero. He illustrates the fact that Bellow's larger-than-life characters do have their counterpart in life. He also illustrates, if only on the surface, the comic primitivism inherent in Bellow's characterization. The slight Joseph suffers emotions in the quiet of his room as gargantuan as those Wilhelm and Henderson suffer in public; the later heroes have bodies to match the subjective size of normal human feeling. Because they have not lost the "expressive power," the size of these heroes reflects the substance of their emotions as well; Wilhelm and Henderson are an externalization of the inner man. If Bellow's technique has changed radically between the quiet of Joseph's room and the chaos of Henderson's pig farm, his intention, the discovery and portrayal of our human nature, hasn't. His comic characterization portrays in broad daylight the agony and guilt that Willard and Leventhal face in private. It provides the distance Bellow needs by objectifying the inner truth of man in a physical image—the human body. It also surmounts the dullness natural to a passive character by making his emotions objects of vision and thus a substitute for action. When Wilhelm "towered and swayed, big and sloven, with his gray eyes red-shot and his honey-colored hair twisted in flaming shapes upward" (50), the emotions which paralyze him become a form of movement or action and embody a suffering which we see rather than share.

Bellow's use of this characterization in "Seize the Day" accounts for his ease in confronting themes he had once found painful. Although the novelette is as well-written as Bellow's first two novels, it has none of their oppressive closeness. The voice of its omniscient narrator, who is both above and within Wilhelm's point of view, is at once hard-headed and sympathetic, reflecting little of Bellow's earlier vacillation between identification and irony. Bellow also finds a simple, uncluttered structure. In the first three sections Wilhelm talks with his retired father, who denies him the moral and financial support he begs. In the second three, during a second breakfast, a trip to the brokerage and then lunch, Wilhelm receives professions of such aid from Tamkin, his substitute father. He returns to the market alone after lunch to find himself wiped out and Tamkin, to whom he lent money, gone. When his wife and his father make their final demands on him, the seventh and last section becomes a simple culmination of Wilhelm's day. His climactic grief in the funeral parlor is a final humiliation, fulfilling the imaginative logic of his defeat, and the only triumph possible, an equal fulfillment, I would argue, of his situation and character.

Wilhelm is first of all, like the other heroes, a victim of society. But Bellow's use of biological terms to define society makes it representative of the physical world. Without a job and unable to pay his hotel bill, Wilhelm needs money—which he has lost to the

sharper people around him. He lacks the shrewd aggression capital-
ism demands. Behind the practical motives of those who cheat him,
however—his wife's need for support, his father's frugality, and
Tamkin's need for capital—lies a purer, deeper malice. Bitter because he left her, Margaret admits that she is out to "murder" him
by her exorbitant demands: "How did you imagine it was going to
be—big shot? Everything made smooth for you?" (114) His father
withholds financial aid because "it was not fair for the better man
of the two, and the more useful, the more admired, to leave the
world first" (54). Tamkin mouths the clichés of the humane man,
but he murders for its own sake. "My real calling is to be a healer,"
he tells Wilhelm. "I get wounded. I suffer from it. I would like to
escape from the sicknesses of others, but I can't" (95). He also suffers when he thinks of others making money: "I get so worked up
and tormented and restless, so restless!" (9) As he tells Wilhelm,
"this type of activity is filled with hostile feeling and lust," for
people "go on the market with murder in their hearts" (10). Because of these motives, money is the weapon and the prize of "the
war of flesh and blood." "When I had it," Wilhelm thinks, "I
flowed money. They bled it away from me. I hemorrhaged money"
(40). When Margaret makes her demands Wilhelm thinks, "we
could not bear . . . to know what we do. Even though blood is
spilled. Even though the breath of life is taken from someone's nos-
trils" (112).

Wilhelm is also the victim of his society's peculiar emotional
sterility. Bellow has said informally that one of his themes in "Seize
the Day" is the city dweller's fulfillment of personal needs on
strangers.[9] The feelings that usually involve private commitment
are now casually exchanged in public. Wilhelm's father finds fulfillment not in his children but in the admiration of his hotel associates. He "created his own praise," Wilhelm thinks. "People
were primed and did not know it. And what did he need praise for?
In a hotel where everyone was busy and contacts were so brief and
had such small weight, how could it satisfy him? . . . He could
never matter much to them" (12). The agent Maurice Venice,
who Wilhelm later learns is a procurer, praises the movie industry

because it supplies the emotional life of the nation. People are "miserable, in trouble, downcast, tired, trying," he tells Wilhelm. "They need a break, right?" The break is the opportunity to "feel" in the movie house: as a movie star, Venice says, "you become a lover to the whole world. . . . One fellow smiles, a billion people also smile" (22). Tamkin, the stranger to whom Wilhelm himself turns, epitomizes this sterility. As a psychologist Tamkin makes his living supplying the emotional needs of strangers, and his claim to work for love rather than money burlesques his patients' dependence on him. When Wilhelm questions Tamkin's claim to have had a consultation before breakfast, he learns that it had been "over the telephone, of course" (62). Seeking emotional support, Wilhelm is driven by his father's impersonality and Tamkin's spurious personalism to achieve his "heart's ultimate need" before the corpse of a stranger.[10]

But Wilhelm is also, and again like the other heroes, a victim of himself. Just as Herzog realizes that his weeping at his father's funeral was a sign of weakness as well as grief, so Wilhelm's emotionalism—his need for what Herzog sneeringly calls *personal relations*—reflects his dependency and his masochism. The people around him are really his weapons for suicide. Bellow uses the philosophy of Tamkin, who is responsible for Wilhelm's bankruptcy, as an ironic revelation of why Wilhelm destroys himself. Tamkin tells Wilhelm that because man is inherently good he has only to "seize the day," or rest content in his own being, to be happy. The desire to murder by means of money making is an artificial trait acquired from society. Wilhelm's belief in Tamkin's philosophy reflects his own denial of human depravity; his partnership with the scoundrel reveals the self-deception—and destruction—that accompanies such a denial. Wilhelm's change of name from Wilhelm Adler to Tommy Wilhelm also embodies his suicidal desire. The change had been "his bid for liberty, Adler being in his mind the title of the species, Tommy the freedom of the person" (25). The "species" which Wilhelm seeks to deny is his racial background; he attempts to deny his Jewish heritage. More important is the human reality that Dr. Adler represents. His father is essentially isolate; he is indifferent to his children except as they reflect his image. "You were set free when Ma died," Wilhelm silently tells him. "You wanted to forget her. You'd like to get rid of [your daughter] Catherine, too. Me, too. You're not kidding anyone" (29). Wilhelm's denial of his father's name is a denial of the impersonality and cruelty of the human species. Because he would destroy these elements within himself, it is also the denial of his own identity.

"Seize the Day" is thus a study in masochism. The "most hopeful and outward-gentle" of all of Bellow's heroes, Wilhelm turns his appetite on himself. When he remembers that he had quit college to go to Hollywood, he realizes that "he was about to make his first great mistake. Like, he sometimes thought, I was going to pick up a weapon and strike myself a blow with it" (17). His gamble with Tamkin on the commodities market was a similar mistake, for having "tasted the peculiar flavor of fatality in Dr. Tamkin, he could no longer keep back the money" (58). Bellow emphasizes Wilhelm's desire to suffer by the irony of his argument with his father. Wilhelm realizes that the elderly man, "with some justice, wanted to be left in peace." He also knows that "when he began to talk about these things he made himself feel worse, he became congested with them and worked himself into a clutch" (43). He warns himself to leave his father alone, but immediately starts a bitter argument. Afterwards, forgetting the old man's initial indifference, he accuses him of torture. "Why do you start up with me if you're not going to help me?" he cries. "What do you want to know about my problems for, Father?" (53) Dr. Adler, clever as he is, is not agile enough to avoid his son's masochistic desire.

In this view of his drowning, Wilhelm must seize the day. Recognizing that "in health we are in the debt of a suffering creation," as Dr. Pep says, he must choose health rather than suffering. Tamkin states a similar idea, and uses water imagery to do it, when he tells Wilhelm that he must accept a mixed nature. "Nature knows only one thing," he says, "and that's the present. Present, present, eternal present, like a big, huge, giant wave—colossal, bright and beautiful, full of life and death" (89). But Bellow also believes—as this pseudo-Whitmanian chant implies—that the present is not enough. Tamkin's advice is too vague, too much what Tamkin wants it to mean at the moment, to be of help. Although "Sermon by Doctor Pep" is sympathetic to them, Bellow here offers a critique on just such fashionable generalities as "seize the day." Wilhelm finds a different and real solution to his problem, I think, in his dream-like passage from the street to a chapel, his confrontation of death, and his ecstatic sense of release—a broadly religious experience. His drowning embodies the meaning and the imagery of William James's description of personal religious conversion: "after the surrender of the personal will," James writes, it seems "as if an extraneous higher power had flooded in and taken possession." [11]

To interpret the conclusion in this way accounts for Wilhelm's sense of triumph and explains away the problem of the relationship of the ending to the rest of the story. As Ihab Hassan defines this issue, "the novelette starts by formulating the problem of success in America in worldly terms, continues to explore the predicament of Wilhelm in the light of the manners and morals of his particular milieu, and suddenly, as it were, resolves the question by rising to a more exalted level of perception." Because he feels that rise is sudden, Hassan wonders if "the particular mode of his illumination does not seem rather gratuitous, rather foreign to the concerns [Bellow] has most steadily expressed throughout the action." [12] While such experiences are naturally sudden and gratuitous—one answer to this complaint—it is also true that Bellow prepares for it in many ways. "Seize the Day" is remarkable among Bellow's works, in fact, for the completeness with which it integrates the social and psychological levels of meaning with the protagonist's religious experience. While Joseph's impulses are confused, Leventhal's "promise" hesitant, and Augie's axial lines lost in external detail, Tommy Wilhelm's climactic breakdown is a religious denouement which Bellow clearly foreshadows.

Bellow prepares for the conclusion by his definition of Wilhelm's need. To accept indifference and murder as the substance of our existence is, for all of Dr. Pep's wisdom, to accept a kind of hell. Wilhelm may be a weakling, but the world he insists upon, and for which he would rather suffer than reject, is a worthy one. Herzog explains Wilhelm's attitude in an early draft of that novel when he says that beating his wife would have helped their marriage, but that "it would have been a sad way to keep the love of your wife." [13] As in the other novels, Bellow advocates a biological health in "Seize the Day" but then defines the biological as intolerable. Bellow also creates a hero who is once more immersed in the world and withdrawn from it, but in either case dependent on it. Wilhelm's plea for help and mercy is a plea that others supply the esteem he cannot give to himself. Tamkin tells him that he must accept his relation to the world, but his problem is that he does just this—he defines himself almost entirely by how he appears in the eyes of others. As an active man, on the other hand, seeking to rise above the average, Wilhelm is equally dependent on the world: he adopts a name that isn't his in order to be accepted by the movie-goers. In either case he needs the same sense of an essential self as Bellow's other heroes. When Tamkin mentions a "true soul" which lies beneath social identity, Wilhelm is intensely interested. "What did it look like?" he wonders. "Does my soul look like me? . . . Where does the true soul get its strength?" (72)

In that Wilhelm is a good man, moreover, his problem is Augie's, the question of how goodness may survive in a world antithetical to it. This is partly a question of psychology or maturity, for to combat evil Wilhelm needs merely to be his own man like Grebe. His interest in where the soul gets its strength is much to the point. But Bellow insists upon a weak "goodness" or a morality that derives its strength from the fact that it is moral. Wilhelm's salvation lies in Grebe's quest for the reality that makes the moral a presence or force in its own right. When Wilhelm wonders what the "true soul" looks like, or how it appears in the practical world, he too searches for Mr. Green. He—and Bellow, I think—find some success in the image of water. Dr. Pep points to the savagery under the surface of man's ideals by revealing that "the fish of first-times loiters offshore somewhere near our loftier thoughts." Bellow uses the same image in "Seize the Day" to suggest the reality of something higher. When Wilhelm thinks of his affection for his parents, Bellow writes, "there was a great pull at the very center of his soul. When a fish strikes the line you feel the live force in your hand. A mysterious being beneath the water, driven by hunger, has taken the hook" (92). Before the funeral scene Wilhelm has felt the power of love within the "cavernous distortion" of his inner consciousness. But, Bellow adds: "Wilhelm never identified what struck within him. It did not reveal itself. It got away" (93).

In several other passages, it does reveal itself to Wilhelm. Defeated by society and an imperfect human nature, Wilhelm begins to see his failure in a new light: he comes to believe that his suffering has a moral purpose. "The spirit, the peculiar burden of his existence lay upon him like an accretion, a load, a hump," Bellow writes. "In any moment of quiet, when sheer fatigue prevented him from struggling, he was apt to feel this mysterious weight . . . which it was the business of his life to carry about. That must be what a man was for." These thoughts are Wilhelm's own, to be taken as we please, and Bellow even undercuts their seriousness when he adds that "Dr. Tamkin had been putting into his mind many suggestions" (38–39). They are also, I think, Bellow's own. By writing as an omniscient narrator who tells most of the story through Wilhelm's eyes, Bellow tends to blur the distinction between his protagonist and himself. And when Bellow speaks out in his own voice, he gives some credence to these thoughts. When Wilhelm "received a suggestion from some remote element in his thoughts that the business of life, the real business—to carry his peculiar burden, to feel shame and impotence, to taste these quelled tears—the only important business, the highest business was being done," Bellow prefaces it with the comment that "there were depths in Wilhelm not unsuspected by himself" (56). As Wilhelm's sense of a moral purpose to his suffering broadens into a sense of the transcendent unity of all life, Bellow treats these thoughts with increasing sympathy. Wilhelm thinks that "when you are like this, dreaming that everybody is outcast, you realize that this must be one of the small matters. There is a larger body, and from this you cannot be separated." Beneath the confusion and the complexity of the world "what Tamkin would call the real soul says plain and understandable things to everyone. . . . There truth for everybody may be found, and confusion is only—only temporary, thought Wilhelm" (84).

But Bellow is also uneasy before such thoughts. This is reflected in the ambiguity and irony with which he treats them in the early novels and in the fact that his new characterization is important to his portrayal of them in "Seize the Day." On another such occasion, while walking in an underground corridor, Wilhelm suddenly feels the unity in love of all minkind. Bellow writes that "in the haste, heat, and darkness which disfigure and make freaks and fragments of nose and eyes and teeth, all of a sudden, unsought, a general love for all these imperfect and lurid-looking people burst out in Wilhelm's breast. He loved them" (84). In his love he is able to accept his limitations: "He was imperfect and disfigured himself, but what difference did that make if he was united with them by this blaze of love?" (84–85) Bellow reveals his embarrassment by converting the vision into comedy. Wilhelm tells himself that the experience is "the right clue and may do me the most good. Something very big. Truth, like." These last words reduce the vision to the pseudo-mysticism of concert hall spiritualists. Not content with a smile, Bellow goes even further. Wilhelm's experience was "only another one of those subway things. Like having a hard-on at random" (85). His sudden crudity after a sentimental but serious vision is funny, but it is also strained, reflecting Bellow's discomfort. Approaching such insights with caution, feeling like Joseph that they are convincing, Bellow needs a distance from them even more than in the depiction of terror—a distance provided by his characterization as well as his comedy. Because it removes his story from the level of common sense and provides the aesthetic distance he needs to relieve and express his doubts, his use of caricature gives him a greater freedom than he found in irony or symbolism.

Wilhelm's final drowning, too, expresses Bellow's ambivalent feelings toward such experiences. But it does so without strain and

in a way that belongs to the experience itself. Wilhelm's drowning
is first of all the climax of his day of failure. The water in which
he drowns is both the world and the masochistic self which have
murdered him. Shortly before Wilhelm enters the funeral home,
Bellow describes the city crowd in terms suggestive of the blind,
impersonal sweep of life, "the inexhaustible current of millions of
every race and kind pouring out, pressing round, of every age, of
every genius" (115).[14] Wilhelm, carried into the funeral home "by
the pressure of the crowd," drowns "in the center of a crowd"—in
the harsh drive of all life for survival (116, 118). If the water
pours into Wilhelm from the outside, it also wells up from within.
Throughout Wilhelm's day, Bellow writes, "he smelled the salt odor
of tears in his nose" (56). When Wilhelm loses everything on the
market, "his unshed tears rose and rose and he looked like a man
about to drown" (104). In the final scene, when "the source of
all tears had suddenly sprung open within him, black, deep, and
hot," Wilhelm drowns in his own tears (117). Within and without,
he drowns in the predatory instincts which the less inhibited direct
toward him and which he directs toward himself. His collapse in a
darkened parlor, before the dead, reflects both his rejection of the
busy street and his wish to destroy himself. The other mourners
batten on his grief, for they find emotional fulfillment in him just
as he does in the corpse: they form a chorus of ironic comment on
his plight—and theirs. Wilhelm is of course "somebody real close"
to the dead man. As he sobs before the stranger the others came to
grieve, Bellow notes that "he, alone of all the people in the chapel,
was sobbing." One man is envious, "Oh my, oh my! To be mourned
like that," and others are excited: "It must be somebody real close
to carry on so." The man who envies the corpse does so with "wide,
glinting, jealous eyes" reminiscent of the force which destroys Wilhelm (118). The corpse itself, as Bellow describes it, reflects the
truth of society and man: "the dead man with his formal shirt and
his tie and silk lapels and his powdered skin looked so proper; only
a little beneath so—black, Wilhelm thought, so fallen in the eyes"
(117).

That Wilhelm's ecstatic collapse is also a triumph, related to his sense of a larger unity to life, is suggested by its similarity to Leventhal's dream in *The Victim*. The harassed editor dreams that he has missed his train and is forcing his way through a crowd to board a second one. He catches a glimpse of the gate he seeks, but, Bellow writes, "there was a recoil of the crowd—the guards must have been pushing it back—and he found himself in a corridor which was freshly paved and plastered." It seems to lead to the tracks, but he is stopped by two men. One of them tells him he can't pass. "You can't go back the way you came, either," he adds. "There's a sign up there. You'll have to leave through here" (168). He pushes Leventhal into an alley where the defeated man unashamedly cries before strangers. Although the details of Wilhelm's experience differ, the pattern is the same. Wilhelm catches a glimpse of Tamkin through a large crowd outside a funeral parlor. If he can get it, the two hundred dollars Tamkin owes him is a second chance. He is suddenly caught by the recoil of the crowd, again caused by the police, and pushed into the funeral home. There, in an atmosphere that is certainly dream-like, he too cries unashamedly before strangers.

Leventhal doesn't understand the literal meaning of his dream, but lying semi-conscious in the dark he experiences "a rare, pure feeling of happiness." His mistakes are unimportant, for "it was supremely plain to him that everything, everything without exception, took place as if within a single soul or person" (169). The stateliness of Bellow's prose in "Seize the Day" suggests a similar joy in Wilhelm's final drowning; the "ultimate need" which is consummated is the transcendence of sorrow by means of a vision of unity lying deeper than the physical world. But, as Leventhal's dream also suggests, this vision comes only in defeat and tears. In the original publication of "Seize the Day," [15] Wilhelm found the "ultimate need" of his heart "by the way that can only be found through the midst of sorrow." If Wilhelm "dies" because he has sought to deny the human condition, he also accepts the pain of his human identity at the same time that he transcends it. Bellow hints at Wilhelm's progress from rejection to acceptance and from destruction to redemption in the poetry that runs through Wilhelm's mind. Early in the story he remembers the line from Shakespeare's 73rd Sonnet, ". . . love that well which thou must leave ere long" (12). He later remembers some lines from Keats' "Endymion": "Come then, Sorrow!/ . . . /I thought to leave thee,/And deceive thee,/But now of all the world I love thee best" (90). Wilhelm takes the line from Shakespeare as an injunction to love his father, but because his father represents the species, it is a command to love the tormented nature of man. When he welcomes sorrow, he welcomes his own identity. He must, as a modern Lycidas, accept the fact that he cannot destroy his true identity—his "sorrow is not dead." In the Jewish funeral home he accepts his racial heritage; before the corpse of a stranger he accepts his human heritage. And behind this lies the larger affirmation, for the sea finds him "where he had hidden himself" in the crowd, seeking to destroy himself by means of its impersonality. As the water pours into him, he sinks "deeper than sorrow," deeper than the emotions of this world to a spiritual center.[16] When he accepts the death within man, Bellow suggests, when he opens himself to grief and surrenders his will, he passes "through torn sobs and cries toward the consummation of his heart's ultimate need" (118).

CHAPTER 6   THE DREAM AND THE JEST

*What does Africa . . . stand for? Is not
our own interior white on the chart? black
though it may prove, like the coast when
discovered.*

THOREAU, *Walden*

The ambiguity of "Seize the Day" reflects the dilemma portrayed in all of Bellow's fiction. "Seize" denotes aggression; to live fully man must assert his will against circumstance. To seize the "Day," however, suggests an acceptance of the present moment. If he accepts the limitations of fate, man finds joy instead of the agony of fruitless rebellion. Tommy Wilhelm ponders this human conflict after reading Tamkin's poem about mountain climbing. "Maybe those guys who climbed Everest were only trying to kill themselves," he thinks, "and if we want peace we should stay at the foot of the mountain. In the here-and-now. But it's also here-and-now on the slope, and on the top, where they climbed to seize the day" (76). In that Wilhelm is a non-climber, he describes the polarity he forms with Bellow's next hero, Henderson. Both characters are burdened by the self, but Wilhelm suffers from the malice of others while Henderson suffers from his own malice toward others. Wilhelm achieves a victory appropriate to his suffering—transcendence of the world he cannot master—while Henderson achieves one appropriate to his aggressiveness—acceptance of the world as it is. "Seize the Day" is quiet, controlled, and sensitive to the ambiguities of suffering and acceptance; *Henderson the Rain King* (1959) is exuberant, spontaneous, and wildly comic about the ambiguities of wrath and rebellion. In *Henderson*

Bellow once again tries to cope with his religious imagination, but he does so not by an ambiguous transcendent vision but by Henderson's lessons in philosophic idealism.

While Wilhelm makes no claims for his final experience, moreover, Henderson boasts of a large thematic victory. He tells us on the first page that "the world which I thought so mighty an oppressor has removed its wrath from me," and later declares that "living proof of something of the highest importance has been presented to me" (3, 22). His difficulty in delivering on these claims—the qualification and ambiguity which he finally insists on—sustains the comic spirit of the novel but creates thematic confusion.[1] As in other Bellow novels, the themes stated by the characters in *Henderson* conflict with those dramatized in the narrative. Henderson professes to have learned the importance of love, but his adventures demonstrate the necessity of will. He claims to have solved a metaphysical problem by embracing society—a reversal of the pattern of the other novels—but his adventures portray a society destructive of the self. Behind these contradictions lies a third, the relationship in the novel between good and evil. Having failed to show that a biological goodness may triumph in *Augie March,* and having settled for an ambivalent vision in "Seize the Day," Bellow unifies good and the sources of evil in the theories of an African king—the "something of the highest importance" which is the chief subject of the novel. Henderson is taught not how to withstand the world's wrath but how to participate in it, converting it to good—a lesson he rejects at the end in favor of a suffering and transcendent goodness.

Henderson exhibits this inconsistency largely because it is a direct portrayal of the conflict in Bellow's imagination. As such, I think, it also demonstrates the negligible importance of such problems to the life and the value of the novel. An imaginative, fantastic story, *Henderson* is the culmination of Bellow's increasing confidence in the subjective and a further development of his ability to contain and use the ambivalence he feels. *Henderson* finds The ideas in the novel remain divided, but Bellow achieves a deeper its value, its meaning and even its geography in its central character.

unity in his metaphor, his comedy, and most importantly, in his characterization—all of which encompass division.[2]

Henderson too would find Mr. Green, and his quest is even more desperate than Wilhelm's. He is not a good man trying to stay alive but a malicious and vengeful one trying to discover how to be good. "Half-finished, original, eccentric," as Scampi describes Weyl, Henderson is at this point the only hero other than Weyl to acknowledge his murderous impulses. While Joseph's bad temper is largely peevishness, and Weyl's malice is embodied in a single act, Henderson's violence is daily and indiscriminate. He fights with police, harasses his wife, and threatens strangers. He wrestles pigs, tries to kill a cat, and threatens suicide. He finally murders when the noise of his rage kills the family cook. While the earlier heroes struggle to confront the fault within them, Henderson—seeking to cure an all too obvious one—travels to the darkest continent—the self. "Maybe every guy has his own Africa," he thinks. "Or if he goes to sea, his own ocean" (275–76). Just as Leventhal's tropical city is a projection of his inner self, so Henderson's Africa is a metaphor of his deepest being—the harsh internal nature he would reject. Henderson's Africa exemplifies the metaphysical cast of Bellow's imagination and his yoking of personality and metaphysical principles. It also embodies, in the two tribes Henderson visits, the elements of love and terror which Bellow's heroes find in themselves.

Bellow's internality and his return to the theme of malice which he once found painful are due in part to his use of caricature. Because Henderson's inner faults are made objects of vision, expressed in the shape and color of the body, Bellow achieves much the same distance from Henderson that he did from Wilhelm. This enables him to celebrate Henderson's violence even as Henderson seeks goodness—to celebrate raw energy as he sought to do in *Augie March*. To the extent that Henderson is a good man, Bellow achieves by caricature what he failed to do by style in *Augie March*: he creates a hero who "matches" the naturalistic world of force. The Machiavellians make caricatures of themselves for the same reason that primitive people, as Augie says, "make themselves masks . . . to anticipate the terror which does not welcome your being" (403). Bellow's willful characters anticipate the city's terror by the forceful exaggeration of personality, and give substance to the hero's fear that he will be dwarfed by the world. Bellow's externalization of Henderson's inner self creates a protagonist who is large enough to "stand before terrible forces," and who clearly dominates his own novel. If Henderson participates in these "terrible forces" as well, Bellow's caricature supplies the distance we need to treat his victims lightly and to enjoy his vitality. *Henderson* is permeated by the hero's moral quest, but Bellow seems to find pleasure in the fact that his middle-aged *picaro* meets the world's wrath with a little anger of his own.

Because it is externalized, Henderson's inner conflict also becomes a source of comedy, another factor in Bellow's return to the theme of malice, and a natural expression of the conflict faced by all of his heroes. Henri Bergson defines the source of comedy as "something mechanical encrusted on the living." We laugh whenever the individual is unable to adapt to circumstance—whenever his behavior is so mechanical that it is inappropriate. One of the mechanical or rigid elements in man is the body. The comic character is often placed in an incongruous position by his natural physical limitations. We laugh, Bergson says, when we see the discrepancy between the flexible, "living energy" or the soul and the "monotonous body, perpetually obstructing everything with its machine-like obstinacy." Oppressed by his physical being, the Bellow hero thus borders on the comic; he represents the greatest source of laughter—"the soul *tantalised* by the needs of the body." But the ideals by which man attempts to surmount physical limitation may also lead to a comic rigidity. Bellow's hero is a typical comic character because he is an idealist or a man with a "dominant idea." His dedication to his "plan" compels him "to keep strictly to one path, to follow it straight along, to shut [his] eyes and refuse to listen." [3] The rigidity of man's denial of the physical may be as comic as his body. The humorous character is funny because his body—his desire for a natural life in the physical world—is tantalized by the rigid obsessions of his soul.

Henderson participates in both forms of rigidity. He explains his militant rejection of fate by his "soldierly rather than . . . civilian temperament" (22). Six feet four, 230 pounds, with suspicious eyes and a "great nose," he epitomizes human desire. Every afternoon, he says, an inner voice nags him with *"I want!"* "When I tried to suppress it it got even stronger. It only said one thing, *I want, I want!"* He tries unsuccessfully to satisfy it with small comforts. "I would walk it, I would trot it. I would sing to it or read to it. No use" (24). He serves in World War II, does combat with two wives, and converts his luxurious estate into a pig farm, but the voice continues to haunt him. "With the bulk of a football player and the color of a gipsy, swearing and crying out," he rushes through life on a rampage of compulsive desire (5). Because this desire is partially physical, Henderson is indeed tantalised by the needs of his body. His nose, his teeth, the "unfinished church" which composes his face—his whole physical existence is "a regular bargain basement of deformities." "Oh, it's miserable to be human," he complains. "You get such queer diseases. Just because you're human and for no other reason" (83). But Henderson's rejection of his humanity causes him even greater pain. His desire is primarily a drive to surmount all human limitation; he finds himself enslaved by his compulsive efforts to demonstrate his freedom. Bellow captures the humor of this obsessive exertion in a checker game the huge father plays with his children. "Regardless how I maneuvered to let them win," Henderson confesses, "and even while their lips trembled with disappointment . . . I would jump all over the board and say rudely, 'King me!' though all the while I would be saying to myself, 'Oh, you fool, you fool, you fool!' " (69) Henderson's inability to lose to his children despite his pugnacious agony suggests his rigid behavior in the world of grownups: he is incapable of either relaxation or acceptance of defeat. His incongruous behavior is a comic version of Joseph's confession in *Dangling Man* that "the fear of lagging pursues and maddens us" (89).

Bellow's use of comedy is particularly suitable to the story of a quest for the self, and so too is the most unique characteristic of the novel, its resemblance to a dream. As Wylie Sypher points out, "Freud interprets the dream and the jest as a discharge of powerful psychic energies, a glimpse into the abyss of the self." [4] Because the dream and the joke are an upsurge from the unconscious, both are a means of exploring that dark realm. Bellow used Joseph's actual dreams in *Dangling Man* to reveal the truth denied by Joseph's conscious mind. His conversion of Leventhal's dream in *The Victim* to Wilhelm's daylight experience in "Seize the Day" anticipated his technique in *Henderson*, the conversion of a whole continent to a waking dream. Because, as Bergson says, the comic figure proceeds "with the certainty and precision of a somnambulist who is acting his dream," Bellow's technique reinforces his comedy. It also illustrates, in its contrast to Joseph's painful "strangeness," Bellow's new ease with ambivalence. The Africa which cures Henderson is dream-like, as we shall see, but so too is the America which drives him to Africa. Henderson's cook, Miss Lenox, lives near a bright blue catalpa tree decorated with mirrors and reflectors. "She liked to climb up there and sit with her cats, drinking a can of beer" (39). Her cottage overflows with the accumulated junk of her daily scavenging. Representative of our culture, Miss Lenox lives in an artificial world because she denies the fact of death. She seeks a symbolic immortality by identifying herself with the inanimate and deathless tokens of life. But she defeats herself, like Bellow's earlier heroes, by sacrificing her life to her pathetic desire to "save" it. In the clutter of junk she suffers a living death. "How can we?" Henderson cries when he visits her house. "Why do we allow ourselves?" (40) He perceives that the accumulated junk and bright artificiality of his culture is a "pestilence" born of man's inability to accept the natural conditions of life.

Henderson too is dying of this pestilence. "What Henderson is really seeking," Bellow has said, "is a remedy to the anxiety over death." [5] Henderson's world is dream-like because he too denies the body and the facts of death and depravity. "If this body, if this flesh of mine were only a dream," he says elsewhere, "then there might be some hope of awakening" (265). In his dedication to this hope he is indeed a dreamer, sacrificing his real life for an artificial one. His living death consists of the many hours he spends in a damp basement study, where he hopes to reach his parents' spirits by playing the violin. "It so happens," he tells us, "that I have never been able to convince myself the dead are utterly dead." Every morning, wearing a red hunting cap, a velvet robe, and dirty farm boots, he retires to demonstrate the immortality of man. "When I learned a few pieces I would whisper, 'Ma, this is "Humoresque" for you.' Or, 'Pa, listen—"Meditation" from *Thaïs*.' I played with dedication, with feeling, with longing, love—played to the point of emotional collapse" (30). Down in the basement he devotes his whole life to his dream of transcending life. The artificiality of his existence illustrates Schlossberg's claim in *The Victim* that "paper grass in the grave makes all the grass paper."

Bellow's meaningful ridicule of Henderson is revealed at the start of Henderson's trip, for it begins as a burlesque of the Hemingway hero. Henderson, who has the same initials as Hemingway, has "always been a sort of Africa buff"; he buys a .375 H and H Magnum rifle because he read about "a fellow from Michigan who had one" (43, 94). He and his companion on the trip, Charlie, have shared the experiences which form the code hero's sub-culture of two. "In 1915 we attended dancing school together," Henderson says, "and such attachments last" (41). In Africa they quarrel over an intruder in the pure male society—Charlie's bride. The wounded Henderson asks, "was this the kid I used to know in dancing class?" Bellow comments on the Hemingway mystique by saying that though time had changed both men, they "were now, as then, in short pants" (43). Henderson requires more discomfort and danger: the war and especially his wound, he says, "gave my heart a large and real emotion. Which I continually require" (22). Henderson is not just a code hero, however, but an unhappy one. He leaves America because it has embraced Hemingway's values, leaving little room for the internal, real issues. His father had expressed the importance of human intangibles, Henderson says, by using "high phrases." "One of my grievances is that they are not said except by cranks and eccentrics to whom social opinion does not matter. Even in such ways there is slavery." He goes to Africa because "I myself to be a man's man have given up such expressions."

Bellow's comic version of Hemingway's strong man is more than criticism. Having created several weak heroes who were not "big enough to fight with life," Bellow now creates a comically strong one. He also overcomes the disadvantages he set himself in his rejection of the Hemingway code in *Dangling Man*. "Most serious matters are closed to the hard-boiled," Joseph says. "They are unpracticed in introspection, and therefore badly equipped to deal with opponents whom they cannot shoot like big game or outdo in daring"—opponents Joseph found formidable indeed (9). By sending his hero after African game, actually symbols of the internal opponents his early heroes confronted, Bellow takes his fiction out of the self-enclosed world of his protagonist's mind. He overcomes the difficulties of subjective issues by converting Hemingway's world into his own. He also acknowledges the underlying affinity between his work and Hemingway's—the fact that the code hero's compulsive action derives from subjective issues. If, as Jake Barnes says, "it is awfully easy to be hard-boiled about everything in the daytime, but at night it is another thing," Bellow's heroes are nocturnal code heroes. Henderson's belief that "Truth comes with blows" and his confrontation of "the biggest problem of all, which was to encounter death," are related to Hemingway's stated ideas (67, 276). Although their styles differ, both Bellow and Hemingway create heroes who vacillate between violent action and passive suffering—between a desperate need for power and an equally desperate need to feel at one with the world. Hemingway too, as Melvin Backman points out, creates a man of will, the matador, and a man of love, the crucified or the sufferer, and unites both modes in a single character.[6] While Hemingway finds a sanction for killing in love, however, Bellow rejects all killing. Hunting is "a strange way to relate to nature," Henderson says. "What I mean is, a man goes into the external world, and all he can do with it is to shoot it?" (94) But Henderson goes to Africa because this "strange way" is his.

Seeking greater danger than he can find with the settled Charlie, Henderson takes a guide and a few provisions and starts for the African interior. He and his new companion, Romilayu, travel by jeep, by a plane flown by an unshod Arab, and then by foot. "I got clean away from everything," Henderson says.

> We came into a region like a floor surrounded by mountains. It was hot, clear, and arid and after several days we saw no human footprints. Nor were there many plants; for that matter there was not much of anything here; it was all simplified and splendid, and I felt I was entering the past—the real past, no history or junk like that. The prehuman past. [46]

Although Bellow's description of this desert is artificial—Keith Waterhouse charged that Bellow "is vividly describing a backdrop" [7]—it conveys an imaginative element that is important to his story. Just as Africa is an analogue to Henderson's character, so the desert captures an element Bellow sees in human nature. Henderson penetrates the "Mongolia, or clear-light desert minus trees," Mintouchian mentions in *Augie March* (480). He travels beyond civilization, beyond humanity, and beyond life itself—to the reality that Leventhal described in *The Victim* as "something inhuman that . . . was implanted in every human being . . . one speck of it, and formed a part of him that responded to the heat and the glare" (51). Henderson also responds to the heat and glare. As he traveled through the hot gases and rock, he says, "I believed that there was something between the stones and me" (46). [8]

The first tribe Henderson visits, the Arnewi, embody the suffering, loving passivity Bellow described in Augie's Mama and brother Georgie. Henderson arrives at their village at a time of great sorrow, for a drought is killing their cattle. They love their dying animals and sit up all night to comfort them. Henderson sympathizes with the Arnewi because, as an ex-pig farmer, he knows "what it is to lose a beloved animal" (51). But he discovers that they have a large reservoir of water. Prince Itelo, who has learned English in a Syrian school, explains that the water is contaminated by frogs, which are taboo. The villagers cannot remove the creatures because it is forbidden to touch them. In their simple acceptance of their fate, the meek and gentle Arnewi resemble the cattle they take as their totem. Their relationship with the harsh desert is to suffer from it. When custom demands that he wrestle Prince Itelo, Henderson throws the fight because he is "trying to stay off violence" (64). But he is unable to accept defeat, wins the rematch, and Itelo assumes the abject position his tribe takes before force. He places Henderson's foot on his head and cries "I know you now. Oh, sir, I know you now" (69).

If the Arnewi accept suffering as their lot, their queen, Willatale, has found joy in the midst of sorrow. Henderson says that she "was typical of a certain class of elderly lady. You will understand what I mean, perhaps, if I say that the flesh of her arm overlapped the elbow." She is missing teeth and has only one eye, but she smiles at him "with many small tremors of benevolence and congratulation and welcome" (71). As Henderson wonders at her happiness during a time of suffering, he realizes that "she had given up such notions, there was no anxious care in her, and she was sustained. Why, nothing bad happened!" (79) She has transcended the world of suffering. Her bad eye, "bluish white," Henderson says, "signified her inwardness to me" (82). Like Augie March turning to the axial lines, the queen has found a way in which the painful chaos of the world passes off as unreal. She has achieved this by reconciling opposites, for she is happily wrapped in a lion skin, which symbolizes wrath, she is believed to be of both sexes, and she is a woman of "Bittah," which means happiness. She finds her joy by accepting the world at the same time that she has "risen above ordinary human limitations" (75). Henderson tells her that he hopes she will share her secret of life with him. Explaining that the "world is strange to a child" she suggests that the sleep of Henderson's spirit is self-imposed. He denies the closeness of death by assuming the attitude of the young, who still have a full life before them. The dream-like quality or "strangeness" which he sees in life is "a thing that makes death more remote, as in childhood" (84). She also tells him that he has "grun-tu-molani," the desire to live. Henderson feels that his "hour of liberation" is near; he foresees that the wise old queen, "grinning with her flat nose and gap teeth, the mother-of-pearl eye and the good eye," may be able to burst his spirit's sleep (79).

True to his obsessive idealism, Henderson destroys his opportunity. The tribe bestows its affection upon him, but he is haunted by the feeling that he hasn't earned it. He is driven to perform some public service—such as destroying the frogs in the reservoir. Since he can't touch them, he decides to blow them out of the water with a home-made bomb. His prudent old guide Romilayu wrings his hands in despair. Prince Itelo shuts his eyes and shakes his head; to change the dictates of fate is impossible. Undaunted, Henderson persists. " 'Prince,' I said, 'let's you and I talk this over.' I grew very intense. . . . I lowered my voice. 'Look here, I'm kind of an irrational person myself, but survival is survival' " (59). He wishes as an American to use his technological knowledge, and as the stranger to cure the plague of the tribe. The role of scapegoat satisfies his need both to give himself—a constructive impulse related to Wilhelm's masochism—and to assert his will against circumstance. But most of all he wishes to vent envy and malice. The frogs are at ease in their world, "stroking along with the water slipping over their backs and their mottles, as if they owned the medium" (60). Henderson's ideal of service coincides with his lust to kill. " 'Poor little bastards' was what I said," he confesses, "but in actual fact I was gloating—yuck-yuck-yuck! . . . We hate death, we fear death, but when you get right down to cases, there's nothing like it. . . . I hungered to let fall the ultimate violence on these creatures in the cistern" (89). He succeeds in killing the frogs, but he destroys the reservoir. The horrified natives watch helplessly as their water pours through the retaining wall and onto the desert floor. In his American exuberance Henderson destroys the very thing he seeks to save. Cows groan, the people gnash their teeth, and Henderson wanders back into the desert, followed by a reluctant Romilayu. In his striving and malice Henderson is a greater threat to the Arnewi than fate. Groaning with remorse, his gums aching with self-pity, Henderson must leave the gentle tribe because of his inability to accept either the limitation or the gift of life.

The bitterness of this failure tempts Henderson to return to America, but he decides to continue his quest. "I haven't got much hope," he says, "but all I know is that at home I'd be a dead man" (113). He starts for another tribe, planning to stay in the desert until he fulfills his original wish, that "all the bad is burned out of me"—a hope the second tribe is suited to fulfill (49). The Wariri tell Henderson that they and the Arnewi had once formed a single people, but that they had parted over the question of "luck." In their language "wariri" means "lucky" and "arnewi" its opposite. Henderson soon discovers that the Wariri, who meet him with guns, earn their name. They too suffer from drought, and Henderson and Romilayu are taken prisoner the evening before a rain ceremony.

In an early version of *Henderson* Bellow imbued the Wariri with the sensuality Leventhal fears. Henderson is aware of the "restlessness of, perhaps, savage customs of the night" and tries "to conceive what abominations were going on." The large umbrella which the king sends him is "like a canopy from the bed of the principal whore of all times." [9] Bellow eliminates these sensual overtones in the finished novel to concentrate on malice and violence. Henderson awakes to find dead bodies hanging from distant scaffolds. "Some of the men wore human jaw bones as neck-pieces under their chins." The villagers are drunken and quarreling, and "some of the older people were particularly abusive and waspish" (146). King Dahfu, with whom Henderson has an audience, speaks across a bowl in which two human skulls lie cheek to cheek. An old schoolmate of Itelo, Dahfu invites Henderson to the rain ceremony and bets him that the "lucky" Wariri will achieve rain in spite of a cloudless sky. During the ceremony a cow is slaughtered, an old man is slashed, and Dahfu risks his life in a deadly game. Under penalty of death if he misses, the king and a gilded priestess play catch with the skulls of his father and grandfather. The destructive will of the Wariri is most vividly portrayed in their treatment of their wooden idols, which they place in the center of the arena and then whip. "It would have been different, perhaps, if this had been a token whipping," Henderson says. "But great violence was loosed on these figures" (201). Instead of cajoling the gods into a bestowal of favor, the most the Arnewi might have dared, the Wariri beat their idols into submission.

At the climax of the ritual the natives carry off their idols one by one. When the strongest man in the tribe fails to lift the heaviest idol, the goddess of the clouds, Henderson is overwhelmed by a desire to try. He obtains permission, succeeds, and after being thrown naked into a stagnant cattle pond, is made Sungo, the Rain King. The heavens pour rain as a result of his effort—and he loses his bet with King Dahfu. He had lost the affection of the Arnewi by violating their religious beliefs, but he achieves community among the Wariri by acting within the context of their ritual. Glorying in his position, Henderson doesn't realize that no one else had wanted to be Sungo because of the danger involved. The gentle cow-people had been reluctant to receive Henderson's aid, and were sorry they had, but the Wariri make quick use of him. The "children of darkness," he will learn, control their fate by enlisting—and sacrificing—their enormous guest.

Before Henderson discovers that his life is in danger, he undergoes a therapeutic danger. Like Willatale, Dahfu has a "gift of life" based upon his intensification of his tribe's manner and values. Henderson finds him on a purple couch: "He seemed all ease," he says, "and I all limitation. He was extended, floating; I was contracted and cramped" (160). While Willatale is battered and yet beyond pain, Dahfu has an athletic grace that reflects his ease in this world. But just as Willatale felt that nothing bad happened, so Dahfu has a theory of how evil may be overcome. "Man is a creature who cannot stand still under blows . . . a creature of revenges," he says. "A brave man will try to make the evil stop with him. He shall keep the blow" (213, 214). Believing that "good exchanged for evil truly is the answer"—a comment that defines the moral stature of the Arnewi—Dahfu explains how one may become strong enough to keep the blows (214–15). He defines a correspondence where Bellow's other heroes see antipathy—a continual interaction between the flesh and the mind. A philosophic idealist, Dahfu believes that "it was not enough that there might be disorders of the body that originated in the brain. *Everything* originated there." Man creates his own body: "He is the artist of suggestions. He himself is his principal work of art, in the body, working in the flesh" (237). The process also works the opposite way, for man may change his mind by physically imitating what he wishes to be. "So you see," Dahfu says, "you came to me speaking of grun-tu-molani. What could be grun-tu-molani upon a background of cows?" (269) The Wariri take the lion as their totem and Dahfu keeps one as a pet in a den beneath the palace. When he proposes that he change Henderson's inner image by means of the lion, the millionaire, remembering his remark that pigs "have become a part of me," agrees (270).

In the den Henderson again meets the reality he denies. He notices that "the light filled up the stony space like a gray and yellow fluid, the surfaces of the wall acting as a filter, for the atmosphere was distributed as evenly as water" (220). Like Tommy Wilhelm, he must drown before he can live. Dahfu treats his tame lioness as if she were a playful puppy, but Henderson panics before her "calm, murderous face and clear eyes" (222). She walks around the two men and then begins to investigate them. "I felt her muzzle touch upward first at my armpits, and then between my legs, which naturally made the member there shrink into the shelter of my paunch" (222). If Henderson can face the lioness without fear, Dahfu claims, he will be able to accept the cruel reality of a naturalistic universe. "She is unavoidable. Test it, and you will find she is unavoidable. And this is what you need, as you are an avoider" (260). Henderson must not only face the fact of "inhuman wrath," or death—he must imitate it. Dahfu has him walk around the den on all fours, pretending to be a lion. Henderson growls and strikes imaginary prey with his paw. "Be the beast!" Dahfu tells him.

"You will recover humanity later" (267). Under Dahfu's instruction, Henderson spends several days as the king of beasts. "I would roar," he says, "and the king would sit with his arm about his lioness, as though they were attending an opera performance" (274).

Dahfu's theory and treatment are shrewdly appropriate to Henderson's weaknesses, and in fact resolve several issues confronted by other Bellow heroes.[10] Dahfu would teach Henderson that "really the danger of life is negligible," even in the lion and the death it symbolizes (258). Because the lion is at home in the world, because it "does not take issue with the inherent. Is one hundred per cent within the given," it exemplifies an acceptance of death which Henderson must emulate (263). The lion is also self-sufficient; Dahfu sees that Henderson, like the heroes before him, fears the world because he is dependent on it for his identity. If he could achieve the lion's autonomy, Henderson would be less frustrated and would have fewer "blows" to pass on: the world's wrath would be removed. While Willatale has learned to transcend pain, Dahfu has learned to derive strength from its sources. Dahfu also resolves Joseph's objection to the imagination and in doing so shows how good may be an actual force. To Dahfu the imagination is not passive, as Joseph believed, but active. "The career of our specie," he says, "is evidence that one imagination after another grows literal. Not dreams. Not mere dreams. I say not mere dreams because they have a way of growing actual. . . . What Homo sapiens imagines, he may slowly convert himself to" (271). By choosing good, man may make his dream of it actual, or part of the flesh: he may make his moral vision a "law of the body." Dahfu finds Mr. Green, places a theoretical foundation under Bellow's use of caricature, and argues, in a synthesis of opposites similar to Willatale's, that Henderson may learn goodness from the wrath or evil of the lion. Dahfu's view that the imagination is capable of influencing matter also answers Donald Malcolm's complaint[11] that Bellow is inconsistent in using an imaginary Africa to argue for creaturely existence. And it explains the fact that Henderson is awakened from his dream by a dream-like Africa. Because dreams "have a way of growing actual," the symptoms of alienation may be "converted into their opposites," as Henderson says at one point, to affirm a world that is ideal. Like Joseph's sense of strangeness, Henderson's dreaming embodies the paradox that the symptom of his illness is proof of the vision that may cure him.[12]

Dahfu appears to live his ideas. If Queen Willatale lives joyously in the midst of sorrow, Dahfu lives calmly in the midst of danger. When Henderson confesses that he envies him because "you are in the bosom of your people," Dahfu describes his duties. "Including also the prerogatives of these many wives. You may not think so on first glance, but it is a most complex existence requiring that I husband myself" (157, 155). If he should fail them, he would be strangled. And he has yet to really earn his throne by capturing the lion which contains his father's soul. The priests fear that the lioness he keeps below the palace is a witch, seducing him from his duty. "They are against me here," Dahfu says (212). Henderson objects to the king's acceptance of these superstitious traditions, but just as Dahfu accepts the principle of wrath, so he accepts the obligations of his culture. When the lion is sighted, Henderson accompanies Dahfu on the hunt. The lion appears "at the very doors of consciousness," Henderson says (306). The beast's roar is "indeed the voice of death." Henderson had boasted to his wife about his love of reality, but he now realizes that "unreality, unreality! That has been my scheme for a troubled but eternal life. . . . Now I was blasted away from this practice by the throat of the lion" (307). The lion forces Henderson to awaken from his dream—to live in the real world.

Dahfu dies in his attempt to capture his father, and Henderson finds that the Sungo is heir to the throne, the reason no one else wanted to be Rain King. Because the throne means sure death, he and Romilayu steal the lion cub which contains Dahfu's soul and flee to civilization. The awakened Henderson is "eager to know how it will be now that the sleep is burst" (335). He changes his name to Leo E. Henderson and plans to fulfill the ambition of his tumultuous fifty-five years by entering medical school. Among the fierce Wariri, it would seem, he had found a reality compatible with his own fierce nature. "I am giving up the violin," he says. "I guess I will never reach my object through it, *'to raise my spirit from the earth, to leave the body of this death'* " (284).

If Henderson abandons his quest for personal immortality, however, he does not abandon it completely, for he professes a faith in the transmigration of souls. He keeps the lion cub because Dahfu has "got to survive in some form" (326). When he looks into the eyes of a Persian orphan on the flight home, he thinks, "why he was still trailing his cloud of glory. God knows, I dragged mine on as long as I could till it got dingy, mere tatters of gray fog. However, I always knew what it was." The orphan's eyes are "new to life altogether. They had that new luster. With it they had ancient power, too. You could never convince me that *this was for the first time*" (339).

That the Wariri cure Henderson suggests the two edges of Bellow's comic sword. Because the rigidity at which we laugh is also the quality we admire in him, Henderson is in the tradition of Don Quixote and Parson Adams. He exemplifies a Kierkegaardian incongruity: that "the infinite may move within a man, and no one, no one be able to discover it through anything appearing outwardly." [13] Man may move in accord with the infinite by accepting his fate, but he demonstrates the infinite within him by struggling against it. Henderson's rage is born of a demand for good. His living death is born of his desire for life. As Dahfu tells him, "men of most powerful appetite have always been the ones to doubt reality the most" (232). Under the careful tutelage of the African king, he learns both the nobility and the relaxation of the lion. "We're supposed to think that nobility is unreal," he says. "But that's just it. The illusion is on the other foot" (318). In Africa he becomes an Ahab cured of his monomania—but with the zeal and courage to assert his will. He acknowledges the ultimate and inevitable limits of his humanity, but retains the nobility of the rebel.

But Dahfu's theory is not as intellectually successful as this cure implies. Although it resolves many issues, it too embodies the conflict in Bellow's imagination. The king rejects grun-tu-molani as insufficient, but admires the goodness of the Arnewi. "Ah, yes, I know the qualities," he tells Henderson. "Generous. Meek. Good. No substitutes should be accepted. On this my agreement is total and complete" (167). He explains the apparent incompatibility between the lion and goodness by the fact that it takes courage to be meek; one must be lion-hearted to accept the blows of fate. But the difference between Bellow's first version of Dahfu's theory, published in *Botteghe Oscure,* and the final one, suggests an incompatibility deeper than Dahfu can reconcile. In both drafts the king denies that the bad is more spectacular than the good. "If it is not spectacular," he claims in the first version, "it is not goodness. . . . Good has to reject bad with passionate intensity." True to the qualities of his tribe and lion, Dahfu insists upon a militant—or willful—rejection of evil. In the final form of the novel, however, Bellow reverses himself. Good "is associated with inspiration, and not conflict, for where a man conflicts there he will fall, and if taking the sword also perishes by the sword" (169). Dahfu's therapy for Henderson is psychologically sound, but it assumes that good may come from evil—which Dahfu here denies. That Dahfu is killed by the lion, having lived by it, further qualifies his theory: he speaks a truth which belies his nature, explains his fate—and justifies the Arnewi.

Henderson, if we can credit him with an identity of his own, rejects Dahfu's theory in spite of Bellow's revision. He senses that Dahfu's denial of conflict is inconsistent with the king's character. He regrets his lion adventures, thinking that under Willatale he "might have been learning about the grun-tu-molani instead." Although he himself would assert an autonomous will, he dismisses Dahfu's theory of the imagination as a "bourgeois idea of the autonomy of the individual mind" (288). During the lion hunt he thinks that "this was all mankind needed, to be conditioned into the image of a ferocious animal like the one below" (307). Bellow's shift in Dahfu's theory, and Henderson's rejection of that theory anyway, reflects Bellow's suspicion of "systems"—despite his delight in theoreticians. It also suggests that the conflict embodied in the two tribes remains unreconciled. Having created a willful Dahfu, Bellow makes him an Arnewi. Having cured Henderson among the Wariri, he establishes the millionaire's intellectual allegiance to Willatale. Bellow's indecision reflects the dilemma in Tamkin's command to "seize the day"—the fact that Ahab cannot enjoy the serenity of home at the same time that he kills the whale. Man cannot climb the mountain and stay at the bottom.

But Henderson too is inconsistent—creating a contradiction which bears upon the complaint that *Henderson* evades social issues.[14] In that Africa is an analogue to his inner self, Henderson goes up Mailer's Amazon of the inner eye to seek personal salvation. His assumption that health grows outward from the inner man reflects Bellow's personalist bias. *Henderson* is still very much about society, however, and finds difficulty in the fact. Dreaming of being socially useful, Henderson discovers African societies that are not only sophisticated, but reminiscent of the American city.[15] The screaming of the native crowd is "like Coney Island or Atlantic City or Times Square on New Year's Eve," and Dahfu's palace garden, like America, is a "vegetable and mineral junkyard" (169, 272). Henderson confronts America in Africa, and then, cured, returns home to serve others as a doctor. But just as society in the previous novels means World War II, a suicide pact, or a war of greed and malice, so Bellow imagines a community in *Henderson* that is destructive. Henderson becomes a Wariri, after all, by virtue of his envy and aggression. And he finds his socially useful position a trap. Because Dahfu had known that Sungo was "too dangerous a position," he too is a Wariri. "What have you pulled on me?" Henderson cries. "I should have been told what I was getting into." Dahfu answers, "It was done to me" (312). He too passes on the blows. Having yearned for community like all of Bellow's heroes, and having achieved it, Henderson discovers that it may cost him his life. He returns to America, which in this case means a flight from society, cured by the Wariri but yearning for the Arnewi— longing, like all of Bellow's heroes, for the secret that will enable him to live with joy in the midst of sorrow. He has learned that love is not the product of will and that good cannot come out of evil. He has also learned that community can be dangerous, a lesson his journey back to his original society obscures.

Although Bellow does not resolve these inconsistencies intellectually, he does I think reconcile the two tribes in his characterization. Just as the two tribes represent the two sides of man's inner reality, so they represent the two sides of Henderson. Bellow's skill in characterization is seen in the fact that while remaining a single individual Henderson appears in the two tribes as two different personalities. Having irreverently blown up the Arnewi frogs, he objects to the Wariri beating of the gods. Too much a man of will to live with the cow-people, he is too much a man of love to accept the Wariri. "Just the same," he says of the gods of the second tribe, "they had dignity—mystery; they were after all the gods, and they made the awards of fate" (181).

Henderson's dual nature is also embodied in Bellow's comedy. We laugh at the millionaire because of his intense physical desire as well as his mental rigidity. In contrast to such events as the checker game and the demolition of the frogs, Bellow portrays Henderson enjoying Willatale's grun-tu-molani. Life is affirmed in these passages by a great sense of physical beauty. When Henderson sees a wall with the sun-lit color of "a clear thin red rose," he tells us: "I pressed my nose to it . . . and knelt there on those old knees, lined and grieved-looking; like carrots; and I inhaled, I snuckered through my nose and caressed the wall with my cheek" (101, 102). Funny among the Arnewi primarily because of his mental rigidity, Henderson is comic in the second tribe because of such physical impulses. His intense fear may be taken as a physical reaction: he is indeed, among the Wariri, a "soul *tantalised* by the needs of the body." As Henderson walks among the savages and corpses, he tries to be a Hemingway hero. "Seem to be a lot of dead people," he comments to his companion nonchalantly. When he must repeat himself in the noise he loses his indifference. " 'Dead people!' I said. And then I told myself, 'Don't ask for information with such despair.' My face was indeed hot and huge and anxious" (150). He is forced to give in to this anxiety again in the lion den.

When Dahfu chastises him for his fear, Henderson says, "I tried to say I wasn't but my face began to work and I couldn't get those words out. Then I began to cough, with my fist placed, thumb in, before my mouth, and my eyes watered. I finally said, 'It's a reflex'" (227). Henderson is funny because of the "machine-like obstinacy" of his body.

The effect of this comedy, too, reflects Bellow's dual vision. As ridicule, Bellow's laughter supplies the criticism and the distance supplied earlier by his irony. As "an overflow of sympathy, an amiable feeling of identity with what is disreputably human," as Wylie Sypher defines the romantic theory of comedy, Bellow's laughter is an act of identification. Bellow uses laughter to express and purge his ambivalence in much the same way that Henderson is purged by his adventures. Just as King Dahfu believes that good may come from evil, and Henderson seeks prestige (and sanctification) by becoming a scapegoat, so, as Wylie Sypher says, "comedy desecrates what it seeks to sanctify." Sypher also points out that "the comic hero and the saint accept the irreconcilables in man's existence." [16] If Wilhelm accepts the dilemma of the human condition by achieving a religious perspective, Henderson does so by being comic. *Henderson* fulfills Augie March's statement that "laughing is an enigma" that includes both man's subservience and his superiority to his physical fate (536).

Thus Bellow leaves his awakened hero on the way home to America and a new life. In the second chapter he had portrayed the reality Henderson denies by a vision of an octopus in an aquarium. As Henderson looked at the creature, he was horrified by "the soft head with its speckles, and the Brownian motion in those speckles, a cosmic coldness in which I felt I was dying" (19). The "cosmic coldness" is the death which awaits him in an inanimate universe and the inhumanity within the human heart. By the end of his African journey Henderson can face both the internal and the external reality. Unlike Augie March, who at the end of *The Adventures* flees a cold "specter of white anger" by the sea, Henderson is at home in the cold. He gets off his plane in a New Found Land. With his lion cub and the young orphan, he runs joyously about the air field. A man of will and a man of love, a rebel and a man of peace, he goes "running—leaping, leaping, pounding, and tingling over the pure white lining of the gray Arctic silence" (341).

CHAPTER 7   THE INSPIRED CONDITION

> *The test of a first-rate intelligence is the ability to hold two opposed ideas in the mind at the same time, and still retain the ability to function.*
>
> FITZGERALD, *"The Crack-Up"*

Although *Herzog* (1964) is a complex novel, each of its individual stories is simple in itself. The frame of the novel is the ecstatic reminiscence of Moses Herzog, a college professor, as he temporarily lives at his country home in the Berkshires. Like Augie March, Herzog does his internal labor: the novel consists of the compulsive reworking of the past by a man who has been deeply hurt. The action which Herzog remembers—the actual present of the novel—is also simple and direct. He decides at the end of the school term in New York to flee from his mistress, Ramona, to some friends at Martha's Vineyard. Once there he decides to return immediately to New York, where he continues the letter writing which has lately become his compulsion. He spends the following evening with Ramona, visits a courtroom the next day, and then flies to Chicago, where he comes close to murdering his ex-wife and her lover—his best friend. He takes his daughter June to an aquarium the next morning, has an auto accident, and appears before a police court for carrying a concealed weapon. He then flies to the Berkshires, returning the novel to its beginning. The past events which he remembers as he travels also form a straightforward story, although they are revealed in fragments. He had divorced his first wife and married the beautiful and neurotic Madeleine, settling with her in the Berkshires to write a book on the Romantics. She had insisted that he could save their marriage only by moving to Chicago and taking their friends, the Gersbachs, with them. Once there she insisted that Herzog see a psychiatrist, saw him herself at the doctor's request, and then one fall morning announced her decision for divorce. Herzog went to Europe to recover from his misery, returned to New York worse off than before, and discovered that Madeleine and Gersbach were lovers even before he moved them all to Chicago.

Each of these story levels repeats the hero's confrontation of an evil in the past—the pattern of all of Bellow's novels. Herzog in the Berkshires remembers the evil he had seen in New York and Chicago, where he remembers the evil he had seen even earlier. In part because of the distance he finds in this triple remove, Bellow once again moves closer to issues and ideas he previously qualified. Herzog is larger than life not because of caricature—although there are some elements of it in his characterization—but because of the intensity of his emotion and the ambition of his thought.[1] More like Willard than Grebe, feeling all the pain and conflict of the other protagonists, Herzog confronts almost every issue raised in Bellow's previous fiction. That he does so in a novel that is realistic rather than picaresque or fantastic makes his struggle a victory over the elements that caused Bellow to abandon "The Crab and the Butterfly." Herzog carries masochism to lengths far greater than Wilhelm, attempts to kill not a cat or a stranger but people close to him, and at the same time arrives at the clearest affirmation in Bellow's fiction of the views that might save him. He makes a complete decision for social service, finding his salvation in a practical, hard-headed manhood, and an unqualified avowal of faith in God, telling us that "this was by no means a 'general idea' with him now" (266). Although twenty-five years and six books separate *Herzog* from Bellow's first short story, "Two Morning Monologues," Herzog embraces the two general views which Bellow then contrasted—the reliance on an inner vision and the determination to act in the social or external world.

If Herzog embraces both the internal and the external, however, he creates a problem by doing so—the chief difficulty in the novel. This issue revolves around the question, as Herzog puts it, of "whether justice on this earth can or cannot be general, social, but must originate within *each heart*" (219). Herzog is divided on this question. When he writes a letter to Eisenhower he tells him that "to Tolstoi, freedom is entirely personal. That man is free whose condition is simple, truthful—real." He suggests that society is a distraction from more important issues. Man must meet his fate, as Joseph tried to do, by discovering the self which is real or autonomous. But Herzog also tells Eisenhower about Hegel who "understood the essence of human life to be derived from history. History, memory—that is what makes us human, that, and our knowledge of death" (162). Herzog rejects both of these ideas at the time because he is "bugging" Ike, but his mention of them in the same breath defines the issue which *Herzog* confronts and embodies. Herzog wants to "renew universal connections"—to lose himself in something larger than personality—and he defines competing universals.

Because of this explicit issue, *Herzog* is Bellow's most detailed examination of love and will so far, and his greatest demonstration of the relevance of that polarity to the contemporary scene. The issue is a universal one, but of particular concern in an era of the enormous state, "other directed" personality, and a tendency to turn from history to the private self. Because "the new fiction, which emerged in the forties, rejected public experience," as Chester Eisinger tells us, Herzog's division corresponds to the division in our recent novels.[2] Thoreau's quest for simplicity, Huck's choice of the river, and Isaac MacCaslin's rejection of his plantation suggest that the issue is perennial in American literature. But as Bellow's own novels reveal, it is one of particular importance to the novel of the fifties and the sixties. Leventhal's affirmation of a deeper "promise" than the social implies that personal experience may have greater significance than the social. Henderson, in contrast, begins his trip with the personal problem of anxiety over death and finds his salvation in the rediscovery of society. In both novels the personal and social make competing claims on the hero and the reader. Eisinger explains the new fiction by saying that "the war drove the writer to withdrawal; the social and political scene served to confirm the wisdom of his retreat," but he uses social or historical terms to do it. The debate which exists over this question is generally recognized, and the ultimately religious nature of the new personalism is becoming so. The "retreat" may be less a disheartened withdrawal from society than an affirmation of a different reality—a religious retreat based on internal experience. Nona Balakian makes a comment that is increasingly typical when she says that the new novelist, "dealing with the redeeming power of love, with the almost mystical need to connect with others and yet preserve the self's inmost truth . . . has bordered on a new spirituality." [3]

As dramatized in the novel, the division between the social and the personal is also an aesthetic one. Herzog's own emotional conflict between the passive and the active corresponds to the division in his thought. In part because Bellow assumes a point of view close to Herzog's—purposely blurring the distinction between narrator and protagonist—our questions about Herzog are questions about the novel's art. Like many personalist novels, *Herzog* appears to be the subjective confusion of a passive hero—a novel that is formless. What action or story exists is obscured by the brilliant letters and disconnected memories which fill the book. "Overcome by the need to explain, to have it out, to justify, to put in perspective, to clarify, to make amends," Herzog writes to everyone—from Marshall Field and Co. to God Himself (2). Bellow reveals a great deal of Herzog's past by these means, but he clearly offers them for their own sake: they are at once intellectual play and a brilliant critique on the values and problems of our society. They seem to be a thread upon which Bellow strings spectacular thoughts and events—a concept which, like that of the dangling man or the victim, threatens to remain static.

There is some question whether Herzog ever changes: circling back upon itself, the novel seems to portray a state of mind rather than a story or a significant event. Thus most critics recognize that Herzog finds peace at the end, but reject it as insignificant or unconvincing. Irving Howe writes that *Herzog* contains a "superbly-realized situation but hardly a developing action" and Marcus Klein argues that the ending "is a little suspect, only a baiting of a resolution." Tony Tanner recognizes a movement from "corrosive restlessness to a point of temporary rest," but holds that we are inside Herzog's mind for the bulk of the novel "—going over things, witnesses of this endless, silent self-examination. It is not systematic: like his life it is mismanaged and patternless." [4] Just as Augie described the form of his novel as "first to knock, first admitted," so Herzog describes the form of his when he says he "might never succeed in becoming systematic" (4).

Although the novel gives this effect, it does contain a definite form, or rather two competing forms.[5] In both, Herzog convincingly changes, does so in a clearly developed action, and in the process unites the letters, his memories, and the present events. Bellow finds form first of all in Herzog's struggle to reject personalism, which he has abandoned at the novel's beginning but which he continues to embody. Herzog defines his rejection and struggle in terms of the contemporary intellectual scene. Our general belief that the modern age is a wasteland, he says—the view that God is dead, society corrupted by size and technology, and the individual overwhelmed—has given rise to a disastrous withdrawal from the world to the private self. We have embraced subjectivity, aestheticism, emotionalism and personalism in an attempt to save the self from the "void." Herzog too, had reacted to this nihilism, though he had assumed he was combating it. Believing that "the strength of a man's virtue or spiritual capacity [is] measured by his ordinary life," Herzog had retired to a private life in the Berkshires in order to demonstrate the reality and the practicality of spiritual virtues (106). "The revolutions of the twentieth century, the liberation of the masses by production," he believed, "created private life but gave nothing to fill it with. This was where such as he came in" (125). Everyone had claimed that "you must sacrifice your poor, squawking, niggardly individuality—which may be nothing anyway (from an analytic viewpoint) but a persistent infantile megalomania, or (from a Marxian point of view) a stinking little bourgeois property—to historical necessity." To assert the value of the individual against this view, Herzog had "tried to be a *marvelous* Herzog, a Herzog who, perhaps clumsily, tried to live out marvelous qualities vaguely comprehended" (93). Herzog sees that this intention had been just another case of the self driven inward by a difficult and apparently meaningless world. It had been not a confrontation of the void but flight from it.

But *Herzog* turns inward as well as outward. If it is an affirmation of society, it is also an affirmation of "the inspired condition," or man's highest subjective experience. The modern world demands our participation, but it also gives special significance to our highest values. "To live in an inspired condition, to know truth, to be free, to love another, to consummate existence, to abide with death in clarity of consciousness . . . is no longer a rarefied project" (165). Herzog's split between the passive and the active finds its parallel in the division in the novel between a traditional structure, recording Herzog's struggle with personalism, and a subjective structure, growing almost unconsciously out of his character. Here too the conclusion grows out of the protagonist's experience, and especially out of the evil he confronts—an evil which belongs to existence rather than society, and which is Herzog's basic problem. Although this story contradicts Herzog's affirmation of society, it exemplifies Bellow's growing ability in his fiction to contain and use the ambivalence he feels. He does this in *Herzog* not by metaphor, comedy or characterization—although Herzog is at once a meek and a "difficult, aggressive man"—but rather by Herzog's own achievement of a hard-headed attitude toward the world. More than in anything else, Herzog earns his salvation by the practical acceptance of the mixture and ambivalence within himself and his faith. This too, Bellow makes clear, is related to our intellectual scene. Like those around him Herzog had assumed that the world was in crisis and that desperate measures were needed to cope with it. He comes to see that this erroneous view leads to cures that compound the problem. Even a writer such as Nietzsche, he says, had "a Christian view of history, seeing the present moment always as some crisis, some fall from classical greatness, some corruption or evil to be saved from." Our retreat from society, our sensationalistic celebration of dread, and our acceptance of violence and obscenity as philosophic truth all derive from our feeling that "we have to recover from some poison, need saving, ransoming" (54). Herzog is aware of our danger, but he rejects the modern sense of crisis to insist upon a modest, level-headed perspective. *Herzog* rejects personalism at the same time that it affirms it, bearing on a central division in our thought, but it is most of all the story of an impulsive man who simultaneously achieves the homely virtue of common sense and the uncommon virtue of religious faith.

In spite of its apparent disunity, *Herzog* is in many ways a more highly organized work than Bellow's previous long novels. Because Herzog's letters and memories suggest a course of action which his present experience clearly reinforces, Bellow unifies *Herzog*—for the first time in his fiction—by means of plot. Herzog's actions are the product and the justification of his thought. When we abstract Bellow's plot from the context of the actual novel, in fact, it seems over-organized or pat—an impression we do not receive from the novel itself. The ideas in Herzog's letters often supply the point to the extended memories the letters awaken. Earl Rovit is right, I think, in seeing "a tendency toward a wearying sameness in the overall texture of the novel," [6] but this tendency is due to Herzog's continual self-examination rather than a lack of evolution in his thought. It is also due to the aesthetic implications of Bellow's rejection of crisis psychology. Lacking an active hero and an external conflict, the novel of revelation finds drama in the quest for insight and its final achievement, a drama found in Bellow's previous novels. But Bellow now rejects momentous insights for a mild, tentative truth. Herzog seeks understanding, and he is excited, but Bellow insists that his quest be modest: Bellow finds drama instead in detail, thought, and characterization, but most of all in the act of reminiscence.

Bellow begins Herzog's story in New York with the memory of Herzog's divorce from Madeleine and those who betrayed him during it. In Chicago, Herzog sees, he had been passive, childish and masochistic. Madeleine's will was triumphant while his was "all converted into passivity" (8). "It had never entered Herzog's mind . . . to stand his ground. He still thought perhaps that he could win by the appeal of passivity, of personality, win on the ground of being, after all, Moses—Moses Elkanah Herzog—a good man, and Madeleine's particular benefactor" (10). As Herzog broods about this, he exhibits these same faults, for he yearns for rest and his painful reworking of the past is self-torture. He had gone to a doctor "hoping for some definite sickness which would send him to a hospital for a while," and he decides to go to Martha's Vineyard where he might "lie down in his bathing trunks, and warm his troubled belly on the sand" (12–13, 17). His friends there will comfort him, and he will escape from Ramona, whose kindness he thinks "was dangerous. He might have to pay with his freedom" (18).

On the way to the train station he writes letters to those who betrayed him during his break-up with Madeleine. He writes to Aunt Zelda, who had lied to him about Madeleine's adultery, to Lucas Asphalter, who had first told him of Madeleine's affair with Gersbach, and to Edvig, the psychiatrist who had helped Madeleine get rid of him: "So, Edvig, . . . you turn out to be a crook too! How pathetic!" (53) Ignorant of Madeleine's adultery, Edvig had advised Herzog to be understanding with her. "As for me," Herzog concludes, "I was your patient" (65). He thinks back to a visit he made to Gersbach, whose strange behavior he now understands. Gersbach had angrily demanded the details of Herzog's fight with Madeleine the previous night, when she had tried to keep Herzog from her bed. Gersbach, who had been with her that afternoon, advises Herzog to let her sleep alone. Gersbach is comic in this scene in the rigidity of his anger while Herzog is comic in his rigid subservience.

> Gersbach sighed and walked along his wall slowly, bending and straightening like a gondolier. "I explained to you last week . . ." he said.
> "You'd better tell me once more. I'm in a state," said Herzog.
> . . . "Let's cut out all the *shtick*," said Gersbach. "Let's say you're a crumb. Let's say even you're a crim-

inal. There's nothing—nothing!—you could do to shake
my friendship. That's no shit, and you know it! I can
take what you've done to me." [60]

Herzog is enraged at himself as well as at these people, for his
childish dependence had made him all too vulnerable. Edvig and
Madeleine had defined their problems in religious terms, and so
Herzog had tried to be meek, "as though such idiotic passivity or
masochistic crawling or cowardice were humility, or obedience, not
terrible decadence" (64). When Herzog later thinks of Ramona he
begs her to marry him—"and was staggered by his rashness, his
weakness" (66). He would again seek salvation in a personal relationship. He suddenly writes to such public figures as Adlai
Stevenson and Martin Luther King, and then he asks himself "since
when have you taken such an interest in social questions, in the
external world?" (68) The two longer letters which follow bear
upon his new political preoccupation. The first is to Shapiro, a
fatuous historian who has written a "merely aesthetic critique of
modern history! After the wars and mass killings!" (75) Shapiro
has retreated into art from the hopeless wasteland. Herzog admits
that "visions of darkness and evil can't be passed over," but he
rejects "the commonplaces of the Wasteland outlook, the cheap
mental stimulants of Alienation. . . . I can't accept this foolish
dreariness. We are talking about the whole life of mankind. The
subject is too great, too deep for such weakness, cowardice—too
deep, too great, Shapiro" (74, 75). But in his next letter Herzog
reveals that he too had been a Shapiro, though he turned to affection rather than art. Herzog writes to Sandor Himmelstein, who
had taken him in after he had moved at Madeleine's request. He
had sought comfort and love from the Himmelsteins and had received what he feels he deserved, a lecture on "reality," or the
empty brutality of existence. Himmelstein had answered his deep
need for affection, had worked him up by discussing Madeleine,
and had ended by discussing his own war wound. After this letter,
Herzog sees the truth of his present holiday at the Vineyard: "What
was he hanging around for? To follow this career of *personal relationships* until his strength at last gave out?" He decides to return

to New York and his problems. "This hugging and heartbreak is for women," he thinks. "The occupation of a man is in duty, in use, in civility, in politics in the Aristotelian sense" (94). Back in his New York apartment that night, he recalls an issue in which he might be of use: Madeleine's babysitter had written that she found June locked alone in the car by Gersbach. He's abusing her, Herzog thinks: "I'll kill him for that—so help me, if I don't!" (101)

Herzog awakes the next morning still obsessed with memories. Having recalled the period of his divorce, he now digs deeper into the past, remembering his courtship of Madeleine, an earlier friendship with Nachman, and then his childhood in LaRoux, Canada. He makes this journey in time in the course of writing to Monsignor Hilton, who had nurtured Madeleine's conversion to Catholicism and who, he says, "may be interested to find out what may happen, or actually does happen, when people want to save themselves from . . . I suppose the word is nihilism" (103). All of the people he now recalls had felt they needed salvation, had sought it in the personal life, and had been ironically self-defeated. Madeleine and her parents told Herzog that he was saving her: her unhappy childhood gave her a deep need for a conventional life with the settled Herzog. Once married, Herzog notes, Madeleine felt trapped by the conventions of housework and family life. The two had turned Herzog's dream of exemplary daily life into private emotional slaughter. Nachman, whom Herzog had known as a boy, had also sought a personal form of salvation: rejecting the modern wasteland, he had fled to lyric poetry, following Blake, and to personal love for a girl who is mentally ill. Nachman's rejection of a squalid age ends in the squalor of his poverty and the pathos of his girl's madness and suicide. Herzog's father had sought desperately to be a successful businessman, had been reduced to bootlegging, and had failed at that. Of course he failed, Herzog thinks: "all of Papa's violence went into the drama of his life, into family strife, and sentiment" (146).

Herzog's exploration of the past is interrupted by a phone call from Ramona, the woman he had fled. "No mere sensualist, but a theoretician, almost a priestess," Ramona invests sex with religious

significance, prescribes it as the only therapy for Herzog's grief—
and becomes a symbol of the personalism Herzog is struggling to
reject (150). Before they had intercourse that evening, Herzog
thinks, Ramona would sympathetically draw him out on his
troubles. "When he was done . . . it would be Ramona's turn.
You treat me right, I treat you right . . . Ramona was highly
experienced at entertaining gentlemen" (157). Herzog's resentment
is that of a man who is pitied, but also that of a man fighting against
his desire, for Ramona offers the rest and the comfort for which he
yearns. Angry and complaining, reluctant and spiteful, Herzog
spends another personal evening. The dinner is delicious, Ramona
attractive, and Herzog finally peaceful. But even as he relaxes, he
rebukes himself for this "feminine game" of hugging and heartbreak. Meditating on the technological age, he accepts the technological impersonality he had once rejected: "The beautiful super-
machinery opening a new life for innumerable mankind. Would
you deny them the right to exist? Would you ask them to labor and
go hungry while you enjoyed delicious old-fashioned Values?"
(201)

Herzog's evening with Ramona (which forms the fifth of nine
sections) is at once the literal and the thematic center of the book,
for in it the novel shifts from Herzog's reliving of the past to his
actions in the present. Bellow continues this new tack when Herzog
is shocked by an evil greater than that done to him by Madeleine.
When he returns from Ramona to his apartment, he suddenly feels
"he must do something, something practical and useful, and must
do it at once" (207). He phones his lawyer Simkin and arranges to
meet him at the courthouse: he might at least save June by taking
her from Madeleine. He arrives early and visits a criminal court.
The cases increase in terror: he witnesses the trials of a robber,
a homosexual medical student, a bragging male prostitute, and then,
in another court, a mother who has murdered her child. Such brutality puts his easy, weepy humanism into a humiliating perspective:
evil requires a more rigorous struggle for good than Herzog had ever
imagined. Having once felt that society's impersonal machinery
could never give real justice, Herzog is surprised at the judge's fair-

ness. The homosexual medical student (who was caught by a policeman loitering as a decoy) is a German immigrant interning in this country. When the judge asks for his plea, he orders the boy's lawyer to advise him that he will not receive a medical license if he pleads guilty. Herzog sees that the judge has, "after all, a human head [and] a human voice" (227). The judge finds room for compassion within the letter of the law: "Social organization, for all its clumsiness and evil," as Herzog said earlier, "has accomplished far more and embodies more good than I do, for at least it sometimes gives justice" (220).

Herzog leaves the first court sick over the evil he has seen and even sicker over his false, ingenuous position. "He felt as though something terrible, inflammatory, bitter, had been grated into his bloodstream and stung and burned his veins, his face, his heart" (230). After witnessing the murder case he is determined to do something about the abuse of his own child. The brutal truth shocks him into action—and into another fault. Having been passive, Herzog now leaps to the opposite extreme; "determined to act without clearly knowing what to do," he flies to Chicago with murder in his heart (241). He will save June, but he will also prove his manhood. As he takes his father's pistol from the desk in his boyhood home, he feels that he is following in his father's footsteps. Papa Herzog had threatened him with that same pistol, "trying to act out the manhood you should have had" (250). But Herzog's new manhood is that of the weak man who falls back on violence. He enacts the very ideas he had rejected, for he views the situation as a crisis, sees violence as the necessary scourge, and most of all bases his actions on the purely subjective. "In spirit she was his murderess," he thinks of Madeleine, "and therefore he was turned loose, could shoot or choke without remorse" (255).

Herzog is saved from committing murder by a scene which embodies Bellow's theme. Peering through the side window of Madeleine's flat, Herzog sees June in the bathtub. "In the rushing water with floating toys his daughter's little body shone. His child! Madeleine had let her black hair grow longer, and now it was tied up for the bath with a rubber band. He melted with tenderness for her." Then he sees a hand turn off the water. "It was Gersbach. He was going to bathe Herzog's daughter! Gersbach!" (256) He watches the man who had cuckolded him perform the father's duty. "Then Gersbach ordered her to stand, and she stooped slightly to allow him to wash her little cleft. Her father stared at this. A pang went through him, but it was quickly done." Once dried, June runs off, leaving Gersbach alone. "There were two bullets in the chamber. . . . But they would stay there. Herzog clearly recognized that" (257). He sees that his rage had been another example of what he elsewhere calls "subjective monstrosity." He also sees that he had been childish and masochistic, for "only self-hatred could lead him to ruin himself because his heart was 'broken'" (258). After the courtroom scene, his feverish flight to Chicago, and his thoughts while getting the pistol, Herzog's decision not to murder is anti-climactic—but a perfect portrayal of Bellow's theme. Herzog learns outside the house of his ex-wife and her lover that the truth may be modest rather than crucial.

This scene could well stand as the turning point of the novel, but Herzog's rush to other activities further exemplifies Bellow's insistence on a modest truth. He attempts to convince Phoebe, Gersbach's wife, to help him get June by testifying to her husband's affair with Madeleine. He accepts her refusal and then tells himself that "the historical process, putting clothes on our backs, shoes on the feet, meat in the mouth, does infinitely more for us by the indifferent method than anyone does by intention" (264). Having recently tried sex and dread, Herzog tells his friend Luke Asphalter that he would replace those values with brotherhood.

> I really believe that brotherhood is what makes a man human. If I owe God a human life, this is where I fall down. . . . When the preachers of dread tell you that others only distract you from metaphysical freedom then you must turn away from them. The real and essential question is one of our employment by other human beings and their employment by us. [272]

Herzog's subsequent experience could also serve as the novel's turning point. He tells himself that he is done with blundering, but another blunder provides a second climax. Herzog picks up June the next morning, has an auto accident, and is arrested for carrying his father's gun. He himself, he thinks bitterly, is the one who endangers June's life. The result of his arrest is even more telling, for Herzog finds himself subject in court to the power he once thought himself immune to: "He could now feel for himself what it was like to be in custody. No one was robbed, no one had died. Still he felt the heavy, deadly shadow lying on him" (286). If he had come close to violence in the previous section, he now comes close to being a criminal. But he is saved from a serious charge by his new poise. He consciously shows the desk sergeant "no defiance, no special pleading, nothing of the slightest personal color" (294). He also handles himself well when Madeleine shows up. She does her best to increase his trouble by implying that he threatened her life. She points to the bullets and exclaims "one of those was for me, wasn't it!" Herzog is neither cowed nor violent. " 'You think so? I wonder where you get such ideas? And who was the other one for?' He was quite cool as he said this, his tone was level. He was doing all he could to bring out the hidden Madeleine." Although he stands before the court at a disadvantage, having been caught with a concealed weapon, Herzog triumphs over Madeleine by receiving a just verdict: like the New York judge, the police sergeant tempers the objective facts with subjective insight. "Her voice went up sharply, and as she spoke, Herzog saw the sergeant take a new look at her, as if he were beginning to make out her haughty peculiarities at last" (301).

Having received a justice he himself could not achieve, Herzog finds his new ideas justified. He sees once again that he has "shown the arbitrary withdrawal of proud subjectivity from the collective and historical progress of mankind" (307). He will give up his quest for personal happiness. Man can suffer anything, he says, "provided there is something great, something into which his being, and all beings, can go" (289). He retires to the Berkshires—a scene which softens the climax of the courtroom—where he feels the ecstasy of his release. He manages enough poise to keep himself out of the hospital his brother Will recommends (and which he had once desired), and even opens himself to Ramona—who has followed him to the country. She is no longer a threat now that he knows his own mind. Although Bellow qualifies Herzog's success, Herzog is anxious to begin the duties he has set himself, and feels that the urge to write his letters has passed.

By embracing society and its values, Bellow comes closer in *Herzog* than he ever has in unifying his drama and his character's thought. That some of Herzog's experience and almost all of Bellow's technique carry implications that contradict this stated theme, however, reflects the conflict that still exists. The most dramatic evidence of this split lies in Herzog's position as a new man. He withdraws from the city to find peace at his country home—which he has established as a symbol of his evasion of society and evil. Cured of passivity, personalism, and solitude, he finds joy while thinking about himself, alone, "lying under the open window with the sun in his face" (313). He has embraced moderation, but his state is ecstatic. He has dedicated himself to social issues, but he enjoys the small sensations of nature rather than the sweep of social forces. His solitude, his absorption with himself, and his internal source of strength ally him with those early American personalists, the Romantics. Like Thoreau he has temporarily withdrawn from society to live alone in nature, where he achieves the joy and simplicity that Augie and Wilhelm only dream of in their cities: "The stars were near like spiritual bodies. Fires, of course; gases—minerals, heat, atoms, but eloquent at five in the morning to a man lying in a hammock, wrapped in his overcoat" (1).

Herzog is a divided novel because its art reflects this happy isolation rather than Herzog's new social affirmation. Herzog's view that "the *whole* was required to redeem every separate spirit" requires an aesthetic different from that which Bellow uses (156). It is true that Bellow laughs at his emotional hero, and that a large number of characters appear, testifying to the color and power of the *whole,* but the value of the novel lies not in the general scene but in Herzog, a brilliantly unique character. *Herzog* finds its subject and structure in the protagonist's quest for insight into himself, and the external events are largely memories—a subjective experience. So too with Bellow's use of time: in that the past overshadows the present in the novel, time is subjective and events are given value by Herzog's emotional needs. Bellow shapes many scenes around Herzog's awareness of the real motives beneath external and social poses, and even the letters, which carry private thought into the public realm (and which are never mailed), give rise to thoughts and memories which are franker and more subjective than the written words. The letters, in fact, may be viewed as a device permitting a novelist to write about the private life of a passive character.

What is true of Bellow's technique is also true of the novel's content. However much Herzog pleads for social service, the novel is about his internal and private experience. Herzog never participates in social service himself, and he embraces that goal in part because society provides him personal justice. He decides to go to Chicago because of the emotional intensity of the evil he views in the courtroom, and he decides not to murder because he sees Gersbach washing June in the bathroom.[7] He proves his new manhood in his private relations with Ramona, and his thought and affection at the end are directed toward family—toward June and his brother Will—rather than toward social issues.[8] Herzog embraces society, but he speaks of it in terms of brotherhood and spiritual community rather than as institutions, causes, or customs.

Although *Herzog* is a statement against personalism, then, it is a personalist novel. In many ways, Herzog's cure lies in his acceptance of the attitudes he intellectually rejects. By pleading that their life in the Berkshires was to be an historic example for the rest of society, Herzog buried his marriage under social and historical concerns. Like Augie fleeing from love to the external world, Herzog fled from marriage to social experiment. Herzog is often less emotional than hyper-analytical. His tendency to remember and to analyze the past reflects not only his self-absorption but his tendency to intellectualize. This removal from himself and his experience derives in part from the novel's framework, but it is also part of Herzog's character. He analyzes Ramona's motives, comments on her ideas, and sends her messages—all in his head while she stands before him. He turns these same powers upon himself as he meditates on the couch in New York. "To his own parents he had been an ungrateful child," he thinks. "To his country, an indifferent citizen. . . . With love, lazy. With brightness, dull. With power, passive. With his own soul, evasive." He makes an object of himself, seeing himself as others see him. But he then makes still another removal from himself: "Satisfied with his own severity, positively enjoying the hardness and factual rigor of his judgment, he lay on his sofa, his arms rising behind him, his legs extended without aim" (4–5). Herzog backs away from himself to review his faults, and then backs away from the reviewer. Bellow finds drama by giving the physical act of meditation and the character's reaction to his own thoughts: self-absorption becomes a form of social activity among the many selves. Herzog supplies in his own character the distance Bellow elsewhere supplies in irony, symbolism, and caricature.

Because Herzog finds his salvation in society, its meaning to him also bears on this conflict. Bellow is caught by the conflict that arises in all his fiction between his dedication to our larger community and his criticism of it. Part of Herzog's self-hate lies in his ascetic distrust of the luxury he associates with personalism—and society. His evening with Ramona shows him to be "powerless to reject the hedonistic joke of a mammoth industrial civilization on the spiritual desires, the high cravings of a Herzog, on his moral suffering, his longing for the good, the true" (166). The values of consumption are one way in which those in power keep their power —and distract us from what is real. But Bellow also equates society with reality. Herzog's cities contain the same naturalistic force as Augie's Chicago and the same sensuality as Leventhal's New York. Because they are built by men, and re-create the universe in which we live, our cities embody the truth about the human as well as the metaphysical. Herzog is oppressed by a chaotic world of sensation which Bellow associates with the confusing numbers and drives of the species. Because the state is the instrument of the species, our self-hate "is undoubtedly a political phenomenon, an action taken against personal impulse or against the personal demand for adequate space and scope" (164). In the subway Herzog sees posters scribbled with "comical genitals like rockets, ridiculous copulations, slogans and exhortations." The marks are "filth, quarrelsome madness, the prayers and wit of the crowd. Minor works of Death" (176). Herzog's taxi ride to the courtroom, where he sees not so minor works of death, is typical of his daily social encounters. The cabbie had seen Herzog kissing Ramona goodbye. "That was a real nice-looking broad," he tells Herzog. "That's the kind that puts down the best stuff." He mentions a girlfriend of his, "a no-good lay. A broad eighteen don't even know how to shit" (223). Herzog finds this amusing—"oratorical lechery"—and does not brood about these elements as do the earlier heroes, but he is disturbed, and they do dominate his world. When they see a derelict waiting to wipe windshields at a stop light, the cabbie is prepared for violence. "I keep a tire tool right here, boy. I'd bust the sonofabitch on the head!" (224)

Bellow's real concern in the novel is evil—a question as metaphysical as it is social.[9] His description of perversion and murder in the courtroom raises issues which are embodied in society but not necessarily caused by it. The mother who beat her son to death was born to poverty, is of low intelligence, and suffers from brain damage. The lawyers describe a scene of terror that makes any explanation difficult. "The child screamed, clung, but with both arms the girl hurled it against the wall. On her legs was ruddy hair. And her lover, too, with long jaws and zooty sideburns, watching on the bed. Lying down to copulate, and standing up to kill" (240). Herzog rejects the theory of depravity, telling Doctor Edvig that his Calvinism is a niggardly view of man, but everyone Herzog meets does him in, and for motives deeper than self-interest. The intermingling of sensuality and violence in Herzog's vision of evil relates it to his attitude toward Ramona. Mulling over his relationship with her with the same intensity he directs toward Madeleine, Herzog feels a threat that goes beyond Ramona's personalism. He suggests this deeper issue as he waits for Ramona to prepare for their love making: when he was ill with pneumonia, he remembers, and Will sent him flowers, "his breath was poisoned by the sweetness of red roses . . . Herzog thought he might be able to stand the roses now. That pernicious thing, fragrant beauty, shapely red. You had to have strength to endure such things or by intensity they might pierce you inside and you might bleed to death" (203).[10]

Herzog's concern with evil is one of the reasons why his new civility is a victory: society is the only instrument with which he can combat evil. If society embodies the destructive principles of the world, a practical, self-assured and knowledgeable social service represents man's ability to live with and perhaps surmount those principles. Herzog turns to social institutions not because he thinks man is perfectible but because only society can cope with a real and intense evil. When he looks within himself to find something for the murdered boy he finds only his *"human feelings."* Wilhelm believes in a moral purpose to his suffering, but does not claim faith in God, while Herzog believes in God but can find no moral justification for pain. When we have said this, however, we must add that there is an element of personal failure in Herzog's new dedication to society. He had failed to disprove the void in his personal life; he finds nothing in his personal vision to meet the evil he witnesses in the courtroom. And his self-doubt makes him all too ready to reject personal effort for that of a larger body. In commenting on T. E. Hulme's criticism of Romanticism, Herzog says that he sympathizes with Hulme's dislike of "spilt religion," but then adds, "bottled religion, on conservative principles—does that intend to deprive the heart of such powers—do you think? Hulme's followers made sterility their truth, confessing their impotence" (129). Although Herzog is not about to give up the "inspired condition," his rejection of the self for society has similar implications. Just as Joseph's search for an essential self was a worthy quest— one Bellow's heroes continued to make for the next twenty years— so Herzog's attempt to work out a life in the Berkshires was a reasonable goal: far from evading society, he was a scholar doing legitimate work, and he faced what Augie March calls "the mystical great things of life" (452).

No one is more aware of these discrepancies than Herzog himself, but by the end of the novel he has learned to live with them. When he embraces a modest truth he embraces one that can tolerate uncertainties. "You gave me good value for my money when you explained that neuroses might be graded by the inability to tolerate ambiguous situations," he writes Edvig. "Allow me modestly to claim that I am much better now at ambiguities" (304). *Herzog* must finally be read in the light of this idea. Much of the story points in two directions at once. Herzog berates himself for masochism with an intensity that is itself masochistic. His letters are at once an expression of will and of impotence, the malady he must cure and his connection with the world. He is in a "whirling ecstasy" as he writes, but his comments reveal the "bossiness and willfulness, the nagging embedded in his mental constitution" (68). So too with the ecstasy he finally feels—the "inspired condition": instead of desperately attempting to affirm it, or berating his society for not recognizing it, Herzog has learned to regard what he knows of it as mixed: "His mind was like that cistern, soft pure water sealed under the iron lid but not entirely safe to drink" (325).

This acceptance of ambivalence is reflected in another source of form in the novel, the cycle of Herzog's masochism. If society represents a healthy confrontation of the destructive world Herzog has ignored, his social consciousness expresses his need to give himself—a desire related to his masochism. Like Henderson, Herzog desires to be a scapegoat. "I fall upon the thorns of life, I bleed," Herzog thinks. "And then? I fall upon the thorns of life, I bleed. And what next? I get laid, I take a short holiday, but very soon after I fall upon those same thorns with gratification in pain, or suffering in joy—who knows what the mixture is!" (206–207). In the last chapter he says again, "I see exactly what I should avoid. Then, all of a sudden, I'm in bed with that very thing, and making love to it." He sees that Madeleine had filled "a very special need. I don't know what. She brought ideology into my life. Something to do with catastrophe" (333–334). The events which reinforce Herzog's new interest in society may be viewed as an expression of this cycle as well, providing Herzog with a purgation that explains his release or with the insight necessary to his transcendent vision. That his purpose in going to Chicago is unconscious is much to the point: just as he had automatically sought comfort from the brutal Himmelstein, had gone to Ramona swearing he shouldn't, and at the end returns to the Berkshires—where his marriage with Madeleine began—so the novel consists of his compulsive return to the scene of his pain. The letters and memories which dominate the story form a parallel to Herzog's return to Chicago: Herzog knows he should forget the past and that his letters merely reawaken his suffering, but he is obsessed with the catastrophe in that past.

Because all of Bellow's heroes feel the same ambivalence toward the world that Herzog feels toward his past, this cycle illustrates and summarizes the form and the meaning of the other novels as well. Each of Bellow's heroes finds the climax of his story —and a sense of great release—in a confrontation with death. Joseph's final walk in the alley is associated with the ancient figure of his dreams, and his subsequent request for induction—itself a confrontation of death—brings relief. Leventhal awakes to find his life in danger, Allbee about to die, and, at the end of their struggle, a sense of completion. Augie too undergoes such an experience in his fight with Basteshaw in the lifeboat and his violent breakup with Thea. Wilhelm breaks down before a corpse and Henderson witnesses Dahfu's death. In each case the hero vacillates before a threat or ordeal and then confronts the source of that threat in the death scene. In each there is a pattern of resistance, embrace and release—reminiscent of Leventhal's description of the swinging door. In all of them the hero identifies with the dead person and comes close to doing violence himself. Although each of these scenes takes its specific meaning from the novel in which it appears, they all point to a single meaning. Even specific chapters and sections within Bellow's novels end on a note of calm after the hero has confronted a lesser form of evil or death.

The several explanations we might make of this confrontation correspond to the distinction between a social view of reality and a religious one. When Herzog asks about his religious preoccupation, "Is it faith? Or is it simply childishness, expecting to be loved for doing your bidden task?" he asks the question which the novel dramatizes (231). From the practical point of view, Herzog is childish and masochistic. The confrontation of the death figure may be viewed as a vicarious release of the hero's masochism or death wish. Leventhal, Joseph, Augie and Henderson all come close to death, and Herzog describes his memories of the dead as his subjugation to death. His temptation to murder is an expression of self-hate and the court in which he appears is associated with the murder case in New York. Masochism may also be accompanied by a wish for the death of the figure who causes pain. Repressing their hostility, "too gentle and abstaining to be predacious at large," the heroes find vicarious fulfillment of their unconscious destructive desires. In that the death figure is often a "double," symbolizing a quality the protagonist represses within himself—perhaps the destructive will itself—the desire to kill is an externalization of the protagonist's inner drives. Herzog's temptation to murder would be a realistic rendering of these drives, of course, and his marriage to Madeleine is related to them. Herzog shows unconscious hostility toward women and gives evidence of seeking a partner who is not only a challenge but a suitable subject for his hostility.[11] His letters are filled with resentment which he releases in the act of writing. But whether he wishes for the death of another or himself, he would achieve in his story a purgation of his desires, related perhaps to the purgative effects of the comedy Bellow now creates.

If Herzog's moral ideas are the expression of masochism, however, he also believes them to be real. "Charity, as if it didn't have enough trouble in this day and age, will always be suspected of morbidity—sado-masochism, perversity of some sort," he thinks. "All higher or moral tendencies lie under suspicion of being rackets" (56). Here the death scene reflects a religious impulse and perhaps a religious experience. Part of Herzog's difficulty is that of Ramona's former lover George Hoberly, who "desperate with longing for reality, for God, could not wait but threw himself wildly upon anything resembling a hope" (208). Like many of the Romantics he studies, Herzog tends to seek religious fulfillment in women—the offer that the love priestess Ramona makes him. He had courted catastrophe out of impulses related to his religious longing. Dahfu "was telling me," Henderson says at one point, "that suffering was the closest thing to worship that I knew anything about" (303–304). As Herzog himself puts it, his suffering has been "a more extended form of life, a striving for true wakefulness and an antidote to illusion, and therefore I can take no moral credit for it" (317). Herzog's elation at the end would derive from the ordeal he has passed through, both in the events of the novel and in his memory.

His comment is related to Wilhelm Reich's description of masochism, which, though posed in sexual terms, bears on religious experience. Just as Herzog strives for wakefulness, so the masochist tries to "burst" the internal pressure of conflict and repression by an external pain. "The masochist *wishes to burst and imagines that the torture will bring this about*." [12] Tommy Wilhelm feels he is about to burst, of course, and Henderson turns to pain to burst his spirit's sleep; the other heroes give themselves to the world in the hope that it will pierce their enclosing armor. All of Bellow's heroes find religious affirmation at the end of pain and struggle—which may "open" them to transcendence. By the end of the novel Herzog has like Henderson been shocked into wakefulness by the truth that "comes with blows." If Herzog's social affirmation is an expression of his will, his religious affirmation is the result of the conflicts which cause him pain. It is also his recognition of the ultimate dependence, the ultimate passivity of man—a perspective which gives release to his willful struggle.

While the ambiguity of Herzog's cycle remains unresolved, Herzog's position is in one sense completely consistent. He claims "belief based on reason," and turns to society because, he says, "I owe God a human life" (165, 272). "Annihilation is no longer a metaphor," he believes. "Good and Evil are real. The inspired condition is therefore no visionary matter" (165). He writes to God that he has made mistakes, "but have desired to do your unknowable will, taking it, and you, without symbols. Everything of intens-est significance. Especially if divested of me" (326). But Herzog has also viewed his inspired condition as a temptation from his duty, a call to illusion, and thus the conflict remains. When he looks into the water at Woods Hole and sees the "stony bottom webbed with golden lines" he is deeply moved. "Herzog sighed and said to himself, 'Praise God—praise God.'" He thinks that "if his soul could cast a reflection so brilliant, and so intensely sweet, he might beg God to make such use of him." He then sees that such a yearning for purity and simplicity is childish. "The actual sphere is not clear like this, but turbulent, angry. A vast human action is going on. Death watches" (91). Herzog's religious consciousness leads him into a joy that has little place in this world. He accepts such joy at the end, but the fact that he is passive and alone as he does so points to its opposition to civil duty. Then too Herzog re-jects "subjective monstrosity" and turns to the external world for reality, but his inner vision, or his soul, is also reality, and might serve as a corrective to external monstrosity.

It is this last point, I think, which is crucial to the largest criti-cal problem in *Herzog*. The chief criticism of the novel, as well as of Bellow's other novels, is that the story is contained within the mind of the protagonist. Stripping away such external supports of the self as wife, job, home, and culture, Bellow throws his pro-tagonist back upon himself, where he threatens to remain. Theodore Solotaroff says that "like Herzog himself, the story of his recovery lacks the true opposition of Otherness," and Irving Howe says that "in the end one feels that *Herzog* is too hermetic a work, the re-sult of a technique which encloses us rigidly in the troubles of a man during his phase of withdrawal from the world."[13] Stephen Spender too feels the novel is self-enclosed and even solipsistic. Although Herzog dedicates himself to the world, as Solotaroff and Howe recognize, his personalism raises the charge that there is not enough of the world to provide a check on his thoughts. Bellow's ability to evoke an intensely real world, even if viewed exclusively through Herzog's eyes, is one answer to this charge. So too is Bel-low's characterization: although Bellow gives only Herzog's view of Madeleine and Gersbach, the thoroughness of his portrayal of Herzog is itself a check on Herzog's views.

But the most important answer, I think, is related to another charge made against Bellow's fiction. Bellow has been criticized not for portraying too little of the world but for not following the dictates of his imagination. Earl Rovit suspects that "Bellow may conceivably surrender too much of his private myth to the exigencies of the world. His intellectual and emotional cosmopolitanism, his commitment to a social good, may cause him to modify the structuring shapes of his own dreams to accord with the world-as-it-is." Reviewing *Henderson,* Dan Jacobson pointedly notes that "the greatness of Melville is that he let [his characters] celebrate what they were, at whatever cost to them, or to himself, or to his own beliefs." [14] Although Bellow has expressed confidence in the imagination as a source of truth, his characters fear that it may be fantasy bordering on madness. Most of his heroes worry about their sanity —Joseph in his feeling of strangeness, Leventhal in his hypochondria, Wilhelm in his trust of Tamkin, and Henderson in his rages and fever. All of them—and Bellow too, I think—are oppressed by the intensity of what they imagine. Just as Leventhal is unable to help Allbee because of what he imagines, so Herzog rushes to Chicago because of what he imagines. The courtroom scenes shock him in part because he envisions the crimes, and he threatens to kill Gersbach because, as he reads about Gersbach's treatment of June, he "can see him mount the stairs while June screams in fright" (100–101).

Herzog does not resolve either of these problems, but Herzog's acceptance of the "inspired condition" is a significant advance in Bellow's struggle with them. One may break out of personality not only by turning outward to society, but by turning inward to a universal truth approached through private imagination. As Dahfu says, nature is a mentality and the imagination a source of truth. Herzog's acceptance of his imaginative vision resolves the other heroes' fear of subjectivity at the same time that it opens the novel to a reality larger than Herzog's consciousness. As Herzog gazes upon himself, his feelings are narcissistic, but they are also full of the mystery of his being. What appears to be self-absorption is really, as in Whitman's poetry, a celebration of the human species and the transcendent Self. Herzog's last letter is a joyful acceptance of the Self—a welcome and well-earned affirmation after his masochistic thrashing. "I look at myself and see chest, thighs, feet—a head. This strange organization. I know it will die. And inside—something, something, happiness . . . 'Thou movest me!' That leaves no choice" (340). Herzog sees himself as an object of wonder he would grant to all. He is imperfect, confused, self-destructive, but his being dwarfs the imperfections of personality. He may continue to turn inward while talking of civility—the image of him lying there talking to himself is somehow definitive—but his acceptance of himself may be the prerequisite to social service.

That Herzog's acceptance of the "inspired condition" is qualified, however, is all important: the visionary is real but mixed—valid, but not to be blindly trusted. Herzog's explicit affirmation of society and faith derives from his ability to live with ambiguity and paradox. He has discovered his interest in the external world by turning inward, has affirmed community by ceasing to write letters, has affirmed the inspired condition by examining society, and has found joy by returning to pain. He is a Moses, who cares deeply about religious faith and a Herzog, or prince, who is interested in society, duty, and power. But he is most of all a man who has accepted the identity that lies within this division.

Because Bellow associates will with the analytic mind, and love with a yielding to the imagination, Herzog's acceptance of a mixed vision reflects a new balance in the hero's personality. The quest for a unified identity in Bellow's fiction usually calls for extreme measures, but Herzog insists that "moderate truthfulness or accuracy seems to have no pull at all. Just what we need now!" (316) Having learned to be levelheaded, to be poised, to keep his mouth closed at the right time, Herzog is convinced of the Self which need not prove its existence by reconciling opposites. Bellow leaves him in a modest state, lying down, thinking about a suggestion to his cleaning lady. But he does so having qualified this moderate tone by the implications of Herzog's final statement:

Something produces intensity, a holy feeling, as oranges produce orange, as grass green, as birds heat. . . . But this intensity, doesn't it mean anything? Is it an idiot joy that makes this animal, the most peculiar animal of all, exclaim something? And he thinks this reaction a sign, a proof, of eternity? And he has it in his breast? But I have no arguments to make about it. "Thou movest me." "But what do you want, Herzog?" "But that's just it— not a solitary thing. I am pretty well satisfied to be, to be just as it is willed, and for as long as I may remain in occupancy." [340]

NOTES   BIBLIOGRAPHY   INDEX

NOTES

INTRODUCTION

1. Lionel Trilling, *The Liberal Imagination* (New York, 1953), 176.
2. "Hemingway and the Image of Man," *Partisan Review,* 20 (May–June 1953), 338.
3. In a letter to the author, March 12, 1961.
4. Saul Bellow, *Henderson the Rain King* (New York: Viking Press, 1959), 22.
5. Saul Bellow, *Herzog* (New York: Viking Press, 1964), 1. These and the following editions of Bellow's other novels are the ones cited in the text: *Dangling Man* (New York: Vanguard, 1944); *The Victim* (New York: Vanguard, 1947); *The Adventures of Augie March* (New York: Viking Press, 1953); *Seize the Day* (New York: Viking Press, 1956).
6. I use the term "religious" broadly, as William James defines it in *The Varieties of Religious Experience* (New York, 1958—p. 42): "the feelings, acts, and experiences of individual men in their solitude, so far as they apprehend themselves to stand in relation to whatever they may consider the divine."
7. Marcus Klein, among others, has commented on Bellow's concern with goodness. See *The Reporter,* 31 (October 22, 1964), 53. Bellow's division is similar to Marcus Klein's definition of "accommodation" as "that simultaneous engagement and disengagement which is the characteristic movement of the novel in these past years." This is "an enterprise of acrobatics" in which the hero fluctuates between isolated freedom and the community which limits the self. (*After Alienation*—New York, 1962—p. 30.) Bellow's division lies deeper than the self's relation with society, I think, for the social is only one of the ways in which the hero may save or throw himself away. Clinging to the self, Bellow's protagonist would dissolve it in the biological, the spiritual, or the social—whatever he considers more purposeful than personality. Bellow seeks to end this conflict by imagining the Self which may enjoy all forms of engagement without loss of selfhood, and this search leads him to the essential or spiritual self. A few critics have mentioned Bellow's religious concern in passing, and some have explicitly denied that it exists. Tony Tanner touches upon the issue in *Saul Bellow* (Edinburgh, 1965).
8. David L. Stevenson, "Styron and the Fiction of the Fifties," *Critique,* 3 (Summer 1960), 56.
9. Bellow resists any attempt to cast him as cultural spokesman, but critics persist in speaking of him as such. Julian Moynahan ends his review of *Herzog* by saying that "its publication now, after the past

terrible year, suggests that things are looking up for America and its civilization" (*New York Times Book Review,* September 20, 1964, p. 41). It is significant that Bellow majored in anthropology at Northwestern, where he founded a socialist club, and that he began graduate work in anthropology at The University of Wisconsin. He is presently associated with the Committee on Social Thought at The University of Chicago.

10. Maxwell Geismar, *American Moderns: From Rebellion to Conformity* (New York, 1958), 217.

11. Malcolm Cowley, *The Literary Situation* (New York, 1954), 83. Chester Eisinger also argues that Bellow achieves a perspective outside of society (in *Fiction of the Forties*—Chicago, 1963); Frederick Hoffman, in contrast, argues that the necessity of living within society is Bellow's major theme (in *Contemporary American Novelists,* ed. Harry T. Moore—Carbondale, Ill., 1964).

12. Alfred Kazin, *Contemporaries* (Boston, 1962), 215.

13. Ihab Hassan, *Radical Innocence* (New York, 1966), 315.

14. *Partisan Review,* 8 (May–June 1941), 230–36.

15. Philip Rieff, *Freud: The Mind of the Moralist* (New York, 1959), 356.

16. Norman Mailer, *Advertisements for Myself* (New York, 1966), 429. Kazin, *Contemporaries,* 222.

17. David L. Stevenson, "Fiction's Unfamiliar Face," *Nation,* 187 (November 1, 1958), 307. Kazin, *Contemporaries,* 208.

18. Henry Thoreau, *Walden* (Cambridge, Mass., 1957), 62.

19. David L. Stevenson makes an important point when he calls the new heroes "the activists." Like the boy, these characters only appear to be passive: "the new activist hero remains to the end an intrepid opportunist of the self. He is an eager, insatiable explorer of his own private experience" (*Daedalus,* 92, Spring, 1963, p. 238). The boy is not quite this energetic, but he foreshadows Joseph of *Dangling Man,* of whom Stevenson speaks.

20. Norman Mailer, "Some Children of the Goddess," *Esquire,* 60 (July, 1963), 69.

21. F. M. Dostoevsky, *Winter Notes on Summer Impressions,* trans. Richard L. Renfield (New York, 1955), 110.

22. William James, *The Varieties of Religious Experience,* 251.

23. "Dora," *Harper's Bazaar,* 83 (November, 1949), 118, 188–90, 198–99.

24. "Dreiser and the Triumph of Art," *Commentary,* 11 (May, 1951), 502–3.

25. "Herzog," *Esquire,* 56 (July, 1961), 117.

26. *Varieties of Religious Experience,* 130, 199.

27. *Contemporaries,* 220.

28. See Sartre's *Nausea* and Camus' *The Myth of Sisyphus.* Bellow's affinity with the Existentialists and the Romantics is generally recognized: it is discussed by Richard Lehan, *Texas Studies in Literature and Language,* 1 (Spring, 1959), 181–202, and Allen Guttmann, *Critique,* 7 (Spring, 1965), 33–42. Bellow's relationship to such broad movements is naturally problematical: the Existentialist Kierkegaard affirms the

soul, for example, while the Romantic Melville is often closer to Sartre than to Emerson. I discuss Sartre and Emerson because their views give focus to the general movements.

29. As William Barrett explains Sartre's position, "if we *exist* our facticity, then we *are* it, and it makes up the total essence of what we are." Barrett goes on to say, "the Self, indeed, is in Sartre's treatment, as in Buddhism, a bubble, and a bubble has nothing at its center" (*Irrational Man*—New York, 1962—pp. 109, 247). When Augie says to Min-touchian, "it is better to die what you are than to live a stranger for-ever" (485), he implies a "you" which is definitive. Henderson seeks such a "you" when he says "I should move from the states that I myself make into the states which are of themselves" (284).

30. "Some Notes on Recent American Fiction," *Encounter*, 21 (November, 1963), 28, 29.

31. "Laughter in the Ghetto," *Saturday Review*, 36 (May 30, 1953), 15.

32. "Introduction," *Great Jewish Short Stories*, ed. Saul Bellow (New York, 1963), 10.

33. Chester Eisinger, *Fiction of the Forties*, 343. In the same book, Eisinger argues that Bellow "gives full expression to a seriously tried yet in-sistently Romantic conception of the self as all in all" (308).

34. Baal Shem Tov, founder of Hasidism, held views strikingly similar to those of the American Transcendentalists. See "Introduction," *A Treas-ury of Yiddish Stories*, ed. Irving Howe and Eliezer Greenberg (New York, 1954), 15.

35. Lionel Trilling, *The Opposing Self* (New York, 1959), 131, 140, 150.

36. *Great Jewish Short Stories*, 10.

37. Martin Buber, *Hasidism and Modern Man*, trans. Maurice Friedman (New York, 1958), 49.

CHAPTER 2

1. Irving Kristol, *Politics*, 1 (June, 1944), 156.

2. "The University as Villain," *Nation*, 185 (November 16, 1957), 363.

3. Fyodor Dostoevsky, *Notes from Underground: The Short Novels of Dostoevsky*, trans. Constance Garnett (New York, 1945), 129, 130.

4. Edmund Wilson, *The New Yorker*, 20 (April 1, 1944), 70.

5. Chester Eisinger, *Fiction of the Forties*, 5.

6. See J. C. Levenson, "Bellow's Dangling Men," *Critique*, 3 (Summer, 1960), 3–14, and Frederick J. Hoffman, "The Fool of Experience," *Contemporary American Novelists*, 80–94. Most critics take Joseph's final comments as ironic, but John Chamberlain claims that Joseph "is profoundly grateful that he is no longer to be held accountable for himself" (*New York Times*, March 25, 1944, p. 13). Frederick J. Hoffman claims "that Joseph should have hastened into the Army is not evidence of the failure of his wish to remain free, but rather a desire to move into the society of his fellows" (85). It would seem that the novel's conclusion may be taken in four ways: Joseph's ad-

mission of failure, in which he is ironic about himself; his straight confession of failure, in which Bellow is ironic; his expression of gratitude, in which Bellow shows sympathy toward his weakness; and his claim to affirmation, in which he recognizes—with Bellow's blessing—that one cannot live without community.

7. *Notes from Underground*, 222.

8. Norman O. Brown, *Life Against Death* (New York, 1959), 286.

9. Lionel Trilling, *The Liberal Imagination*, 263.

10. Joseph's friends embody the malice and self-defeat which Dostoevsky interprets as proof of the need for religious belief. The ideal construction is broadly religious in function, of course. Bellow's debt to *Notes from Underground* is extensive: both Joseph and the Underground Man are baffled by their paralysis and each tries to explain, as Dostoevsky says, why he was "bound to make his appearance in our midst" (*Notes from Underground*, 129). Both alternate between legitimate complaint and self-pity, victimization and personal weakness. Both are sickened by their inability to do good, by boredom, by the vagueness of their "enemy," and by their need for a redeeming ideal (which they are unable to accept). Both embody the illness they attribute to society and excuse their faults by pleading a determinism which they otherwise abhor. Both reject rational utopianism, although Joseph insists upon the rationalism which the Underground Man (intellectually) rejects. The Russian revels in his pain, however, and his self-loathing is unrestrained; Joseph, less diseased than demoralized, seeks the means to end his paralysis.

11. *Notes from Underground*, 153.

12. *Time*, 43 (May 8, 1944), 104. Herbert Kupferberg, *New York Herald Tribune Book Review*, 20 (April 9, 1944), 11. N. L. Rothman, *Saturday Review of Literature*, 27 (April 15, 1944), 27. Rueben Frank, "Saul Bellow: The Evolution of a Contemporary Novelist," *Western Review*, 18 (Winter, 1954), 103.

13. "Sermon by Dr. Pep," *Partisan Review*, 16 (May, 1949), 462.

14. *Notes from Underground*, 136.

15. To Michael Dostoevsky, March 26, 1864. Quoted by Ralph Matlaw, "Structure and Integration in *Notes from Underground*," *PMLA*, 73 (March, 1958), 109.

16. Joseph's dream also finds "fulfillment" in Herzog's childhood memory of a homosexual rape which occurred in a mud alley, with dogs barking, by a man who is unshaven. *Herzog*, 288.

17. Just as Bellow relates Joseph's dreams to his experience, so he relates Joseph himself to several characters in the novel. As Mark Schorer has noted, Joseph is paralleled by his landlady, who lingers with a fatal illness until Joseph's induction, and by Vanaker, a noisy alcoholic neighbor who moves from the rooming house shortly before Joseph leaves (*Kenyon Review*, 6, Summer, 1944, p. 461). Joseph actually identifies with almost everyone around him—with such friends as Abt and the unemployed Steidler, with Etta, his father-in-law and his grandfather, and with the dead man in the street and the guide in his dream. This tendency suggests that Joseph is in danger of losing himself by identify-

ing with others, or it reflects his desperate need for community. Joseph would need a strong sense of self in either case, but Bellow does not develop the idea. He does so, rather, in *The Victim,* which finds its center in the fact that the opposites Leventhal and Allbee identify with one another.

18. Saul Bellow, "Address by Gooley MacDowell to the Hasbeens Club of Chicago," *Hudson Review,* 4 (Summer, 1951), 227.

19. Jean-Paul Sartre, *Nausea,* trans. Lloyd Alexander (Norfolk, Conn., 1959), 237.

20. "The Sealed Treasure," *Times Literary Supplement* (July 1, 1960), 414.

CHAPTER 3

1. See Bruce Cook, "Saul Bellow: A Mood of Protest," *Perspective,* 12 (February, 1963), 49.

2. Jean-Paul Sartre, *Anti-Semite and Jew,* trans. George J. Becker (New York, 1960), 40, 54, 148.

3. Diana Trilling, *Nation,* 166 (January 3, 1948), 25. Rueben Frank, *Time,* 50 (December 1, 1947), 111, Rueben Frank, "Saul Bellow: The Evolution of a Contemporary Novelist," *Western Review,* 18 (Winter, 1954), 108. Alan S. Downer, *New York Times Book Review,* 52 (November 30, 1947), 29. Leslie Fiedler feels that *The Victim* "suffers somewhat because of its ending" (*Kenyon Review,* 10, Summer, 1948, p. 520). Jonathan Baumbach finds the last chapter "somewhat unsatisfying" (*The Landscape of Nightmare*—New York, 1965—p. 46).

4. Although they recognize its problems, some critics feel that *The Victim* is Bellow's best novel. V. S. Pritchett says it "is the best novel to come out of America—or England—for a generation" (*New York Review of Books,* 3, October 22, 1964, p. 4). It has received new attention in articles by Malcolm Bradbury and Karl Miller, and Jonathan Baumbach devotes a chapter to it in *The Landscape of Nightmare.*

5. Fyodor Dostoevsky, *The Eternal Husband: The Short Novels of Dostoevsky,* trans. Constance Garnett (New York, 1945), 460.

6. Although Bellow makes Dostoevsky's story his own, his debt, noted by several critics, is extensive. Mickey's death finds its source in the death of Pavel's daughter. Velchaninov takes her away from Pavel because he suspects she is his own, while Leventhal, prejudiced against the Italians, feels Mickey is his "own." Bellow makes two important changes in Dostoevsky's story: he blurs the moral issue, raising the all important ambiguity of Leventhal's guilt, and he presents characters who are not as malicious or masochistic as Dostoevsky's. Bellow does not use the sexual issue Dostoevsky raises (Pavel is a cuckold and seeks help in remarrying), but he does sustain Dostoevsky's sexual overtone: the oppressive, homosexual affection felt by Dostoevsky's characters is a natural parallel to the bigot's emotional obsession with the Jew. Taken as more innocent affection, paralleling the affection between Leventhal and Max, the feeling may point to a sense of kinship transcending racial differences.

7. For an elaboration of this interpretation see "The Double Vision," in Jonathan Baumbach's *The Landscape of Nightmare.*

8. "A Father-to-Be," *Seize the Day,* 130.

9. Norman O. Brown, *Life Against Death,* 252.

10. Saul Bellow, "By the Rock Wall," *Harper's Bazaar,* 85 (April, 1951), 215.

11. As a "double" novel, likened by several critics to "The Secret Sharer" and *The Double, The Victim* naturally implies a divided or incomplete self. As Leventhal's alter-ego, representing what Leventhal fears in himself, Allbee must symbolically die if Leventhal is to find peace. It is significant, however, that Leventhal saves Allbee in the suicide scene, for this too may be a source of his serenity. Marcus Klein says that Leventhal gives up ultimate questioning at the end, but if Allbee represents the questioning perspective which Leventhal needs to be fully human, then the embrace of the two represents, on a deeper imaginative level, the unification of alter-egos. Leventhal does ask Allbee "who runs things." In any case, Leventhal and Allbee play out the split Joseph suffers in his room and the conflict, completely objectified, between Augie and two dozen Allbees spread across two continents.

CHAPTER 4

1. *Seize the Day,* 154. Bellow's heroine in the story "Leaving the Yellow House," makes a similar comment about the desert wastes: "They drew you from yourself. But after they had drawn you, what did they do with you? . . . Maybe something too cruel for women or for any woman, young or old" (*Esquire,* 49, January, 1958, p. 123).

2. Irving Kristol, *Encounter,* 3 (July, 1954), 74.

3. J. B. Priestley, *Sunday Times* [London], May 9, 1954, p. 5. Norman Podhoretz, "The New Nihilism and the Novel," *Partisan Review,* 25 (Fall, 1958), 579.

4. "Isaac Rosenfeld," *Partisan Review,* 23 (Fall, 1956), 567.

5. John Aldridge, too, says that Bellow's failure in the novel "is as much a fault of his experience of his time as it is of his talent" (*In Search of Heresy*—New York, 1956—p. 139). Marcus Klein defines this experience as well as Augie's character when he says of fiction since World War II: "The hero chooses community—he assumes racial obligations, or he declares himself a patriot, or he makes love—and he discovers that he has sacrificed his identity, and his adventures begin all over again" (*After Alienation,* 30).

6. Chester Eisinger, *Fiction of the Forties,* 355. Norman Podhoretz, *Doings and Undoings* (New York, 1964) 218. V. S. Pritchett, *New Statesman and Nation,* n.s. 47 (June 19, 1954), 803.

7. John Aldridge summarizes this problem when he charges that "as a man committed to nothing, [Augie] can have no dramatic centrality; his conflict with society can never be really intense or meaningful because there is nothing at stake, no piece of spiritual opposition which might endow him with tragic or pathetic value" (*In Search of Heresy,*

135). Aldridge argues that *Augie March* is not a *Bildungsroman* because Augie, unchanged at the end, plays out what he is in the manner of the *picaro*. In a sense Bellow's definition of the Machiavellian drove him into a corner, for the Machiavellian's inhumanity derives from his commitment. To provide a contrast, Augie must forego commitment or discover a way not to be defined by it—creating problems of characterization in either case.

8. Beatrice Kalb, "Biographical Sketch," *Saturday Review of Literature,* 36 (September 19, 1953), 13.

9. J. C. Levenson, R. D. Crozier, and Robert Alter have touched on this idea. Dorothy Rosenberg says that as Augie's "external symbols fail him and he begins to travel inwardly, then Saul Bellow's tale takes on meaning and direction" (San Francisco *Sunday Chronicle,* October 25, 1953, p. 18). Tom Hopkinson says that Augie comes to look "more for truth and less for enjoyment, more for consciousness and less for self-immersion" (*London Magazine,* 1, August, 1954, p. 84).

10. Beatrice Kalb, "Biographical Sketch."

11. In *Partisan Review,* 17 (November–December, 1950), 779–94.

12. *Hudson Review,* 4 (Summer, 1951), 226.

13. Another parallel between "Trip to Galena" and *Augie March* is Bellow's contrast of the hero's rejection of the middle class with a brother or sister's acceptance of it. In both stories the brother and sister marry into money out of fear and try to recruit the hero who chooses to risk ruin for the sake of his ideal.

14. Dallas Wiebe, University of Cincinnati, brought this fact about the cultural references to my attention.

15. Robert Heilman, "Variations on Picaresque," *Sewanee Review,* 66 (October–December, 1958), 547–77). Part of the difficulty in categorizing *Augie March* lies in the term "picaresque." Heilman says that the picaresque novel reflects "a diminution, if not total elimination, of emotional depths and moral concerns" (548), while Robert Alter claims that the *picaro,* embodying a true morality, feels compassion but not bitterness. Alter categorizes *Augie March* as a *Bildungsroman* because Augie seeks selfhood. John Aldridge posits a "spiritual picaresque," in which the hero develops as in the *Bildungsroman,* but excludes *Augie March* from even this category.

16. Marcus Klein, "A Discipline of Nobility: Saul Bellow's Fiction," *Kenyon Review,* 24 (Spring, 1962), 217.

17. Bellow has to work at Augie's optimism from the beginning. Chapter I threatens to become a complaint about Grandma Lausch: "Still the old lady had a heart," Augie says. "I don't mean to say she didn't." Bellow begins the next paragraph, "the old *grande dame,* I don't want to be misrepresenting her" (10, 11). Augie's mixed attitude toward the Machiavellians is found in the combination of his love for them and an unconscious satisfaction with the fact that they are destroyed by the principles they advocate. Grandma's hard-boiled sons send her to a home, and Einhorn loses his fortune partially because of his vindictiveness.

18. "Pleasures and Pains of Playgoing," *Partisan Review,* 21 (May–June, 1954), 313.

19. See Laura Hobson, "Trade Winds," *Saturday Review of Literature,* 36 (August 22, 1953), 6.

20. In a letter to the author Bellow said, "the affectionate characters are stubborn too, and go their own way. They have a powerful will, and affection suits them because it removes obstacles and resistances. They have their own will to power, I've never been in any doubt about that." (March 12, 1961.) Augie speaks of a love of power which "afflicted practically everyone I had ever known in some fashion, and which in my degree, though in a different place, I had too" (337).

21. John Aldridge makes a similar comment in *In Search of Heresy,* p. 134.

CHAPTER 5

1. Bellow's water imagery seems more contrived in summary than in the text, but it permeates the novelette, sometimes with humor. The agent Maurice Venice is engaged to a bathing beauty, and Tamkin has designed equipment to walk under water. Wilhelm, who envisions himself as a bull eaten by piranha, uses an electric razor to avoid water. As Dr. Adler sits among glasses of water in a sunny bay, he tells Wilhelm that "there's nothing better than hydrotherapy when you come right down to it. Simple water has a calming effect and would do you more good than all the barbiturates and alcohol in the world" (44). The final break between father and son occurs near the hotel swimming pool.

2. "Sermon by Doctor Pep," *Partisan Review,* 16 (May, 1949), 460. Brendan Gill, *The New Yorker,* 32 (January 5, 1957), 70.

3. Harvey Swados is correct in saying that "Seize the Day" "culminates in an extraordinary ending which is going to be read and argued over for a long time to come" (*New York Post Magazine,* November 18, 1956, p. 11). The conclusion has been described variously as unclear but brilliant, or all too clear and maudlin. Bellow is said to be brutally ironic or sentimentally sympathetic, and the conclusion is taken as an example of his difficulty in ending his stories or—because he makes us sympathize with a despicable character—as a demonstration of his skill. As Wilhelm's failure, the end portrays an orgy of self-pity, a reversion to childhood, an image of the ultimate anti-hero. As a triumph, it is explained in many ways: Wilhelm undergoes catharsis; he finds himself or transcends himself; he grows from self-pity to grief for mankind, or from self-deception to self-knowledge; he finds the courage to live his plight.

4. John A. Lynch, *Commonweal,* 65 (November 30, 1956), 238.

5. First published in *Commentary,* 11 (March, 1951), 251–61. Citations are to *Seize the Day.*

6. *Harper's Bazaar,* 85 (April, 1951), 135, 205, 207–8, 214–16.

7. "Hemingway and the Image of Man," *Partisan Review,* 20 (May–June, 1953), 341.

8. "Literary Notes on Khrushchev," *Esquire,* 55 (March, 1961), 107.

9. In a class discussion, Spring, 1962.

10. While Wilhelm suffers from the public emotional life of his father and Tamkin, he also suffers from his attempt to hide his own emotions. Others conceal themselves from public view, but Wilhelm, choked by his effort, needs to break down openly. He begins his day hiding behind a cigar and wearing a hat because "it is harder to find out how [one] feels" (3). Tamkin traps Wilhelm into lending money by appealing to just this need for a prosperous, unworried appearance: "Neither of them needed an income from the market, of course. This was only a sporting proposition anyhow, Tamkin said" (58). Wilhelm lies when he is wiped out, but "his need to cry, like someone in a crowd, pushed and jostled and abused him from behind, and Wilhelm did not dare turn" (104). When he breaks down in the funeral parlor, he discovers a kind of strength: no longer caring what the public thinks of him, he is no longer—for a time, anyway—dependent on it.

11. William James, *The Varieties of Religious Experience,* 185.

12. Ihab Hassan, *Radical Innocence,* 315, 316.

13. "Letter to Doctor Edvig," *Esquire,* 60 (July, 1963), 62.

14. Herzog too equates the pressure of the crowd with water, noting "the pressure of human millions who have discovered what concerted efforts and thoughts can do. As megatons of water shape organisms on the ocean floor. As tides polish stones" (201).

15. *Partisan Review,* 23 (Summer, 1956), 432.

16. If Bellow's other heroes struggle to accept a destructive world and then are shocked by a final experience they cannot accept, Wilhelm breaks the pattern by accepting his final defeat. His drowning is related to Augie's vision of the axial lines, which comes only after the horrors of Mexico. Augie does not live up to his vision, but we feel that Wilhelm will.

CHAPTER 6

1. John Wain, for example, says "Mr. Bellow is deliberately not supplying any answers. He is supplying questions" (*Observer,* May 24, 1959, p. 21). Donald Malcolm complains that Henderson "takes refuge in statements so general as to be meaningless" (*The New Yorker,* 35, March 14, 1959, p. 173).

2. See Wylie Sypher, "Appendix: The Meaning of Comedy," *Comedy,* ed. Wylie Sypher (New York, 1956), 219. Sypher paraphrases Cornford's view "that if tragedy requires plot first of all, comedy is rooted so firmly in 'character' its plot seems derivative, auxiliary, perhaps incidental." Bellow's emphasis on character at the expense of plot may also be related to his emphasis on the essential self.

3. Henri Bergson, "Laughter," *Comedy,* 84, 93.

4. Wylie Sypher, *Comedy,* 198.

5. Nina A. Steers, " 'Successor' to Faulkner?" *Show,* 4 (September, 1964), 38.

6. Melvin Backman, "Hemingway: The Matador and the Crucified," *Hemingway and His Critics,* ed. Carlos Baker (New York, 1961), 245–58.

7. Keith Waterhouse, *New Statesman,* n.s. 57 (June 6, 1959), 806.

8. See Marcus Klein, *After Alienation.* Bellow obviously uses the waste-land theme in *Henderson:* the desert contains limestone rocks, suggest-ing water once was present, and both tribes seek water through sacrifice —of either themselves or others. More important is the meaning of the desert to Bellow's imagination. Lionel Trilling says that "it may be taken as very nearly a rule that the more the author disguises the per-sonal nature of his fantasy, the greater its force will be" (*The Liberal Imagination,* p. 80). *Henderson* is openly fantastic, but Trilling's com-ment applies: the desert embodies not only the contrasting tribes but the same destructive force as the mink in "By the Rock Wall," the city and Mexico in *Augie March,* and the character of Henderson.

9. "Henderson in Africa," *Botteghe Oscure,* 21 (1958), 187, 198, 219.

10. Several critics have noted the influence of Wilhelm Reich in Dahfu's theory. It is also present in Bellow's attempt to envisage the good as a physical force or a "law of the body."

11. *The New Yorker,* 35 (March 14, 1959), 171–73.

12. Henderson says that the old native who directs him to the Wariri re-sembles the man who directed the Biblical Joseph to Dolthan, the pit and slavery. When he later sees the native he remembers that Joseph's brothers had said, "behold, the dreamer cometh" (171). Both Joseph and Henderson rage at their fellow man because of their anxiety over their dreams, and just as the dreams of the Biblical Joseph come true, so do theirs. Richard Stern notes that Bellow's straight narration of the story without special explanation implies that it is real. If the imagina-tion is a real force in the world, as Bellows argues, then a purely imaginative novel may be real—as *Henderson* is in its description of internal human experience.

13. Quoted by Wylie Sypher, *Comedy,* 197.

14. See Dan Jacobson, *Spectator,* 202 (May 22, 1959), 735; and Carlos Baker, *New York Times Book Review,* 64 (February 22, 1959), 4–5.

15. See Marcus Klein, *After Alienation.* Klein argues that the city imagery exists "despite Bellow's first intention," but I think that the destructive force it portrays, belonging to both nature and society, is central to Bellow's purpose.

16. Sypher, *Comedy,* 204, 224, 237.

CHAPTER 7

1. Bellow's earlier version of *Herzog,* a part of which was published in 1961 (one of many drafts), is closer to caricature than the final version. Between 1961 and 1964 Bellow shifted from exaggerated detail and emotion to a realistic treatment of an excited hero, a shift made pos-sible, I think, by the distance supplied by Herzog's reminiscence. Her-zog's letters are an elaboration of Henderson's letter to Lily, in which Bellow intersperses the letter with Henderson's italicized thoughts. Bel-low says he wrote the last fifty pages of *Henderson,* which include the letter, at a feverish, exultant pitch.

2. Chester Eisinger, *Fiction of the Forties,* 19. As Richard Ellmann and Charles Feidelson, Jr. describe the issue, "committed to everything in human experience that militates against custom, abstract order, and even reason itself, modern literature has elevated individual existence over social man, unconscious feeling over self-conscious perception, passion and will over intellection and systematic morals, dynamic vision over the static image, dense actuality over practical reality" (*The Modern Tradition*—New York, 1965—p. vi).

3. Nona Balakian, "Introduction," *The Creative Present,* ed. N. Balakian and C. Simmons (Garden City, N. Y., 1963), xv, xvi.

4. Irving Howe, *New Republic,* 151 (September 19, 1964), 23. Marcus Klein, *The Reporter,* 31 (October 22, 1964), 54. Tony Tanner, *Saul Bellow* (Edinburgh, 1965), 88, 89.

5. Bellow promises some order when he says that "at first there was no pattern to the notes he made" (2), and then later that Herzog "was busy, busy, in pursuit of objects he was only now, and dimly, beginning to understand" (102).

6. Earl Rovit, *American Scholar,* 34 (Spring, 1965), 296.

7. See Bell Gale Chevigny, *Village Voice,* October 8, 1964, p. 17.

8. Recognizing that Herzog had cast off responsibility for Daisy and Marco, his first wife and child, Maurice Samuel claims that Herzog really goes to Chicago to rid himself of responsibility for June. Herzog at the Berkshires is thus the happily irresponsible American hero. Moses Herzog is a minor character in *Ulysses,* but Samuel likens Bellow's Herzog to Bloom, claiming that the masochism of both characters derives from their rejection of their Jewishness. See *Midstream,* 12 (April, 1966), 3–25.

9. Richard Ellmann suggests that Herzog's struggle to understand Madeleine's cruelty is a meditation on human evil. "Her ultimate malevolence is a mystery that refuses solution" but in the police station Herzog finally "understands the pointless, destructive rage which she directs against him. It is the emblem, in little, of the cruelty, the mad urge for corpses, that generated concentration camps." (Chicago *Sun-Times Book Week,* September 27, 1964, pp. 1, 2.)

10. Augie too describes a red "which in the greater strength of the day would make you giddy and attack your heart with a power almost like a sickness, some sickness causing spat blood, spasm, and rot just as much and as rich as pleasure" (302).

11. V. S. Pritchett says that "Moses is looking for easily punishable women without his or Mr. Bellow's knowing it" (*New York Review of Books,* October 22, 1964, p. 5).

12. Wilhelm Reich, *Wilhelm Reich, Selected Writings* (New York, 1960), 105.

13. Theodore Solotaroff, *Commentary,* 38 (December, 1964), 66 and Howe, *New Republic,* 24.

14. Rovit, *American Scholar,* 248. Daniel Jacobson, *Spectator,* 202 (May 22, 1959), 735.

BIBLIOGRAPHY

For an annotated bibliography see that compiled by Harold W. Schneider in *Critique*, 3 (Summer, 1960), 72–86. I have found it helpful. Abbreviations used are: *NYTBR* for *New York Times Book Review, NYHTBR* for *New York Herald Tribune Book Review, SRL* for *Saturday Review of Literature,* and *TLS* for *Times Literary Supplement.*

BY SAUL BELLOW

LONGER WORKS

Dangling Man. New York: Vanguard, 1944.
The Victim. New York: Vanguard, 1947.
The Adventures of Augie March. New York: Viking Press, 1953.
Seize the Day. New York: Viking Press, 1956.
Henderson the Rain King. New York: Viking Press, 1959.
Herzog. New York: Viking Press, 1964.
The Last Analysis [play]. New York: Viking Press, 1965.

SHORT FICTION

Asterisks indicate items not republished as novel chapters or in *Seize the Day.*

1941	* "Two Morning Monologues," *Partisan Review,* 8 (May–June, 1941), 230–36. Reprinted in *Partisan Reader* (New York, 1946), 91–96.
1942	* "The Mexican General," *Partisan Review,* 9 (May–June, 1942), 178–94. Reprinted in *More Stories in the Modern Manner* (New York, 1954), 235–52.
1943	"Notes of a Dangling Man," *Partisan Review,* 10 (September–October, 1943), 402–9, 429–38. Reprinted in *Best American Short Stories, 1944,* ed. Martha Foley (Boston, 1944), 21–40.
1949	* "Sermon by Doctor Pep," *Partisan Review,* 16 (May, 1949), 455–62. Reprinted in *Best American Short Stories, 1950,* ed. Martha Foley (Boston, 1950), 59–66; in *The New Partisan Reader, 1945–1953* (New York, 1953), 99–105; in *Fiction of the*

Fifties, ed. Herbert Gold (New York, 1959), 66–73.
* "Dora," *Harper's Bazaar,* 83 (November, 1949), 118, 188–90, 198–99.
"From the Life of Augie March," *Partisan Review,* 16 (November, 1949), 1077–89.

1950   * "Trip to Galena," *Partisan Review,* 17 (November–December, 1950), 779–94.

1951   "Looking for Mr. Green," *Commentary,* 11 (March, 1951), 251–61.
* "By the Rock Wall," *Harper's Bazaar,* 85 (April, 1951), 135, 205, 207–8, 214–16.
* "Address by Gooley MacDowell to the Hasbeens Club of Chicago," *Hudson Review,* 4 (Summer, 1951), 222–27.
"The Coblins," *Sewanee Review,* 59 (Autumn, 1951), 635–53.
"The Einhorns," *Partisan Review,* 18 (November–December, 1951), 619–45. Reprinted in *Perspectives USA,* 2 (Winter, 1953), 101–29.

1952   "Interval in a Lifeboat," *The New Yorker,* 28 (December 27, 1952), 24–28, 33–39.

1953   "The Eagle," *Harper's Bazaar,* 87 (February, 1953), 126–27, 196, 203–4, 206.
"Mintouchian," *Hudson Review,* 6 (Summer, 1953), 239–49.

1954   "The Wrecker" [play], *New World Writing,* 6 (1954), 271–87.

1955   "A Father-to-Be," *The New Yorker,* 30 (February 5, 1955), 26–30.

1956   "Seize the Day," *Partisan Review,* 23 (Summer, 1956), 295–319, 376–424, 426–28, 431–32.
"The Gonzaga Manuscripts," *Discovery No. 4,* ed. Vance Bourjaily (New York, 1956). Reprinted in *Prize Stories 1956: The O. Henry Awards* (Garden City, 1956), 76–102.

1958   "Henderson in Africa," *Botteghe Oscure,* 21 (1958), 187–225.
"Henderson the Rain King," *Hudson Review,* 11 (Spring, 1958), 11–28.
* "Leaving the Yellow House," *Esquire,* 49 (January, 1958), 112–26.

1961   "Herzog," *Esquire,* 56 (July, 1961), 116–30.

1962   "Scenes from Humanitis—A Farce" [play], *Partisan Review,* 29 (Summer, 1962), 327–49. (Early version of *The Last Analysis.*)

1963   "Letter to Doctor Edvig," *Esquire,* 60 (July, 1963), 61–62, 103–5.

1964   "Herzog Visits Chicago," *The Saturday Evening Post,* 237 (August 8, 1964), 44–45 ff.

"Napoleon Street," *Commentary,* 38 (July, 1964), 30–38.

1965   * "A Wen" [play], *Esquire,* 63 (January, 1965), 72–74, 111.

REVIEWS

"Beatrice Webb's America," *Nation,* 197 (September 7, 1963), 116. [*Beatrice Webb's American Diary (1898),* ed. David A. Shannon.]

"Dreiser and the Triumph of Art," *Commentary,* 11 (May, 1951), 502–3. Reprinted in *The Stature of Theodore Dreiser,* ed. Alfred Kazin and C. Shapiro (Bloomington, Indiana, 1955), 146–48. [F. O. Matthiessen, *Theodore Dreiser.*]

"Gide as Autobiographer," *New Leader,* June 4, 1951, p. 24. [André Gide, *The Counterfeiters.*]

"Hemingway and the Image of Man," *Partisan Review,* 20 (May–June, 1953), 338–42. [Philip Young, *Ernest Hemingway.*]

"Italian Fiction: Without Hope," *New Leader,* December 11, 1950, 21–22. [*New Italian Writers,* ed. Marguerite Caetani.]

"Laughter in the Ghetto," *SRL,* 36 (May 30, 1953), 15. [Sholom Aleichem, *The Adventures of Mottel the Cantor's Son.*]

"Movies," *Horizon,* 5 (September, 1962), 108-10.

"Movies," *Horizon,* 5 (November, 1962), 110–12.

"Movies," *Horizon,* 5 (January, 1963), 111–13.

"Movies," *Horizon,* 5 (March, 1963), 109–11.

"A Personal Record," *New Republic,* 130 (February 22, 1954), 20. [Joyce Cary, *Except the Lord.*]

"Pleasures and Pains of Playgoing," *Partisan Review,* 21 (May–June, 1954), 312–17. [Four plays, including T. S. Eliot's, *Confidential Clerk.*]

"Rabbi's Boy in Edinburgh," *SRL,* 39 (March 24, 1956), 19. [David Daiches, *Two Worlds.*]

"The Riddle of Shakespeare's Sonnets," *The Griffin,* 11 (June, 1962), 4–8. [*The Riddle of Shakespeare's Sonnets*; text of the sonnets and essays by Spender, Fiedler, Blackmur, Frye and Hubler.]

"The Swamp of Prosperity," *Commentary,* 28 (July, 1959), 77–79. [Philip Roth, *Goodbye, Columbus.*]

"Two Faces of a Hostile World," *NYTBR,* 61 (August 26, 1956), 4–5. [Jean Dutourd, *5 A.M.*]

"The Uses of Adversity," *The Reporter,* 21 (October 1, 1959), 42–44. [Oscar Lewis, *Five Families.*]

ARTICLES

"Deep Readers of the World, Beware!" *NYTBR,* 64 (February 15, 1959), 1, 34.

"Distractions of a Fiction Writer," *The Living Novel,* ed. Granville Hicks (New York, 1957), 1–20. Also in *New World Writing,* 12 (New York, 1957), 229–43.

"Foreword," Isaac Rosenfeld, *An Age of Enormity,* ed. Theodore Solotaroff (Cleveland, Ohio, 1962), 11–14.

"The French as Dostoevsky Saw Them," *New Republic,* 132 (May 23, 1955), 17–20. Reprinted as "Foreword," F. M. Dostoevsky, *Winter Notes on Summer Impressions,* trans. Richard Lee Renfield (New York, 1955), 9–27.

"How I Wrote Augie March's Story," *NYTBR,* 59 (January 31, 1954), 3, 17.

"Illinois Journey," *Holiday,* 22 (September, 1959), 62, 102–7.

"Introduction," *Great Jewish Short Stories, ed.* Saul Bellow (New York: Dell, 1963), 9–16.

"Isaac Rosenfeld," *Partisan Review,* 23 (Fall, 1956), 565–67.

"The Jewish Writer and the English Literary Tradition," *Commentary,* 8 (October, 1949), 366–67.

"Literary Notes on Khrushchev," *Esquire,* 55 (March, 1961), 106–7. Reprinted in *First Person Singular,* ed. Herbert Gold (New York, 1963), 46–54.

"Literature," *The Great Ideas Today* (New York: Encyclopaedia Britannica, Inc., 1963), 135–79.

"My Man Bummidge," *New York Times,* September 27, 1964, Section 2, p. 1.

"Recent American Fiction," Lecture delivered under the auspices of the Gertrude Clarke Whittal Poetry and Literature Fund (Washington: Library of Congress, 1963). Reprinted in *Encounter,* 21 (November, 1963), 22–29.

"The Sealed Treasure," *TLS,* July 1, 1960, p. 414.

"Spanish Letter," *Partisan Review,* 15 (February, 1948), 217–30.

"A Talk with the Yellow Kid," *The Reporter,* 15 (September 6, 1956), 41–44.

"Thinking Man's Wasteland" [excerpt from address], *Saturday Review,* 48 (April 3, 1965), 20.

Translation of I. B. Singer's "Gimpel the Fool," *Partisan Review,* 20 (May–June, 1953), 300–13. Reprinted in *A Treasury of Yiddish Stories,* ed. Irving Howe and Eliezer Greenberg (New York, 1954), 401–14; also in *Gimpel, the Fool and Other Stories* by Isaac Bashevis Singer (New York, 1957), 3–21.

"The University as Villain," *Nation,* 185 (November 16, 1957), 361–63.

"Where Do We Go from Here: The Future of Fiction," *Michigan Quarterly Review,* 1 (Winter, 1962), 27–33.

"A Word from Writer Directly to Reader," *Fiction of the Fifties,* ed. Herbert Gold (New York, 1959), 19.

"The Writer and the Audience," *Perspectives USA,* 9 (Autumn, 1954), 99–102.

"The Writer as Moralist," *Atlantic,* 211 (March, 1963), 58–62.

THE NOBLE SAVAGE

Edited by Saul Bellow, this periodical contains unsigned articles by him.

"Number One," eds. Saul Bellow, Keith Botsford, and Jack Ludwig (New York, 1960).

"Number Two," eds. Saul Bellow, Keith Botsford, and Jack Ludwig (New York, 1960).

"Number Three," eds. Saul Bellow and Keith Botsford (New York, 1961).

"Number Four," eds. Saul Bellow and Keith Botsford (New York, 1961).

"Number Five," eds. Saul Bellow, Keith Botsford, and Aaron Asher (New York, 1962).

ABOUT SAUL BELLOW

BIOGRAPHICAL MATERIAL

Boroff, David, "About the Author," *SRL,* 47 (September 19, 1964), 38–39 ff.

Breit, Harvey, "Saul Bellow," *The Writer Observed* (New York, 1961), 176–78.

Current Biography, February, 1965, pp. 3–5.

Davis, Robert G., "Readers and Writers Face to Face," *NYTBR,* 63 (November 9, 1958), 4, 40–41.

Galloway, David D., "An Interview with Saul Bellow," *Audit,* 3 (Spring, 1963), 19–23.

Gutwillig, Robert, "Talk with Saul Bellow," *NYTBR,* 69 (September 20, 1964), 40–41.

Hamill, Pete, "A Look at Saul Bellow, Writer at the Top," *NYHT,* September 27, 1964, p. 35.

Hobson, Laura, "Trade Winds," *SRL,* 36 (August 22, 1953), 6.

Kalb, Beatrice, "Biographical Sketch," *SRL,* 36 (September 19, 1953), 13.

Kazin, Alfred, "My Friend Saul Bellow," *Atlantic,* 215 (January, 1965), 51–54.

Kunitz, Stanley J., ed., *Twentieth Century Authors,* First Supplement (New York, 1955), 72–73.

MacGregor, Martha, *New York Post,* September 13, 1964, p. 47.

Nachman, Gerald, "A Talk with Saul Bellow," *New York Post Magazine,* October 4, 1964, p. 6.

NYHTBR, 58 (October 11, 1953), 18.

"People are Talking About," *Vogue,* 144 (November 15, 1964), 110–11.

"Portrait," *SRL,* 40 (November 16, 1957), 20.

"Saul Bellow: An Interview," *Wisconsin Studies in Contemporary Literature,* 6 (Summer, 1965), 156–60.

Steers, Nina A., " 'Successor' to Faulkner?" *Show,* 4 (September, 1964), 36–38.

Warfel, Harry R., ed. *American Novelists of Today* (New York, 1951), 32–33.

Who's Who in America, 34 (Chicago, 1966–67), 153.

GENERAL CRITICISM

Aldridge, John W., "The Society of Three Novels," *In Search of Heresy* (New York, 1956), 126–48.

Alter, Robert, "Heirs of the Tradition," *Rogues' Progress: Studies in the Picaresque Novel* (Cambridge, Mass., 1964), 106–32.

––––––. "The Stature of Saul Bellow," *Midstream,* 10 (December, 1964), 3–15.

Baumbach, Jonathan, "The Double Vision: *The Victim* by Saul Bellow," *The Landscape of Nightmare* (New York, 1965), 35–54.

Bergler, Edmund, "Writers of Half-Talent," *American Imago,* 14 (Summer, 1957), 155–64.

Booth, Wayne, *The Rhetoric of Fiction* (Chicago, 1961), 369.

Bradbury, Malcolm, "Saul Bellow's *The Victim,*" *The Critical Quarterly,* 5 (Summer, 1963), 119–27.

––––––. "Saul Bellow and the Naturalist Tradition," *Review of English Literature,* 4 (October, 1963), 80–92.

Chase, Richard, "The Adventures of Saul Bellow: Progress of a Novelist," *Commentary,* 27 (April, 1959), 323–30.

Clay, George R., "Jewish Hero in American Fiction," *The Reporter,* 17 (September 19, 1956), 43–46.

Cook, Bruce, "Saul Bellow: A Mood of Protest," *Perspective,* 12 (February, 1963), 47–50).

Cowley, Malcolm, "Naturalism: No Teacup Tragedies," *The Literary Situation* (New York, 1954), 74–95.

Crozier, R. D., "Theme in *Augie March,*" *Critique,* 7 (Spring, 1965), 18–32.

Davis, Robert G., "The American Individualist Tradition: Bellow and Styron," *The Creative Present,* ed. N. Balakian and C. Simmons (Garden City, N. Y., 1963), 111–41.

Donoghue, Denis, "Commitment and the Dangling Man," *Studies,* 53 (Summer, 1964), 174–87.

Eisinger, Chester E., "Saul Bellow: Love and Identity," *Accent,* 18 (Summer, 1958), 179–203. Also in *Fiction of the Forties* (Chicago, 1963), 341–62.

Ellison, Ralph, "Society, Morality and the Novel," *The Living Novel,* ed. Granville Hicks (New York, 1957), 76.

Fiedler, Leslie A., "The Breakthrough: The American Jewish Novelist and the Fictional Image of the Jew," *Midstream,* 4 (Winter, 1958), 15–35. Also in *Recent American Fiction: Some Critical Views,* ed. Joseph J. Waldmeir (Boston, 1963), 84–109.

––––––. *Love and Death in the American Novel* (New York, 1960), 360.

———. "Saul Bellow," *Prairie Schooner,* 31 (Summer, 1957), 103–10. Also in *The Modern Critical Spectrum,* ed. Gerald J. Goldberg and Nancy M. Goldberg (Englewood Cliffs, N. J., 1962), 155–61.

Frank, Rueben, "Saul Bellow: The Evolution of a Contemporary Novelist," *Western Review,* 18 (Winter, 1954), 101–12.

Freedman, Ralph, "Saul Bellow: The Illusion of Environment," *Wisconsin Studies in Contemporary Literature,* 1 (Winter, 1960), 50–65.

Galloway, David D., "The Absurd Man as Picaro: The Novels of Saul Bellow," *Texas Studies in Literature and Language,* 6 (Summer, 1964), 226–54.

Geismar, Maxwell, "Saul Bellow: Novelist of the Intellectuals," *American Moderns: From Rebellion to Conformity* (New York, 1958), 210–24.

Glicksberg, Charles I., "The Theme of Alienation in the American Jewish Novel," *Reconstructionist,* 23 (September 29, 1957), 8–23.

Gold, Herbert, "Introduction," *Fiction of the Fifties,* ed. Herbert Gold (New York, 1959), 7–17. Reprinted in "Fiction of the Fifties," *Hudson Review,* 12 (Summer, 1959), 192–201; in *Recent American Fiction,* ed. Joseph J. Waldmeir (Boston, 1963), 36–44.

Goldberg, Gerald J., "Life's Customer, Augie March," *Critique,* 3 (Summer, 1960), 15–27.

Goldfinch, Michael A., "Journey to the Interior," *English Studies,* 43 (October, 1962), 439–43.

Guttmann, Allen, "Bellow's *Henderson,*" *Critique,* 7 (Spring, 1965), 33–42.

Handy, William J., "Saul Bellow and the Naturalistic Hero," *Texas Studies in Literature and Language,* 5 (Winter, 1964), 538–45.

Hassan, Ihab H., *Radical Innocence: Studies in the Contemporary American Novel* (New York, 1966), 290–324.

———. "Saul Bellow: Five Faces of a Hero," *Critique,* 3 (Summer, 1960), 28–36.

Hoffman, Frederick J., "The Fool of Experience," *Contemporary American Novelists,* ed. Harry T. Moore (Carbondale, Ill., 1964), 80–94.

———. *The Modern Novel in America: 1900–1950* (Chicago, 1951), 188–89.

Howe, Irving, "Mass Society and Post-Modern Fiction," *Partisan Review,* 26 (Summer, 1959), 420–36. Reprinted in *A World More Attractive* (New York, 1963), 77–97; in *Recent American Fiction,* ed. Joseph J. Waldmeir (Boston, 1963), 3–17.

Hughes, Daniel, "Reality and the Hero: *Lolita* and *Henderson the Rain King,*" *Modern Fiction Studies,* 6 (Winter, 1960–61), 345–64.

Kazin, Alfred, "The Alone Generation," *Harper's,* 219 (October, 1959), 127–31. Reprinted in *Contemporaries* (Boston, 1962), 207–17; in *Recent American Fiction,* ed. Joseph J. Waldmeir (Boston, 1963), 18–26.

———. "The World of Saul Bellow," *The Griffin,* June, 1959, pp. 4–9. Also in *Contemporaries* (Boston, 1962), 217–23.

Klein, Marcus, "A Discipline of Nobility: Saul Bellow's Fiction," *Kenyon Review,* 24 (Spring, 1962), 203–26. Reprinted in *After Alienation* (New York, 1962), 33–70; in *Recent American Fiction,* ed. Joseph J. Waldmeir (Boston, 1963), 121–38.

Lehan, Richard, "Existentialism in Recent American Fiction: The Demonic Quest," *Texas Studies in Literature* and *Language,* 1 (Spring, 1959), 181–202. Also in *Recent American Fiction,* ed. Joseph J. Waldmeir (Boston, 1963), 63–83.

Levenson, J. C., "Bellow's Dangling Men," *Critique,* 3 (Summer, 1960), 3–14.

Levine, Paul, "Saul Bellow: The Affirmation of the Philosophical Fool," *Perspective,* 10 (Winter, 1959), 163–76.

Lewis, R. W. B., *The American Adam* (Chicago, 1955), 199–200.

Ludwig, Jack, *Recent American Novelists* (Minneapolis, Minn., 1962).

Mailer, Norman, *Advertisements for Myself* (New York, 1966), 426–36.

———. "Modes and Mutations: Quick Comments on the Modern American Novel," *Commentary,* 41 (March, 1966), 37–40.

———. "Some Children of the Goddess," *Esquire,* 60 (July, 1963), 63–69, 105. Also in *Cannibals and Christians* (New York, 1966), 104–30.

Malin, Irving, "Saul Bellow," *London Magazine,* 14 (January, 1965), 43–54.

Mathis, J. C., "Theme of 'Seize the Day,'" *Critique,* 7 (Spring, 1965), 43–45.

Miller, Karl, "Leventhal," *New Statesman,* 70 (September 10, 1965), 360–61.

Podhoretz, Norman, "The Adventures of Saul Bellow," *Doings and Undoings* (New York, 1964), 205–27.

———. "The New Nihilism and the Novel," *Partisan Review,* 25 (Fall, 1958), 576–90. Also in *Doings and Undoings,* 159–78.

Quinton, Anthony, "The Adventures of Saul Bellow," *London Magazine,* 6 (December, 1959), 55–59.

Rans, Geoffrey, "The Novels of Saul Bellow," *Review of English Literature,* 4 (October, 1963), 18–30.

Ross, Theodore J., "Notes on Saul Bellow," *Chicago Jewish Forum,* 18 (Fall, 1959), 21–27.

Samuel, Maurice, "My Friend, the Late Moses Herzog," *Midstream,* 12 (April, 1966), 3–25.

Spender, Stephen, "Literature," *The Great Ideas of Today,* ed. Robert M. Hutchens and Mortimer J. Adler (Chicago, 1965), 167–210.

Stevenson, David L., "The Activists," *Daedalus,* 92 (Spring, 1963), 238–49.

———. "Fiction's Unfamiliar Face," *Nation,* 187 (November 1, 1958), 307–9.

Tanner, Tony, *Saul Bellow* (Edinburgh, 1965). An extract appears in *Encounter,* 24 (February, 1965), 58–70.

"A Vocal Group: The Jewish Part in American Letters," *TLS,* November 6, 1959, p. xxxv.

Wasserstrom, William, *Heiress of All the Ages* (Minneapolis, Minn., 1959), 120.

Weiss, Daniel, "Caliban on Prospero: A Psychoanalytic Study on the Novel 'Seize the Day,'" *American Imago,* 19 (Fall, 1962), 277–306.

Widmer, Kingsey, "Poetic Naturalism in the Contemporary Novel," *Partisan Review,* 26 (Summer, 1959), 467–72.

Young, J. D., "Bellow's View of the Heart," *Critique,* 7 (Spring, 1965), 5–17.

SPECIFIC CRITICISM

Reviews of *Dangling Man*:

Chamberlain, John, *New York Times,* March 25, 1944, p. 13.

De Vries, Peter, *Chicago Sun Bookweek,* April 9, 1944, p. 3.

Fearing, Kenneth, *NYTBR,* 49 (March 26, 1944), 5, 15.

Hale, Lionel, *Observer,* January 12, 1947, p. 3.

Heppenstall, Rayner, *New Statesman and Nation,* n.s. 32 (December 28, 1946), 488–89.

Kristol, Irving, *Politics,* 1 (June, 1944), 156.

Kupferberg, Herbert, *NYHTBR,* 20 (April 9, 1944), 11.

Mayberry, George, *New Republic,* 110 (April 3, 1944), 473–74.

O'Brien, Kate, *Spectator,* 178 (January 3, 1947), 26.

Rothman, N. L., *SRL,* 27 (April 15, 1944), 27.

Schorer, Mark, *Kenyon Review,* 6 (Summer, 1944), 459–61.

Schwartz, Delmore, *Partisan Review,* 11 (Summer, 1944), 348–50.

Time, 43 (May 8, 1944), 104.

TLS, January 11, 1947, p. 21.

Trilling, Diana, *Nation,* 158 (April 15, 1944), 455.

Wilson, Edmund, *The New Yorker,* 20 (April 1, 1944), 70, 73–74.

Reviews of *The Victim*:

Downer, Alan S. *NYTBR,* 52 (November 30, 1947), 29.

Farrelly, John, *New Republic,* 117 (December 8, 1947), 27–28.

Fiedler, Leslie, *Kenyon Review,* 10 (Summer, 1948), 519–27.

Gibbs, Wolcott, *The New Yorker,* 28 (May 10, 1952), 58 [drama].

Greenberg, Martin, *Commentary,* 5 (January, 1948), 86–87.

Hale, Lionel, *Observer,* June 13, 1948, p. 3.

Hardwick, Elizabeth, *Partisan Review,* 15 (January, 1948), 108–17.

Match, Richard, *NYHTBR,* 24 (November 23, 1947), 10.

Poore, Charles, *New York Times,* November 22, 1947, p. 13.

Smith, R. D., *Spectator,* 180 (June 4, 1948), 686, 688.

Straus, Ralph, *Sunday Times* [London], June 6, 1948, p. 3.

Time, 50 (December 1, 1947), 111–12.

Trilling, Diana, *Nation,* 166 (January 3, 1948), 24–25.

Wilson, Edmund, *The New Yorker,* 23 (December 13, 1947), 139–40.

Reviews of *The Adventures of Augie March*:

American Scholar, 23 (Winter, 1953–54), 126.

Amis, Kingsley, *Spectator,* 192 (May 21, 1954), 626.

Cassidy, T. E., *Commonweal,* 58 (October 2, 1953), 636.

Connole, John, *America,* 90 (October 31, 1953), 133.

Crane, Milton, Chicago *Sunday Tribune Magazine of Books,* September 20, 1953, p. 4.

Davis, Robert Gorham, *NYTBR,* 58 (September 20, 1953), 1, 36.

Finn, James, *Chicago Review,* 8 (Spring–Summer, 1954), 104–11.

Geismar, Maxwell, *Nation,* 177 (November 14, 1953), 404.

Harwell, Meade, *Southwest Review,* 39 (Summer, 1954), 273–76.

Hicks, Granville, *New Leader,* 36 (September 21, 1953), 23–24.

Hopkinson, Tom, *London Magazine,* 1 (August, 1954), 82, 84, 86.

Hughes, Riley, *Catholic World,* 178 (December, 1953), 233–34.

Kristol, Irving, *Encounter,* 3 (July, 1954), 74–75.

Mizener, Arthur, *NYHTBR,* 30 (September 20, 1953), 2.

Newsweek, 42 (September 21, 1953), 102, 104.

Pickrel, Paul, *Yale Review,* n.s. 43 (Autumn, 1953), x.

Podhoretz, Norman, *Commentary,* 16 (October, 1953), 378–80.

Popkin, Henry, *Kenyon Review,* 16 (Spring, 1954), 329–34.

Prescott, Orville, *New York Times,* September 18, 1953, p. 21.

Priestley, J. B., *Sunday Times* [London], May 9, 1954, p. 5.

Pritchett, V. S., *New Statesman and Nation,* n.s. 47 (June 19, 1954), 803.

Rolo, Charles J., *Atlantic,* 192 (October, 1953), 86–87.

Rosenberg, Dorothy, San Francisco *Sunday Chronicle,* October 25, 1953, p. 18.

Schorer, Mark, *Hudson Review,* 7 (Spring, 1954), 136–41.

Schwartz, Delmore, *Partisan Review,* 21 (January–February, 1954), 112–15.

Time, 62 (September 21, 1953), 114, 117.

TLS, June 4, 1954, p. 357.

Warren, Robert Penn, *New Republic,* 129 (November 2, 1953), 22–23.

Webster, Harvey Curtis, *SRL,* 36 (September 19, 1953), 13–14.

West, Anthony, *The New Yorker,* 29 (September 26, 1953), 140, 142, 145.

West, Ray B., Jr., *Shenandoah,* 5 (Winter, 1953), 85–90.

Wilson, Angus, *Observer,* May 9, 1954, p. 9.

Reviews of *Seize the Day*:

Allen, Walter, *New Statesman and Nation,* n.s. 53 (April 27, 1957), 547–48.

Alpert, Hollis, *SRL,* 39 (November 24, 1956), 18, 34.

Baker, Robert, *Chicago Review,* 11 (Spring, 1957), 107–10.

Bayley, John, *Spectator,* 198 (June 7, 1957), 758.

Bowen, Robert, *Northwest Review,* 1 (Spring, 1957), 52–56.

Crane, Milton, Chicago *Sunday Tribune Magazine of Books,* December 30, 1956, p. 7.

Fenton, Charles A., *Yale Review,* 46 (Spring, 1957), 452.

Fiedler, Leslie, *The Reporter,* 15 (December 13, 1956), 45–46.

Flint, R. W., *Partisan Review,* 24 (Winter, 1957), 139–45.

Gill, Brendan, *The New Yorker,* 32 (January 5, 1957), 69–70.

Gilman, Richard, *Commonweal,* 78 (March 29, 1963), 21 [drama].

Gold, Herbert, *Nation,* 183 (November 17, 1956), 435–36.

Hicks, Granville, *New Leader,* 39 (November 26, 1956), 24–25.

Hogan, William, San Francisco *Chronicle,* November 15, 1956, p. 27.

Hopkinson, Tom, *Observer,* April 21, 1957, p. 11.

Kazin, Alfred, *NYTBR,* 61 (November 18, 1956), 5, 36.

Lynch, John, *Commonweal,* 65 (November 30, 1956), 238–39.

Newsweek, 48 (November 19, 1956), 142–43.

Pickrel, Paul, *Harper's,* 213 (December, 1956), 100.

Rolo, Charles J., *Atlantic,* 199 (January, 1957), 86–87.

Rugoff, Milton, *NYHTBR,* 33 (November 18, 1956), 3.

Schwartz, Edward, *New Republic,* 135 (December 3, 1956), 20–21.

Swados, Harvey, *New York Post Weekend Magazine,* November 18, 1956, p. 11.

Swan, Michael, *Sunday Times* [London], April 21, 1957, p. 7.

Time, 68 (November 19, 1956), 122.

TLS, May 10, 1957, p. 285.

West, Ray B., Jr., *Sewanee Review,* 65 (Summer, 1957), 498–508.

Wyndham, Francis, *London Magazine,* 4 (August, 1957), 66.

Reviews of *Henderson the Rain King*:

Baker, Carlos, *NYTBR,* 64 (February 22, 1959), 4–5.

Cruttwell, Patrick, *Hudson Review,* 12 (Summer, 1959), 286–95.

Curley, T. F., *Commonweal,* 70 (April 17, 1959), 84.

Gold, Herbert, *Nation,* 188 (February 21, 1959), 169–72.

Hardwick, Elizabeth, *Partisan Review,* 26 (Spring, 1959), 299–303.

Hicks, Granville, *SRL,* 42 (February 21, 1959), 20.

Hogan, William, San Francisco *Chronicle,* February 23, 1959, p. 25.

Jacobson, Dan, *Spectator,* 202 (May 22, 1959), 735.

Kogan, Herman, Chicago *Sunday Tribune Magazine of Books,* February 22, 1959, p. 3.

Leach, Elsie, *Western Humanities Review,* 14 (Spring, 1960), 223–24.

Maddocks, Melvin, *Christian Science Monitor,* February 26, 1959, p. 11.

Malcolm, Donald, *The New Yorker,* 35 (March 14, 1959), 171–73.

Newsweek, 53 (February 23, 1959), 106.

Pickrel, Paul, *Harper's,* 218 (March, 1959), 104.

Podhoretz, Norman, *NYHTBR,* 35 (February 22, 1959), 3.

Prescott, Orville, *New York Times,* February 23, 1959, p. 21.

Price, Martin, *Yale Review,* n.s. 48 (Spring, 1959), 453–56.

Rolo, Charles J., *Atlantic,* 203 (March, 1959), 88.

Scott, J. D., *Sunday Times* [London], May 24, 1959, p. 15.

Stern, Richard G., *Kenyon Review,* 21 (Autumn, 1959), 655–56.

Swados, Harvey, *New Leader,* 42 (March 23, 1959), 23–24.

Time, 73 (February 23, 1959), 102.

TLS, June 12, 1959, p. 352.

Wain, John, *Observer,* May 24, 1959, p. 21.

Waterhouse, Keith, *New Statesman,* n.s. 57 (June 6, 1959), 805–6.

Weales, Gerald, *The Reporter,* 20 (March 19, 1959), 46–47.

Whittemore, Reed, *New Republic,* 140 (March 16, 1959), 17–18.

Wilson, Angus, *Observer,* "Books of the Year," December 27, 1959, p. 8.

Reviews of *Herzog*:

Barrett, William, *Atlantic,* 214 (November, 1964), 192, 196.

Battaglia, Frank, San Francisco *Chronicle,* March 7, 1965, p. 43.

Capon, Robert F., *America,* 112 (March 27, 1964), 425–27.

Chevigny, Bell Gale, *Village Voice,* October 8, 1964, pp. 6, 17.

Curley, Thomas, *Commonweal,* 81 (October 23, 1964), 137–38.

Davenport, Guy, *National Review,* 16 (November 3, 1964), 978–79.

Elliott, George P., *Nation,* 199 (October 19, 1964), 252–54.

Ellmann, Richard, *Chicago Sun-Times Bookweek,* September 27, 1964, p. 1.

Gill, Brendan, *The New Yorker,* 40 (October 3, 1964), 218–22.

Gross, J., *Encounter,* 25 (July, 1965), 64–65.

Hicks, Granville, *SRL,* 47 (September 19, 1964), 37–38.

Howe, Irving, *New Republic,* 151 (September 19, 1964), 21–26.

Kermode, F. *New Statesman,* 69 (February 5, 1965), 200–201.

Klein, Marcus, *The Reporter,* 31 (October 22, 1964), 53–54.

Maddocks, Melvin, *Christian Science Monitor,* September 24, 1964, p. 7.

Moynahan, Julian, *NYTBR,* 69 (September 20, 1964), 1, 41.

Newsweek, 64 (September 21, 1964), 114.

Pickrel, Paul, *Harper's,* 229 (October, 1964), 128.

Poirier, R., *Partisan Review,* 32 (Spring, 1965), 264–71.

Pritchett, V. S., *New York Review of Books,* 3 (October 22, 1964), 4–5.

Rahv, Philip, *New York Herald Tribune Book Week,* September 20, 1964, pp. 1, 14, 16.

Rovit, Earl, *American Scholar,* 34 (Spring, 1965), 292, 294 ff.

Scott, N. A., *Christian Science Century,* 81 (December 16, 1964), 1562–63.

Solotaroff, Theodore, *Commentary,* 38 (December, 1964), 63–66.

Time, 84 (September 25, 1964), 105.

TLS, February 4, 1965, p. 81.

INDEX